Richard Wilkinson is the author of *Louis XIV* (2017) and a contributor to *History Today*. He holds a PhD from University of Hull and is a former teacher.

'Richard Wilkinson has penned a highly readable study which makes full use of the available rich archival material. The author has fully entered into the spirit of the man, fully comprehending the manifold complexities of a unique human being and public figure who undoubtedly made a towering contribution to the development of Britain.'

– J. Graham Jones, former Head of the Welsh Political Archive at the National Library of Wales

LLOYD GEORGE

Statesman or Scoundrel

RICHARD WILKINSON

I.B. TAURIS
LONDON · NEW YORK

Published in 2018 by
I.B.Tauris & Co. Ltd
London • New York
www.ibtauris.com

ISBN: 978 1 78076 389 7
eISBN: 978 1 78672 182 2
ePDF: 978 1 78673 182 1

A full CIP record for this book is available from the British Library
A full CIP record is available from the Library of Congress

Library of Congress Catalog Card Number: available

Typeset by Riverside Publishing Solutions, Salisbury, UK
Printed and bound in Sweden by ScandBook, AB

For James Rothwell

Contents

Illustrations

Acknowledgements

THE FOLLOWING libraries have been invariably helpful:

The National Library of Wales
The British Library
The House of Lords
The Bodleian Library
Doctor Williams' Library
Leyburn Public Library

I am grateful to the following:

Dr J. Graham Jones for writing the foreword and for introducing me to the wonders of the National Library of Wales. Professor Robert Pearce for guiding me through the early stages of my research. Julian Sandham for driving me round Criccieth.

Baroness Shirley Williams and Lord Kenneth Morgan have answered my letters, so have Ffion Hague and Huw Edwards.

My wife has corrected my style, my taste and my computing errors. I.B.Tauris have been pleasant to work for, notably Jo Godfrey, Paul Beancy and (especially) Sophie Campbell.

Foreword

IT IS a delight to be able to welcome yet another brief outline biography and critical analysis of David Lloyd George. One might indeed justifiably question the need for a further biographical study of a man who is already the subject of dozens of biographies of varying size and merit and vastly contrasting standpoints, and an array of more specialised studies – both scholarly monographs and journal articles – dealing with certain aspects of a wholly unique life and positively complex political career spanning more than six decades, from the Gladstonian heyday of the 1880s almost to the end of World War II. Yet, as will at once become apparent to the discriminating reader, Richard Wilkinson has penned a highly readable study which makes full use of the rich archival material in the custody of both the Parliamentary Archive at the House of Lords in London and the Welsh Political Archive at the National Library of Wales, Aberystwyth (recently the venue of an impressive exhibition to mark the 150th anniversary of the birth of David Lloyd George at Chorlton-upon-Medlock, Manchester, in January 1863). Although not previously a Lloyd George specialist, the author has certainly mastered the great volume of Lloyd George's published literature, scholarly monographs and periodical articles alike, and has fully entered into the spirit of the man, fully comprehending the manifold complexities of a unique human being and public figure who undoubtedly made a towering contribution to the development of Britain throughout the period 1906–1922 and, although subsequently firmly out of office, remained a politician of some consequence for years afterwards. In the words of his friend and fellow war leader Winston Churchill:

> He was the greatest Welshman that unconquerable race has produced
> since the age of the Tudors ... When the English history of the first
> quarter of the twentieth century is written, it will be seen that the
> greater part of our fortunes in peace and in war were shaped by this
> one man.[1]

Among those who also paid tribute in the House of Commons on
28 March 1945, two days after Lloyd George's death, was Aneurin
Bevan, the Labour MP for Ebbw Vale, who had famously crossed
swords with Lloyd George on more than one occasion, 'We have lost
our most distinguished member and Wales her greatest son ... We
have lost in his death the most irredescent figure that ever illumined
the British political scene'.[2] Richard Wilkinson has certainly not
accepted these funereal judgements uncritically. On the contrary, he
has produced a meticulously balanced 'warts and all' reassessment
and re-evaluation based on a fresh and rigorous examination of the
disparate source materials.

The story of published biographies of Lloyd George now extends
back over a century – to 1908 when J. Hugh Edwards, soon to be
elected a Liberal MP himself, published his *From Village Green to
Downing Street* which appeared to coincide neatly with Lloyd George's
promotion to become Chancellor of the Exchequer under Asquith
that April.[3] Edwards later published a substantial four-volume biography of Lloyd George, as indeed did Herbert du Parcq in 1912, a
still useful work for which the author, uniquely, was granted access to
the extensive archive of papers which had been carefully assembled by
Lloyd George's younger brother William George, a Criccieth solicitor,
at the family home at Garthcelyn, Criccieth. These early biographers
were generally sympathetic to their subject, as indeed were slightly
later writers like the journalists Harold Spender and E. T. Raymond in
the early 1920s. The dramatic fall of Lloyd George from power in the
autumn of 1922, however, led to a marked change of emphasis which
became apparent in the generally hostile, critical works of biographers
like J. A. Spender, A. G. Gardiner and, above all, Charles Mallet, all
of these by then disgruntled, embittered Asquithian Liberals. Above
all, in his *Essays in Biography* (1933), the distinguished economist
J. M. Keynes, whose radical, reformist ideas had so appealed to Lloyd
George in the late 1920s, described the former Prime Minister as 'this
siren, this goat-footed bard, this half-human visitor to our age from

the hag-ridden magic and enchanted woods of Celtic antiquity'.[4] Even the works of more sympathetic writers like the Barmouth-born W. Watkin Davies – whose biography is still a major source of information for Lloyd George's life and career before 1914 – and Lord Beaverbrook contained some elements of hostility and bitterness towards Lloyd George.

After Lloyd George's death and the end of World War II in 1945, a number of important biographies appeared, including works by Sir Alfred T. Davies (1948), Malcolm Thomson (1948) – the official biography published with the full collaboration of the Dowager Countess Lloyd-George of Dwyfor and unrestricted access to the papers in her custody – and Frank Owen (1954). A pioneering volume published by Lloyd George's long-suffering Principal Private Secretary, A. J. Sylvester, *The Real Lloyd George* (1947) also portrayed the former Prime Minister in rather a bad light as 'a soured, autocratic and peevish old man'.[5] Even greater hostility was, predictably, apparent in the tone and contents of a biographical volume by Lloyd George's eldest son Major Richard, the second Earl Lloyd-George of Dwyfor, which appeared in 1960. A previous volume written by 'Dick' Lloyd-George about his mother, whom he adored, back in 1947 and entitled *Dame Margaret* was, predictably, much more sympathetic and indeed idolatrous. Generally critical, too, was the tone of Donald McCormick's *The Mask of Merlin* (1963). This attitude of criticism was also perpetuated in the more general works of historical interpretation published in the first half of the 1960s.

From this point on, however, a more sympathetic, revisionist, rehabilitation-orientated, attitude emerged to Lloyd George, reflected in the major works of eminent historians like Martin Gilbert, Cameron Hazlehurst, Robert Skidelsky and Peter Clarke. This was in part the result of the availability of exciting new source materials, notably the magnificent archive held at the Beaverbrook Library, later transferred to the custody of the Parliamentary Archive at the House of Lords, and the so-called 'Brynawelon' group of papers purchased by the National Library of Wales in 1969 – the first of seven major Lloyd George archives eventually to be acquired by the National Library by the year 2000. As a result, important published works flowed from the press – extracts from Frances Stevenson's diary in 1971, *Lloyd George: Family Letters, 1885–1936* (1973), and the letters between Lloyd George and Frances Stevenson in 1975. The first volume of John Grigg's outstandingly accomplished multi-volume biography *The Young Lloyd George* saw the light of day in 1973, to be followed in due course by three further substantial, authoritative volumes which take the story down to the end of World War I. A similar long-term project by a distinguished American historian, Bentley B. Gilbert, yielded two impressive volumes, but came to an end in the year 1916. The deaths of both these biographers brought the promising series to a sadly premature end. Important thematic works included Chris Wrigley's *David Lloyd George and the British Labour Movement: Peace and War* (1976). A massive, comprehensive single-volume biography was published by Peter Rowland in 1975 and has generally stood the test of time. Lloyd George's only nephew, the late Dr W. R. P. George, published in 1976 and 1983 two important works which traced his uncle's career down to his entry into the Cabinet in December 1905, and based primarily on the superb archive then in his private possession, subsequently purchased by the National Library in 1989.

Thereafter there ensued something of a lull in Lloyd George studies – in spite of the favourable, wide-scale publicity engendered by a BBC1 television series scripted by the late Elaine Morgan in which Lloyd George was played to huge commendation by the distinguished actor Philip Madoc. Interest has, however, certainly revived during the last decade or so when a spate of seminal works has seen the light of day. John Campbell, author of an authoritative study of Lloyd George's so-called 'wilderness years' *The Goat in the Wilderness, 1922–1931* (1977), has re-examined in commendable detail the complex, long-term relationship between Lloyd George and Frances Stevenson in *If Love Were All …* (2007). Richard Toye published a comprehensive study of *Lloyd George & Churchill: Rivals for Greatness* (2008), while Ffion Hague broke new ground in a meticulously researched volume on Lloyd George's private life entitled *The Pain and the Privilege: the Women in Lloyd George's Life* (2008). The following year, Roy Hattersley published *David Lloyd George: the Great Outsider*, the first substantial one-volume biography of Lloyd George to be published for decades. The present writer brought together his journal articles in *David Lloyd George and Welsh Liberalism*, published by the National Library of Wales in June 2010. A number of television series, including one scripted and presented by the Welsh-born BBC newscaster Huw Edwards, and several individual documentary programmes, have also helped to create an increased awareness of Lloyd George. So, too, did the unveiling by the Prince of Wales in October 2007 of a statue of him in Parliament Square near the House of Commons, after a protracted campaign to amass the necessary resources, and the on-going activities and array of impressive accessions at the enterprising Lloyd George Museum at Llanystumdwy. The celebration of the 150th anniversary in January 2013 of the birth of Lloyd George has also led to a renewed interest and some reassessment of his many lasting achievements and towering contribution.

Richard Wilkinson, while preparing this impressive, eminently readable volume, has read voraciously and quarried with extraordinary industry and commendable insight, the great mass of published volumes and scholarly articles on David Lloyd George. He has distilled their contents, a great welter of complex material, into a concise, readily digestible narrative, certain to be appreciated by a wide and disparate readership. The volume also benefits from the author's impressive background knowledge of a crowded, involved period in British political history, and from the use of a nice balance of printed sources and the wide range of archival sources now available in the various repositories. He is prepared to challenge some of the accepted 'truths' and assertions about Lloyd George and to discuss others in a questioning, interrogative spirit. He clearly has an eagle eye for the telling quotation, many of which he has deftly woven into his narrative, and his conclusions and conjecture are certain to invite further questioning and provoke lively, intelligent speculation and informed debate. This is a positive measure of the book's undoubted success. The result of Richard Wilkinson's labours is a cohesive, compelling narrative, certain to be well-received and warmly appreciated. I commend it most highly as the latest most valuable addition to the burgeoning scholarly literature on David Lloyd George.

J. GRAHAM JONES
Aberystwyth

Introduction

H. H. ASQUITH, Prime Minister of Great Britain, was acutely disturbed. Only seven weeks previously he had executed his finest political achievement to date when he successfully committed a virtually united nation to war with Germany. Now, on 19 September 1914, the war had lasted seven weeks without any of the combatant powers achieving a decisive breakthrough, least of all Great Britain. Meanwhile thousands were dying every day, making Kitchener's prediction that the war would last at least another three years chilling indeed. Armageddon – the titanic conflict between good and evil – had arrived. Asquith, humane, civilised, tolerant, peered over the edge of the abyss and did not like what he saw. His immediate priority was to uphold morale and confidence in the government's ability to survive this crisis. More men were needed, but where could they be found? A morale boosting speech was required, defending the government's record and commitment to victory. Could a flag-waving meeting at the Queen's Hall, in central London, attended by the great and the good and a crowd of Welshmen singing 'Men of Harlech' be the answer? Much depended on Asquith's choice of the man to pull off this oratorical coup. It was not something he could manage himself, nor pass on to the Foreign Secretary: Sir Edward Grey was far too judicious. Winston Churchill was widely distrusted. Who else was there from Asquith's star-studded but pacific cabinet but the Welsh wizard? Lloyd George got the nod.

David Lloyd George, the Chancellor of the Exchequer and Asquith's right-hand man, did not let the premier down. A stumpy, dapper figure with a fine head of hair, a virulent moustache and

1

piercing blue eyes, Lloyd George was by no means an automatic choice, although he was at the height of his powers as a social reformer. Unlike his friend Winston Churchill, who had been born in Blenheim Palace, Lloyd George was a cottage-bred Welshman with no social or educational pretensions. Many of his own colleagues, never mind the Tory opposition, regarded him as a provincial pleb. When he had made his name nationally 14 years earlier, it was as an opponent of the Boer War. In July 1901 he was nearly lynched when he tried and failed to address an anti-war meeting in Birmingham Town Hall, ironically summoned to cement Liberal Party unity. Now he would certainly be listened to, though Lord Riddell,[1] Lloyd George's tame Press magnate, agreed with Frances Stevenson,[2] Lloyd George's secretary-cum-mistress that on this occasion he was acutely nervous before speaking. Riddell records Lloyd George walking in the countryside near Walton Heath until nightfall, agonising over what to say. Most contemporaries thought that Lloyd George was a talented but unreliable speaker, while historians have agreed ever since with this viewpoint. Certainly he was an unusual orator, who succeeded through hard work and meticulous preparation, as the Queen's Hall speech indicates. It was, in fact, a brilliant – though tendentious – masterpiece.

Anyone studying Lloyd George's life can, with profit, examine this speech in which his strengths and weaknesses are apparent. Here we can make the acquaintance of a fascinating hero, with glaring flaws. Speaking softly at first so that the audience had to lean forward to catch every syllable, gradually he warmed to his theme. He was keen to defend the government's decision to go to war, in particular on moral grounds. The German invasion and exploitation of Belgium was central to his argument. The German military elite, he claimed, was 'the road hog of Europe', driving smaller vehicles into the ditch. Lloyd George showed commendable broadmindedness in stressing the decency of German civilians, pointing out that German merchants and traders had the reputation of being as upright and straightforward as any in the world. But it was the aggression of the Kaiser's warlords that had to be resisted. 'They think we cannot beat them. It will not be easy. It will be a long job; it will be a terrible war; but in the end we shall march through terror to triumph.'[3] Here was the supreme test of British idealism, given the sacrifice demanded.

Now Lloyd George shamelessly gripped his audience by the lapels:

I envy you young people your opportunity. They have put up the age limit for the Army, but I am sorry to say I have marched a good many years even beyond that [Lloyd George was 51]. It is a great opportunity, an opportunity that comes only once in many centuries to the children of men. For most generations sacrifice comes in drab and weariness of spirit. It comes to you today and comes to us all in the form of the glow and thrill of a great movement for liberty ... There is something infinitely greater and more enduring which is emerging out of this great conflict – a new patriotism, richer, nobler and more exalted than the old ... May I tell you in a simple parable what I think this war is doing for us? I know a valley in North Wales, between the mountains and the sea. It is a beautiful valley, but it is very enervating. We have been living in a sheltered valley for generations. We have been too comfortable and too indulgent, many perhaps too selfish, and the stern hand of Fate has scourged us to an elevation where we can see the great everlasting things which matter for a nation – the great peaks which we had forgotten of Honour, Duty, Patriotism, and, clad in glittering white, the great pinnacle of Sacrifice pointing like a rugged finger to Heaven.[4]

It was certainly brilliant, if you were impressed by challenging rhetoric verging on moral blackmail. In his sadly unfinished four volume biography, however, John Grigg asks: 'What are we to make of the Queen's Hall speech? Was it a masterpiece of genuine patriotism, or a masterpiece of hypocrisy?'[5] It attracted praise and admiration from a tearful Sir Edward Grey the Foreign Secretary and an equally lacrimose Prime Minister. Accolades poured in from hitherto unsympathetic Tories and from the press. However there were some embarrassing secrets which, fortunately for Lloyd George, were not widely known. On 11 August 1914 he had written to his wife Margaret suggesting that she should prevent their younger son Gwilym from volunteering: 'I am not going to sacrifice my nice boy.'[6] What, then, of envying young people their opportunity? What of sacrifice? Why could not Lloyd George tackle his own sons, as opposed to expecting his wife to deputise for him? Lloyd George did not truly envy people who volunteered because he himself was a physical coward, scared of shells and bombs. Nor did he come clean about Britain's strategic desire to preserve the Belgian coast from German domination, arguably a more pressing priority than the defence of small nations.

Another dishonest note was struck by the claim that 'we have been too comfortable'. Lloyd George had championed those living in acute poverty, especially the miners, farm labourers and the other victims of capitalism in London's East End. He knew too well that their lives were far from 'comfortable'.

A dispassionate reading of Lloyd George's speech at the Queen's Hall reveals his qualities. He had a job to do and he did it well. No other cabinet minister could have done it so well, not even his friend and colleague Winston Churchill. His choice of phrase, his impassioned delivery were almost irresistible.[7] But not to all, as this popular jingle demonstrates:

> Lloyd George no doubt when his life ebbs out will ride on a blazing chariot.
> He'll ride in state on a red hot plate twixt the Devil and Judas Iscariot.
> Ananias that day to the Devil will say 'My right to precedence fails.
> Move up a bit higher away from the fire, make way for that bounder from Wales.[8]

Ananias, it will be recalled,[9] was a thief and a liar. So was the bounder from Wales. He was also infuriatingly elusive, very hard to pin down, as the economist John Maynard Keynes famously observed:

> How can I convey to the reader who does not know him any just impression of this extraordinary figure of our time, this siren, this goat-footed bard, this half-human visitor to our age from the hag-ridden magic and enchanted woods of Celtic antiquity ... Who can paint the chameleon or tether the broomstick? Lloyd George is rooted in nothing ... a vampire and medium in one.[10]

It may read as fanciful character-assassination, but many acknowledged the justice of these comments, recognising in particular Lloyd George's inability to speak the truth. Harold Nicolson, politician and diplomat, believed that 'the good fairies gave him everything at his christening, but a bad fairy said: "People won't trust him"'.[11]

To descend from the mystical to the earthy, Lloyd George was a sexual predator who cheated on both his wife and his mistress. He was widely distrusted as a politician. On his own admission he destroyed the Liberal party. His record as a social reformer was flawed.

When he finally became 'the man who won the war', he only did so by betraying Asquith, his leader, and the soldiers who trusted him to protect them from the idiocy of some British generals. Lloyd George was indeed a bounder who gambled with other people's money and with their lives. He enriched himself by selling honours. His religion was hypocritical, and at the end of his life, the great radical accepted a peerage. As Emanuel Shinwell said to Lloyd George's grandson, 'he was a scoundrel'. How did he get away with it?[12]

Charm is partly the answer. Lloyd George was a most attractive man, both to women and to men. Women agreed with the society lady who exclaimed 'he's eight feet tall' when Lloyd George was described as 'a little man.'[13] His Tory opponent and later his ally, A. J. Balfour referred to him as 'the little man', but this was in affection and admiration; he was indeed a great little man. Everyone responded to his cheerfulness, wit and good humour. He was lively company, a vivacious conversationalist, the life and soul of any party who brought noise and laughter to any gathering. He was an attentive listener who conveyed the impression that you were the only person in the world whose opinions interested him. There was no side to him. He loved children and was at his best with them and, for what it is worth, was a great animal lover, surrounded by his favourite dogs and cats.

But *Prenez garde!* as the French say. This book is exceptional in questioning Lloyd George's record as a war-leader and identifying him as a sex-pest. It acknowledges him with some reservations as a social reformer and also, bizarrely, as a hymn specialist – which other biographers ignore. His relationship with Germany culminated in his visit to Hitler in September 1936 which other biographers condemn, perhaps too harshly.[14] He was the most controversial as well as the most colourful figure in modern British history. According to Lord Beaverbrook, 'Churchill was the greater man, but George was more fun.'[15] As a young man he began his life in politics by promising to 'promote myself by honest endeavour to benefit others,'[16] but was he honest? Did he live up to this apparently laudable ambition of benefiting others? Did he have any basic integrity? Was his sympathy for the underdog sincere, and what did he do about it?[17] This introduction offers guidance to readers on what to expect and when to be on their guard. Charm and fun can be dangerous.[18]

1

The Rise of the Cottage-Bred Man (1863–1890)

The Tories have not yet realised that the day of the cottage-bred man has at last dawned.

— Lloyd George, April 1890[1]

Loyd GEORGE's progress from the remote village of Llanystumdwy in north Wales to Westminster was the most remarkable chapter in his remarkable career. Once established as an MP, at the age of 27, he certainly had to struggle to make his name in the Liberal Party and to become a national figure. Then he had to meet demanding challenges for another 11 years as a Cabinet Minister before acquiring the premiership in December 1916. Yet the handicaps he confronted were at their steepest in the years before he was elected an MP – as an inexperienced, obscure country-boy struggling to qualify as a lawyer with scant financial backing, educational or social qualifications.

David Lloyd George was born on 17 January 1863 at New York Place, Chorlton-upon-Wedlock, Manchester. This might seem paradoxical for 'the greatest Welshman of all time', but it did not bother Lloyd George who regarded geography as less important than 'stock'. And indeed his parents, William and Elizabeth George, were descendants of respectable Welsh stock, part intellectual, part farming. William was a headmaster when David was born. He was on friendly terms with the Congregationlist J. D. Morell and Lancashire philosophers such as James Martineau. He had a reputation for speaking the truth.[2] Maybe it was his truthfulness which alienated his governors, whom William described as 'working men to whom

I would prefer to give orders'. As it happened, things did not pan out. William became unwell. The Georges therefore decided to return to the traditional family occupation of farming in Pembrokeshire. There in 1864 William George died from pneumonia at the age of 43. Left in reduced circumstances with two infants and a third on the way, Elizabeth sent a pregnant telegram to the northern extremity of Cardigan Bay: 'Come Richard.'

'Richard' was her brother, Richard Lloyd, the master shoemaker of Llanystumdwy, a couple of miles from Criccieth. Known to the family as Uncle Lloyd, he was an amazing man who, not for the last time, played a crucial role in Lloyd George's life. Because then as now, north–south communications in Wales were poor, it took Uncle Lloyd two days, walking 20 miles to the nearest rail-head, taking a train, stage-coach and finally a horse-and-trap, to reach his bereaved sister. But he came as requested. Together they sold as many of the family's possessions as they could carry, despite the two toddlers' attempts to prevent this by blocking the entrance to the farm with piles of stones. Then they returned to the north end of Cardigan Bay, with the late headmaster's books. David's home for the next 16 years was to be at Highgate, Llanystumdwy where Uncle Lloyd gave him food, shelter, companionship, self-belief and much more. Indeed he was a virtual father to the two children, who were joined a few weeks later by David's younger brother, William.

Anyone interested in Lloyd George's career should visit Llanystumdwy (which means 'the church on the bend in the Dwyfor'). It is vital to appreciate what an unprepossessing place the great man came from. It is quite a pretty – though rather nondescript – village in the back of beyond, amid mountain scenery boasting Snowdon in the distance. Llanystumdwy lies on the road from Criccieth to Pwllheli, clustered round the bridge over the River Dwyfor. There are an Anglican church, two chapels, a shop and a pub. Lloyd George's grave lies in the village overlooking the Dwyfor. It is covered by a large boulder above a ravine through which the river plunges on its way to the sea, two miles away. Highgate is still there, faithfully preserved by Lloyd George's relatives and admirers. It is part of a fine museum, full of Lloyd George memorabilia. Welsh is spoken by virtually everyone. As Lloyd George frequently complained, it rains a lot.

In Lloyd George's boyhood, Uncle Lloyd's workshop dominated the main street. It was all very well for Lloyd George to complain about the handicap of being a cottage-bred boy – but Uncle Lloyd's was no ordinary cottage. He employed two assistants while Uncle Lloyd's mother kept the books. It was a thriving concern. The children were adequately if not luxuriously fed. The two boys were the only members of their school to wear knickerbockers, while their sister Mary Ellen, known as Polly, was sent away to a finishing school. Books and newspapers were everywhere. In the main room downstairs, an informal debating society frequently met where Lloyd George listened and learned. Uncle Lloyd was fascinated by politics. For him his nephew was to be a surrogate player in local and national politics. His encouragement of David's ambitions and self-belief was to be of profound significance. The boy was to go where his uncle could not penetrate, for Uncle Lloyd was only a village craftsman and an unpaid minister in a breakaway Baptist church, the Disciples of Christ.

Uncle Lloyd was an attractive and impressive Christian. For all his enthusiasm and devotion to this obscure sect, he was generous and charitable. He even tolerated Anglicans, despite being deaf in one ear because in his childhood an Anglican teacher had struck him for speaking Welsh. He knew the Bible backwards, and expected his nephews and niece to do the same. He remained philosophical even when his older nephew told him that he could not accept Christianity after he had been baptised in the Dwyfor. Uncle Lloyd realised that such scepticism was probably transient and would be no handicap in the wider world beyond Llanystumdwy. That was what really mattered.

It is customary to represent Uncle Lloyd as a saint.[3] His bedroom wall was stained with his sweat as he wrestled with his God in prayer. He certainly comes across as a genuinely humble man when we learn how he taught his nephews French so that they could qualify in their legal training: every night he prepared the next day's lesson, though one can't help but wonder what their pronunciation was like. No trouble was too great for 'his' Daffyd. John Grigg, however, is refreshingly critical.[4] He argues that his worst offence was to favour his older nephew at the expense of his younger. David was literally his blue-eyed boy and he would see no fault in him. Uncle and nephew doted on each other. William, the younger brother, had this to say: 'Whether this unrestrained admiration was wholly good for the lad upon whom it was lavished, and indeed for the man who evolved out of him, is a matter upon which opinions may differ.'[5] The women of the household followed Uncle Lloyd's lead and ministered to the boy's every need. Consequently, David never had to learn the most elementary skills such as doing up his shoes or tying his tie. In later life, his wife Maggie always carved. In a word, he was spoilt, and remained so for the rest of his life.[6]

Meanwhile poor William was not even allowed to include 'Lloyd' in his surname so that when the brothers went into legal partnership the firm was called 'Lloyd George and George'. When William was given an important commission by their employer, Randal Casson, Uncle Lloyd's reaction was, 'I would rather have seen D. Ll. G. being asked' – though he graciously added that he was pleased for William. Grigg wrongly compares William with the self-pitying and uncharitable older brother in Christ's parable of the prodigal son,[7] for truly William was astonishingly patient and loyal both to his uncle and to his brother. He cheerfully accepted that by avuncular decree, David was to take the high road and he the low. This involved him in working hard as a solicitor so as to pay for Uncle Lloyd and brother David's upkeep for many a year – a touching story entirely to William's credit. His granddaughter, Anita George, is not the only relative to regard him as a saint.

Unlike virtually all his contemporary political allies and rivals, Lloyd George did not attend university – although neither did Churchill or MacDonald. The village elementary school, Uncle Lloyd's workshop and the Criccieth Debating Society substituted. There he learned to listen, to argue and to speak. His old schoolfellow, William Williams, drove past a youthful figure on the Portmadoc Road one winter's evening, vigorously gesticulating as he rehearsed a speech. The future statesman already recognised the need to prepare thoroughly for confrontation with authority. So the *North Wales Express* praised Lloyd George's attack on the Liberal government's invasion of Egypt (24 November 1882): 'Arabi Paha was a man that had risen from amongst them – a man who knew all about their wants, because he had felt their wants himself.'[8]

Lloyd George did not attend secondary school, let alone university, for there was no such thing in most of the towns and villages of both England and Wales at the time. But here, again, Lloyd George was not wholly at a disadvantage. There was a school in Llanystumdwy, and a very good one. We would call it a primary school, or more accurately an elementary school, in that the boys and girls were able to remain until the age of 13. Privileged, gifted pupils stayed on until age 14 or even 15, if they received the approval and support of the head-teacher. Often they served as pupil-teachers before qualifying for teacher-training. Fortunately for Lloyd George, the head of Llanystumdwy School was outstanding. David Evans was a genuine academic, an enthusiast and a brilliant communicator who loved children. But he was an Anglican: he had to be to qualify for his job, for the school was a National School, owned by the Church of England and committed to teaching Anglican doctrine.

While Lloyd George enjoyed school, all the while he was encouraged by his uncle William to become a political animal. He was carried on his uncle's shoulders during the 'great' 1868 general election when Gladstonian Liberalism triumphed in Wales. He absorbed Welsh nonconformist and nationalist prejudices against squires, brewers and parsons. The Anglican establishment was the victim of one of Lloyd George's first organised protests. Every year Squire Ellis Nanney whose great house dwarfed the village, the rector and various local bigwigs descended on the school to hear the children recite the Apostles' Creed, the Lord's Prayer and the Catechism. Possibly today's historians are unaware how deeply deferential and indeed obsequious the Catechism is. The child has to promise 'to order myself lowly and reverently to all my betters and to do my duty in that state of life, unto which it shall please God to call me'. No wonder this stuck in Lloyd George's throat. First, however, came the Creed. Lloyd George's protest began when all the children remained silent. The rector and the bigwigs looked daggers, while the poor headmaster was covered in confusion. After several minutes silence, brother William took pity on David Evans who after all had not deserved this public humiliation and disloyalty. He started his fellow pupils off by shouting, 'I believe …' Afterwards Dafydd gave his brother a beating. But the point had been made and the ceremony was not repeated.

Although in later life Lloyd George would grumble about the tedium of his boyhood days in Llanystumdwy, he seems to have been happy enough, for instance, leading gangs of local boys in poaching expeditions in the grounds of Plas Gwynfryn, Squire Nanney's palatial residence. The Squire was quite tolerant provided the boys kept the dog Bismarck[9] on its lead so that it could not chase the sheep. Lloyd George never learnt to swim or ride a bicycle – he was too ill-coordinated. But he enjoyed walking and was not too exhausted by the half a dozen walks in all weathers to and from chapel on Sundays.

However, while he appreciated the Welsh hymns and a good sermon, he was bored by the repetitive nature of nonconformist worship. He joined the local militia but had to keep his uniform hidden from Uncle Lloyd. Once he got drunk – probably the only time in his life.[10]

His chief relaxation was the opposite sex. Described by contemporaries and historians as a flirt, sexual predator would be more accurate. With his good looks and bewitching smile, even as a teenager he was irresistible to women. According to his Private Secretary A. J. Sylvester: 'He was born with the biggest organ I have ever seen. No wonder the women are always after him, and he after them.'[11] But they loved him for his personality as well. When an Irish labourer descended on the school in order to thrash some boys who had mocked his sister, the girl intervened on David's behalf: 'Not that one!' When Lloyd George gave Dick, his eldest son, some money so that he could take a girl out, he complained:

> 'The art of courtship is a lost art – how would you fancy trying your hand with a girl when you've only got thruppence in your breeches and the only place you can take her is for a walk in the rain?'
> 'What did you do?'
> 'We got wet.'[12]

He enjoyed philandering with Jennie Evans when he was 17. His diary conveys his self-centred approach to his girlfriends: 'Jennie has been flirting with other boys … All the same I mean to carry on with her … Was reserved with Jennie. I want to get rid of her – we are being talked about. Uncle knows it this long time.' Actually Uncle was a problem. Lloyd George's relationships with several girls were the subject of local gossip of which not only Uncle Lloyd but Lloyd George's mother and sister were aware. They did not approve. Uncle Lloyd commented censoriously 'on the many young people at Criccieth Fair openly cuddling and wandering around like summer ducks'. When Lloyd George was out in the evening, Uncle Lloyd took to trailing him. If he could not find his wandering boy, he would question passers-by. Lloyd George was annoyed by this intrusion and hid his uncle's boots. He began to refer to him behind his back as 'the bishop'. Just how promiscuous Lloyd George was – now and in the years ahead – is anyone's guess.[13] Some of his biographers, particularly those related to him, are fiercely loyal, but he certainly got into hot water. A sympathetic commentator, J. Graham Jones, is probably not too wide of the mark when he compares the great man's vulnerability to scandalous gossip with that of Irish politician, Charles Parnell (1846–1891), the exposed adulterer. Lloyd George's social problems were indeed formidable. His innate sympathy for Parnell was, in part at least, a reflection of his own awareness of the potential disaster awaiting him if one of his numerous extra-marital affairs should erupt into scandal.[14]

Lloyd George now faced up to the challenge of earning a living and making a career for himself. David Evans would have been delighted to welcome his star pupil into the teaching profession, if only adherence to the Anglican creed had not been required. Similarly Uncle Lloyd would have gladly supported his nephew's entry into the full-time Baptist ministry. Medicine was another possibility, but Lloyd George was squeamish about blood. So the law beckoned. Lloyd George was duly articled to the Portmadoc firm of Breese, Jones & Casson, where he made himself useful as an office clerk and general messenger before graduating to higher responsibilities. He lived in cheap lodgings in Portmadoc, enjoying the greater freedom – for instance, he and his friend Moses Roberts ended up in bed with two Irish girls. In the meantime, he worked fairly hard at his studies so as to qualify as a solicitor. He acquired a sound working knowledge of the laws of property, insurance, trespass and libel which was to stand him in good stead in his later career. Lloyd George had no intention of finishing his days as a country attorney. He totally accepted Uncle Lloyd's plans for him to enter politics. As a genuine idealist he intended to benefit his fellow human beings, especially the poor, the downtrodden and the underprivileged, by rising to the political heights on their behalf. Aged 17 he defined his chief ambition as, 'To promote myself by honest endeavour to benefit others.'[15]

In 1880 opportunities for political involvement emerged. Uncle Lloyd retired from his shoemaking business in order to devote himself to the Lord's service – and his favourite nephew's. The whole family moved to Morvin House, Criccieth whence Lloyd George could more easily walk to work every morning, and Uncle Lloyd and his mother could once again keep an eye on him. Lloyd George wrote in his diary that he 'left Llanystumdwy without a feeling of remorse, regret or longing'.[16] He was actively involved as Casson's assistant during the general election of April 1880. Casson worked hard as Liberal Party Agent for Caernarvonshire. The Liberals triumphed here and across Wales. Lloyd George branched out as a political journalist under the pseudonym 'Brutus'. He contributed a slashing attack on Lord Salisbury in the North Wales Express – incidentally no parish pump stuff for our ambitious hero but the wider world of the Tory foreign secretary.

Having qualified as a solicitor with third class honours in 1884, Lloyd George left Breese, Jones & Casson and set up on his own, soon to be joined by his brother, William, who infuriated both Uncle Lloyd and his brother by getting a first. These were hard times. Their mother worked as the receptionist, while Uncle Lloyd served the writs. What was needed was success in court and publicity in the world of Welsh politics and society. Here there was excitement and controversy. The Reform Acts of 1867 and 1884 had gone far to challenge the Tory-Anglican monopoly of power as newly enfranchised Welshmen campaigned for political and religious justice. Why should landlords continue to dominate and bully? After the 1868 general election, Lord Penrhyn evicted tenants who had dared to vote Liberal. However, the Secret Ballot Act of 1872 put an end to such victimisation. Men were now free to vote, if not to speak, as they pleased. Why should the Anglican Church be subsidised by the hard earned incomes of nonconformists who had to pay tithe? The ultimate solution was clearly the disestablishment of the Anglican Church in Wales. It had happened in Ireland, so why not elsewhere? Why should the brewing industry dominate politics by extracting money from the villagers who flocked to the pub to their own impoverishment and degradation – and to the benefit of the Tory Party? Here Lloyd George was in his element. He spoke in public against his favourite enemies: the landlord, the brewer, the publican and the parson. He was elected Secretary of the Caernarvonshire Anti-Tithe League. He made speeches at the Portmadoc Debating Society, he wrote to the newspapers, he preached in chapels in favour of public houses closing on Sundays.

Lloyd George joined a number of active young Welshmen in forming an exciting new movement, Cymru Fydd (Young Wales). This was partly cultural, partly political. The idea, never fulfilled, was to unite south and north Wales, but the contrasts were too marked between the rural north and the anglicised, industrial, rugby-playing south. The movement agitated for Home Rule for Wales and the disestablishment of the Anglican Church. Kenneth O. Morgan doubts whether Lloyd George's enthusiasm for Welsh home rule was as forthright as some historians, Emyr Price for instance, have maintained.[17] Nevertheless,

Lloyd George spoke aggressively in public, especially advocating the widespread use of the Welsh language. He appeared on the same platform with Michael Davitt, the Irish nationalist to whom he proposed an eloquent vote of thanks, prompting Davitt's forecast that he would soon be in Parliament. This was Lloyd George's first speech before a wide public audience. Significantly, he displayed greater concern for Welsh agrarian interests than for Irish Home Rule. Equally significant was his exploitation of Luke, Chapter X, when he compared Davitt to the Samaritan foreigner binding up the wounds of victimised Welsh farmers. However, Lloyd George was curiously laid back about Davitt's prediction that he would soon be in Parliament, having been unimpressed by the House of Commons when he had visited London a few months before: 'Went to the Houses of Parliament, very much disappointed with them – great buildings outside, but inside they are crabbed, small and suffocating, especially the House of Commons.'[18] Nor did he relish being an MP without the necessary wealth 'in a house of snobs'. Still, his time would come. He confided to his diary his satisfaction 'that his speech had gone like wildfire thro' Festiniog. Going to make me MP'. In the meantime, he crossed swords with a curate who challenged his audience to look critically at 'this little attorney': 'If you go to his office you'll pay six and eight pence for him to speak a word with you'. The 'little attorney' pointed out that the curate was lavishly paid for his sermons whether anyone went to listen to him or not.[19]

Lloyd George made a local reputation for himself as a speaker on public platforms and in court. His wit and overall know-how enabled him to deal with hecklers. When he advocated 'Home Rule All Round', he was interrupted by a shout, 'Home Rule for Hell'. 'Yes indeed', he responded, 'I like everyman to speak for his own country.'[20] With regard to his orations in chapel and Sunday school, Uncle Lloyd's diary was predictably enthusiastic: 'Wednesday Night. Excellent meeting. D. Ll. G. speaking for the first time – O, my dear boy, he did speak well!' Lloyd George was delighted when the chairman of a disestablishment meeting introduced him as follows: 'In my opinion, gentlemen, that Bishop of St. Asaph ish one of the biggest liars in creashon; but, thank God – yes, thank God – we haff in Mr Lloyd George a match for him tonight [*sic*].'[21]

Meanwhile, two successes in court advanced his career. First, he successfully defended the relatives of a Nonconformist quarryman whom they had buried in the graveyard at Llanfrothen in accordance with the Burials Act of 1880. The intolerant rector had tried to prevent this by locking the gates. Lloyd George advised the family that they were entitled to break in and conduct the burial by their own non-Anglican rites. The rector took them to court. On Lloyd George's advice the family demanded a trial by jury. Unfortunately, a dishonest and prejudiced judge misrepresented the jury's verdict and found for the rector. Lloyd George appealed to the High Court in London where Lord Justice Coleridge reversed the county court judge's ruling, making critical comments on his conduct. Lloyd George became the most popular man in Wales.

A couple of years later he successfully defended four quarrymen who were accused of illegally fishing in Nantlle Lake. The issue in dispute was whether the men had been fishing in a lake or a river. The Chairman of the Caernarvonshire County Bench ruled that the question would have to be decided in a higher court. The following newspaper account gives an accurate impression of Lloyd George's style:

Mr George: Yes, Sir, and in a perfectly just and unbiased court too.

The Chairman: If that remark of Mr George's is meant as a reflection upon any magistrate sitting on this Bench, I hope that he will name him. A more insulting and ungentlemanly remark to the Bench I have never heard during the course of my experience as a magistrate.

Mr George: But a more true remark was never made in a Court of Justice.

The Chairman: Tell me to whom you are referring? I must insist upon you referring to any magistrate or magistrates sitting in this Court.

Mr George: I refer to you in particular, Sir.

The Chairman: Then I retire from the Chair. Good-bye, gentlemen. This is the first time that I have ever been insulted in a Court of Justice.[22]

Lloyd George's total lack of deference no doubt made him enemies. But on this occasion two of the quarrymen were acquitted and the other two given a derisory fine of one shilling each.

It was while David Lloyd George was making a name for himself as a rising star in the Welsh political and legal firmament that he got married. His bride was Margaret Owen, the only child of prosperous, middle class Welsh landowners who lived at Mynydd Ednyfed, an imposing farmhouse overlooking Cardigan Bay. Richard Owen farmed a hundred acres, invested in Portmadoc fishing fleets and drove cattle to Barnet Fair on the northern outskirts of London every autumn. Mary Owen was illiterate, but nonetheless formidable, determined to protect her daughter from unworthy suitors. 'Maggie', as Lloyd George called her, was a young woman of character and ability, four years younger than her lover, handsome rather than beautiful. Historians have claimed that she could satisfy Lloyd George neither physically nor intellectually,[23] but this is nonsense. During the years of their courtship they were very much in love and, indeed, fascinated by each other. She was considered to be the best catch of the neighbourhood and all agreed that he would be lucky to have her. Her parents, however, took some convincing. Lloyd George's good looks, charm and promising ability were not to be doubted. But they had pencilled in a highly suitable Methodist minister, John Owen, as Maggie's husband. Not only was Lloyd George a Baptist, but he had a bad reputation as a philanderer or worse. They therefore had no hesitation in ordering him to keep away from their daughter, while Maggie was forbidden to see him. So began a long series of clandestine meetings and furtive correspondence. Fortunately she kept his letters which give us a valuable window into his ambitions and values. Maggie once complained that she had thought that she was marrying just a Caernarvonshire lawyer. But she really had little excuse for getting him wrong. Take this for instance as a declaration of intent:

> My supreme idea is to get on. To this idea I shall sacrifice everything – except, I trust, honesty. I am prepared to thrust even love itself under the wheels of my juggernaut if it obstructs the way – that is if love is so much trumpery child's play as your mother deems courtship to be ... My love for you is sincere and strong. In this I shall never waver. But I must not forget that I have a purpose in life. And however painful the sacrifice I may have to make to attain my ambition, I must not flinch.[24]

If Maggie had any doubt as to the role she would be expected to play as Mrs Lloyd George, what about this estimate of the wife's role? He apparently had little sympathy for women's emancipation.

> You seem to think that the supreme function of a wife is to amuse her husband – to be to him a kind of twin or plaything to enable him to while away with enjoyment his leisure hours. Frankly that is simply prostituting marriage. My ideas are very different – if not superior – to

yours. I am of opinion that woman's function is to soothe and sympathise and not to amuse. Men's lives are a perpetual conflict. The life I have mapped out will be especially so – as lawyer and politician. Woman's function is to pour oil on the wounds – to heal the bruises of spirit received in past conflicts and to stimulate to renewed exertion. Am I not right? If I am, then you are pre-eminently the girl for me. I have a thorough belief in your kindliness and affection.[25]

While several of his letters were complaints that she had been late or had failed to arrive as promised, every now and again he set out his stall deliberately and provocatively. The question of his susceptibility to pretty young women was faced before their marriage, for instance when Maggie objected to her lover's friend-ship with Miss Jones, a Portmadoc fishmonger's daughter. He had the effrontery to quote Jesus Christ as his role model, for had not the first disciples been fishermen? Ultimately Maggie simply had to take him on trust: 'If you will be as faithful to me as I shall be to you, it will be all right.'[26] Alas for Maggie, he was not faithful to her, and the marriage was far from all right. But her parents' consent was eventually extracted by a mixture of their daughter's pleading and Lloyd George's plausibility.

They were married on 24 January 1888 at Pencaenewydd's remote Methodist chapel, a few miles from Criccieth. The ceremony was conducted jointly by the Rev. John Owen and Uncle Lloyd. This admirable venture in ecumenicalism was presumably too provoc-ative to be held nearer to civilisation. But they left Criccieth to a noisy send-off from friends and neighbours including fireworks and bonfires, for a honeymoon in London. They saw *Hamlet* and *HMS Pinafore*. Maggie had to intervene when her husband was involved in fisticuffs with a cabbie over a disputed fare. They eventually returned to Maggie's parents' house in Criccieth and remained married for 53 years until Maggie's death in 1941. When Maggie became pregnant with Richard and again soon afterwards with Mair Eluned, Lloyd George was left unfulfilled and had a liaison with a Caernarvon widow. She too became pregnant and had to be bought off. Maggie was kept in the dark.[27] But for an ambitious politician it was a time-bomb fully primed.

No doubt such an apparently sound marriage benefited Lloyd George socially and politically. At any rate, now feeling ready for Westminster, he was adopted as the Liberal Party candidate for Caernarvon Boroughs (Caernarvon, Bangor, Conwy, Nefyn, Pwllheli and Criccieth). This was a marginal seat in which there were too many pubs for Liberal comfort. It had been won for the Conservatives in the 1886 general election by an elderly, widely respected barrister, Edmund Swetenham. Lloyd George was not an automatic choice by any means. True, his allies had engineered his election as a Caernarvonshire Alderman and as a Nonconformist he cashed in on the late nineteenth century revival in North Wales. Furthermore, his triumphs in the court room and his spell-binding oratory (when appropriate in Welsh) were famous. However, his insolence to establishment figures and his assaults on the Anglican Church were unlikely to go down well in a cathedral city (Bangor) or anglicised tourist centres (Caernarvon or Conwy). Just how remarkable his success was indicated by the calibre of his defeated rivals for the Liberal Party nomination: a famous Irish professor, a prominent preacher and a wealthy Montgomeryshire landowner. Still, having been adopted, Lloyd George worked hard mobilising support. The electorate, despite the 1884 Reform Bill, was only 4,000 – small enough for the Liberal candidate to exercise his charm and persuasion at a personal level.

The Tories sat back complacently as the next election was not due until 1892. But on 20 March 1890 when Lloyd George and Maggie were setting off for a day out in Caernarvon, an electrifying telegram arrived: 'Swetenham died last night'. It was indeed so. After an energetic day shooting game, the barrister had felt unwell over dinner and shortly afterwards had a heart attack in his library. Maggie wrote: 'The sunshine seemed to have gone from the day.' She was right. Her husband's juggernaut was about to roll.

Lloyd George threw himself into campaigning, visiting parts of the scattered, sprawling constituency hitherto ignored by politicians. He travelled by train and pony-trap, shaking hands and distributing Liberal leaflets everywhere. He even wrote a campaign song entitled '*George and Gladstone*', sung to '*Marching through Georgia*'. He was helped by prominent Welsh Liberal MPs such as S. T. Evans and W. Abraham ('Mabon') who spoke on his behalf. He was helped too by the Tories' selection of none other than the genial squire of Llanystumdwy, Ellis Nanney. He was not to be underestimated, but was hardly an automatic winner, for he was none too bright, had poor health and had no Welsh. Did he remember the village boy who led the refusal to say the Creed? Fortunately, Lloyd George's potentially lethal sex life remained hidden. In a speech in the Caernarvon Guild Hall, Lloyd George took the offensive. He had recently heard his colleague T. E. Ellis denigrated by a Tory opponent because he had been brought up in a cottage. But the Tories had not yet realised that 'the day of the cottage-bred man has at last dawned'.[28] Nevertheless, while Lloyd George had consistently put Wales before Liberalism, for instance advocating Welsh home rule, disestablishment and the Welsh language, he now 'trimmed' his nationalism so as not to alarm his more cautious Liberal supporters. He was not the only opponent of Ellis Nanney to fear a Tory victory in what was clearly going to be a tight contest.[29]

Excitement was feverish when the 3,908 votes cast were counted. Lloyd George wrote to his brother that the Tories were doing their level best, and indeed 'beneath their level best'. Sure enough when the voting papers were counted, Lloyd George's sharp-sighted agent spotted some Liberal votes concealed in the Tory pile. A recount produced the revised and final tally: Lloyd George, 1963; Ellis Nanney, 1945; Liberal majority, 18 – close, but enough. A riotous crowd escorted the victor to Mynydd Edynfed where a nursemaid on her mistress's behalf sent them packing lest they wake the baby. Lloyd George's triumph and Maggie's dereliction had begun. For she did not enjoy the life of a politician's wife or relish the triumph of the cottage-bred man, however brilliant.

2

An Unusual Backbencher (1890–1905)

I had my war-paint on.

– Lloyd George[1]

Fighting for Wales

DAVID LLOYD George spent the next 15 and a half years on the back benches with the rest of the Liberal MPs. Apart from a brief, inglorious interlude (1892–1895) when Gladstone followed by Rosebery ruled unhappily and ineffectually, the Tories monopolised power. Lloyd George eventually rose from obscurity to become a national figure and a key player in the Liberal revival which brought the Party to power in December 1905, and a seat in the Cabinet for the irrepressible member for the Caernarfon Boroughs. But it took time, patience and determination. How did Lloyd George manage it, given his lack of wealth and connections? He is frequently called an outsider, and so he was in an English context – truly another handicap.

However he was less of an outsider in Wales where he concentrated on building up a power-base before 'invading' England. His dazzling oratory, considerable journalistic ability and flair for publicity soon brought him before the Welsh public's attention. The Liberal Party leadership found that they could not ignore him. Paradoxically, Lloyd George spent comparatively little time in Wales. Not for him the nursing of his constituency by living there and getting to know his constituents. As he once remarked to J. Hugh Edwards, a fellow Liberal MP, 'John Hugh, you and I, we would do anything for Wales – except live there'. He disliked Criccieth which he described as 'a miserable, down-at-heel backwater'. Wales and its people bored him, compared to the bright lights of London and the wider world. There were periods in his political career when his constituents complained that they were virtually disenfranchised. Consequently Lloyd George depended on his wife, his uncle and his brother to represent him in the Caernarfon Boroughs and keep him informed as to what was going on, such as the prevalence of damaging gossip. They kept him up to date with the strength of the local political parties relevant in 1890 as the next general election was only two years away and the Tories had selected as their candidate the popular and experienced Sir John Puleston.

Lloyd George attracted support by campaigning for the disestablishment and disendowment of the Anglican Church in Wales, the improvement of education and better terms for tenant farmers. He defended Welsh-speaking employees of the London and North Western Railway who were threatened with dismissal if they could not speak English. He advocated the curtailment of the powers and privileges of brewers and publicans (mostly Tories). This last was the subject of his maiden speech in the Commons in which he supported A. H. D. Acland's suggestion that compensation for the closure of public houses in Wales should be devoted to educational causes. He spoke wittily and concisely for 17 minutes. He wrote to Maggie that 'he had scored a success and a great one, and had been overwhelmed with congratulations'.[2] He enjoyed boasting to his nearest and dearest, taking praise at face value, however fulsome. All in all he made a fair fist of battling for the downtrodden. He pinpointed the millions living in degradation and poverty, when £200 was spent on a steamer, which conveyed the new Lord Lieutenant of Ireland, Lord Zetland, to Dublin, and £2,000 on rigging him up in all his finery.[3]

Since MPs were then unpaid, he relied on William for financial support, especially on the profits made by Lloyd George and George, never very substantial at the best of times and now reduced by the senior partner's frequent absences. Easily resisting the euphoria of David's by-election victory, William grasped the financial implications of his brother's success if indeed he was now to live for most of the time in London. He wrote in his diary: 'For the village lad to have beaten the parish county squire is a great honour. Two practical questions present themselves: (a) How is D. to live there? (b) How am I to live down here?'[4]

Maggie's parents built a couple of solid semi-detached houses on the seafront at Criccieth, living in one themselves and donating the other to their daughter and her famous but improvident husband. Maggie infinitely preferred Criccieth to London. On the healthy and inexpensive edge of Cardigan Bay she bore David's children – Richard (1889), Mair Eluned (1890), Olwen (1892), Gwilym (1894) and Megan (1902). She lived on her parents' charity and on the generosity of her saintly brother-in-law. Even Uncle Lloyd was critical of David's exploitation of William, noting in his diary how William commuted between Porthmadoc, Pwllheli, Festiniog, Criccieth, Caernarfon and all stations in between, often getting home on the milk train in the small hours.

David, meanwhile, opened a branch of the family firm in London, but he never devoted enough time or effort to make it a success. His priorities were political. He triumphed in the 1892 general election, polling 2,154 votes against Puleston's 1,958, a creditable majority of 196 as against the recount two years previously. When the result was announced, Lloyd George made a witty and gracious speech, claiming that his victory was not to be attributed to him but to the popularity of Liberal principles. He promised not to be a political partisan, but a true representative of the Boroughs of Caernarfon. According to the North Wales Chronicle 'he was willing to represent even Sir John Puleston (laughter)'.[5]

Unfortunately for his marriage, Lloyd George believed that he could best serve his constituents' interests in London. This he no doubt genuinely believed, though it was what he wanted to believe. It was not simply that the southeast was the centre of government and of the empire. In other respects London, the city of sin, fascinated the country boy from Llanystumdwy. To be fair to Lloyd George, one of his most traumatic experiences was a visit to the east end of London where his eyes were opened to real poverty and exploitation. Furthermore, William George vigorously defends his brother from the charge of neglecting Wales, detailing the time, effort and speeches delivered to the House of Commons on such issues as Welsh harbours and 'questions affecting Wales and the Welsh Language', plus 'Railway Rates and Light Railways'.

Between 1890 when he entered Parliament and 1899 when the Boer War transformed his political prospects, Lloyd George was actively involved in Welsh politics, especially the Cymru Fydd movement.

Emyr Price, in his engaging biography, argues that during these years Lloyd George was a genuine Welsh nationalist who believed that the Principality could be united in the pursuit of justice for all, Welsh devolution, the disestablishment of the Anglican Church in Wales, and the common use of the Welsh language. Other historians such as J. Graham Jones and Kenneth Morgan suggest that Lloyd George to a certain extent used Wales as a springboard for his parliamentary career at Westminster and beyond. What is beyond dispute is that Cymru Fydd and its dynamic leader hit the buffers in South Wales in early 1896 when Lloyd George was shouted down by 'people sunk into a morbid footballism' at a meeting in Newport – a defeat which a follow-up gathering of party officials at Cardiff could not erase. It was the end of Cymru Fydd. Lloyd George now became convinced that he could only achieve justice for Wales from an established platform in the House of Commons.

Whatever alibis Lloyd George could quote for his absences from North Wales, the marriage was soon under strain. The first major crisis was caused by a flirtatious, bored doctor's wife, Catherine Edwards who publicly claimed that Lloyd George was the father of her illegitimate child. The resulting court case went Lloyd George's way due to brother William's expertise and Maggie's loyalty. Lloyd George's great-nephew W. R. P. George was convinced of his great-uncle's innocence, though Ffion Haig is inclined to acquit Lloyd George on the paternity charge but condemn him on the accusation of adultery. We shall never know for sure. But Maggie was deeply distressed, especially when a more formidable rival than Catherine Edwards ensnared her husband in London.

It was cheaper for Lloyd George to accept hospitality from colleagues such as Sir Charles Henry or Timothy Davies, a prosperous Welsh businessman who established a comfortable home in Putney at his house called Pantycelyn, after a Welsh hymn-tune. Lloyd George, for all his enthusiasm for Welsh hymn-tunes, especially appreciated good food, warm fires and the charms of his hostess, Elizabeth Davies (always referred to as 'Mrs Tim' in the frequently acrimonious correspondence between Lloyd George and his wife). Lloyd George sometimes stayed at the Liberal Club, sometimes in a set of rooms he rented near Grey's Inn, sometimes in cheap 'digs' nearer Parliament. But he often found accommodation with friends and colleagues who were married to susceptible wives. Lloyd George was soon writing self-pitying and offensive diatribes to his wife, far away in North Wales – though not far enough for her to be conned by her husband who defended himself from her accusation that he was far too kind to Mrs Timothy Davies, giving her his seats at the opera and neglecting his professional duties in order to spend time with her. This handwritten letter, dated 27 May 1897 in the National Library of Wales, is a masterpiece of dishonesty and plausibility:

> My Dearest Jealous Maggie,
>   What a jealous little wife I have got to be sure! Now let me prove to her how groundless her suspicions are – as usual. So much was I in agreement as to the prior claims of the Grossgarth Davies's (another Welsh family) that I offered them my extra seat last night ... so poor Mrs Tim only came third or even fourth. But still I don't wish to occupy that back seat if you object. Is there anyone you would like me to convey my seat to? And now for the next point. You say I have done nothing and might as well have been down at Criccieth. Well, I was under the delusion until I received your letter that I had accomplished a good deal. I have just put through the scheme for organising Wales. D. A. (D. A. Thomas, later Lord Rhonnda) is also under the impression that I have done it. For all that you may be right and I may have had nothing to do with it after all ... But I think I must add fuel to your jealousy and warn you that unless you turn up, I'll go gallivanting with Mrs Tim or some other Miss or Mrs.[6]

Maggie's reluctance to come to London was indeed a problem. In her absence her husband could get up to all kinds of tricks. Ever the tactician, Lloyd George acted on the principle that attack was the best form of defence. Because no one was there to look after his creature comforts, he claimed that he never had clean underwear – indeed he had worn the same drawers for a fortnight. In a letter written at about the same time he accused Maggie of being a bad wife:

> Be candid with yourself – drop that infernal Methodism which is the curse of your better nature and reflect whether you have not rather neglected your husband. I have more than once gone without break-fast. I have scores of times come home in the dead of night to a cold, dark and comfortless flat without a soul to greet me. I am not the nature either physically or morally that I ought to have been left like this. You have been a good mother. You have not – and I say this now not in anger – always been a good wife. My soul as well as my body

has been committed to your charge and in many respects I am helpless as a child.[7]

This was all very well, and indeed there was an element of truth in Lloyd George's indignant self-pity. One can perhaps sympathise with him when he defied his wife to expose him in public, if that was what she really wanted, or when he assured her that he could quote dozens of his contemporaries who slept around. But it is surely significant that all the children of the marriage sided with their mother. Olwen offers the following account of how Maggie's suspicions of Mrs Tim were confirmed: Lloyd George invited his children to guess who had given him a new pen – the correct answer being Maggie. 'Is it a lady?' 'Yes.' 'Do you kiss her?' 'Yes.' Here, the tactless Olwen asked, 'Is it Mrs Timothy Davies?' The following embarrassing silence said it all.

It is only fair to Lloyd George to record that he did his best to compensate for his infidelities by becoming a regular correspondent with not only Uncle Lloyd and William, but with Maggie to whom he frequently wrote in affection and trust, only occasionally quarrelling with her. His letters were usually chatty, loving and somewhat self-preening, this, for example from a meeting in Cardiff where one wonders if his South Wales critics were quite as enthusiastic as he claimed:

> Well, last night was an immense success. Place crowded to the bung with a highly intelligent audience. Splendid reception when I rose – all the audience rose and cheered and still finer reception when I sat down, they rose again and cheered frantically. There is a leading article on it in the South Wales Daily News about the impression I made. How I raised the audience to a high level and highly eulogistic. The editor was present.[8]

Lloyd George's letters home were frequently demanding. In July 1890 he asked Maggie to tell William and Uncle Lloyd that he would be 'very disappointed' if he did not receive long letters from both of them. He requested clothes, documents, shaving tackle – and always sandwiched between great gobbets of self-praise. The marriage remained firm, though often tempestuous, as long as Lloyd George merely fell in lust with his many lady friends. Maggie did not like or approve of these affairs, but ultimately knew that she remained his girl.[9] 'Come on, you wouldn't want me any different, would you?', he impenitently chided her. Not surprisingly, given their personalities, there were frequent rows between the couple, which certainly upset Dick who recalled one occasion when he shouted at his father, 'Don't hurt Mamie!'[10] But even Maggie recognised that, in October 1905, Mrs Tim saved Lloyd George's life when she summoned a doctor to deal with a nasty haemorrhage in his throat.

Alas, all was to change when Miss Stevenson arrived on the scene in summer 1912. Before that cataclysmic event, Lloyd George's infidelities were typical of many a professional couple's marriages where man and wife jogged along, more or less. Lloyd George remained a doting father, discussing with Maggie the health of their children in a concerned way, even at a distance of 250 miles. He was clearly fond of Dick, telling Maggie how 'the poor little fellow slept before his dada got up and did not see the great reception he met with'.[11] His eldest daughter, Mair Eluned, was always his favourite; he was delighted with the way she jumped over hedges and stiles on a country walk. However, there is no reason to doubt the sincerity of his affection for all of his children and his regret that he could not see more of them. Unfortunately, there was no doubt about his ultimate priority, as he had warned Maggie before they were engaged. Now his juggernaut rolled on:

> I do hope Will can get on without me the coming week. If not it can't be helped. I must get down there [presumably Criccieth] Monday night's mail, and that is all. My blood is up and I am in for it. I care not for anything or anybody – except my pets of course – a thousand kisses to them all.[12]

Unfortunately money remained as big a problem as marriage. Lloyd George succumbed as many impoverished adventurers have done to the temptation of a fast buck. It was not that he was grossly extravagant: unlike his friend Winston Churchill ('My tastes are simple: I am easily satisfied with the best.') he was neither a drunkard nor a glutton. Granted, he sent his children to fee-paying schools, he was always nattily dressed and he liked a cigar – though he probably received as complimentary dinner gifts more than he needed, once inviting a young visitor to help himself from a collection on his desk – 'Choose a good one, mind'. Perhaps his greatest extravagance was a taste for foreign travel. We catch a glimpse of him holidaying in Normandy with his friends who tried in vain to teach him to ride a bicycle; his co-ordination was so hopeless that he fell off on several painful occasions and eventually wrecked the machine.

Not an expensive mistake perhaps, but he was interested enough to invest when some North Wales acquaintances headed by Harlech mining engineer, David Richards, believed that there was gold to be mined in Patagonia, where Welsh folk had settled for half a century. The venture was a failure: if there was any gold there, Richards never found it. Lloyd George foolishly wasted his own money and, more culpably, persuaded his brother and several of his friends to follow him. Typically his chief concern was that Uncle Lloyd should not find out that his beloved nephew was a failed gambler. For several months only Will and Maggie knew about the scheme, as Lloyd George's letter to Maggie, dated 16 August 1893 implies:

> Patagonia is, I fear, a failure. Don't let uncle or anyone else know a word. Hoefer wires that 'the property falls short of representations ... He will be here in a month and will let us know whether it is worthwhile going on with the matter any further. Will and I may be able to save ourselves to a great extent by a stiff lawyers' bill but we must of course lose a lot of money. Just like our luck.[13]

Lloyd George's eventual progress from rags to riches was uneven. He died worth £139,855 which a modern scholar equates to about £6.5 million in today's values. But his extremely welcome ministerial salary at the Board of Trade in 1906 did not save him from gambling unwisely in Marconi shares six years later. He bought shares in the *Daily Chronicle*, but otherwise confined his speculative ventures to authorship (see Chapter 9) at which he was modestly successful, and farming at Churt and Ty Newydd where his profits were much less than he liked to claim (see Chapter 12). Unfortunately, he meddled and interfered with his reasonably competent farm managers.

During his first decade as an MP Lloyd George developed the necessary skills as a parliamentary debater. He learnt the rules of the House and became skilful at thinking on his feet. He was not easily discomposed by the good and the great, for example defying Gladstone's famous glare when he opposed a bill for disciplining errant Anglican clergy – he flippantly preferred drunken to sober priests, anticipating his future colleague Clemenceau's adage that 'there was only one thing worse than a bad priest and that was a good priest'. Lloyd George and three fellow Welsh MPs were wrongly blamed for bringing down Rosebery's administration by siding with the Tories, but truly Rosebery needed little demolition. ('As you know,' he once wrote to a friend, 'I am not a supporter of the government.') Not that unpopularity ever bothered Lloyd George overmuch: his chief political crusade was the Cymru Fydd movement which was dedicated to Welsh culture, the Welsh language and ultimately Welsh self-government. But, as we have seen, he failed to unite North and South Wales, on one occasion in January 1896 suffering the indignity of being shouted down at a meeting in Newport when a Cardiff Englishman defeated him in argument.

An Unlikely Pro-Boer

Lloyd George's real breakthrough in national politics came as a result of the Boer War. When it began in October 1899 he was in Canada as a guest of the government there, and had to come hurriedly home. By the end of December, the British armies in South Africa had been humiliated. Salisbury's government had to replace the incompetent General Sir Redvers Buller as Commander-in-Chief with Field Marshal Roberts, supported by Kitchener as Chief of Staff. Even these paladins of Empire with 450,000 troops behind them could not defeat the Boer army of 70,000 well-equipped and well-led farmers, soon reduced to 2,000 irregulars. Until the summer of 1902 when a compromise peace was signed at Vereeniging, Lloyd George had a field day – diplomatic, military and moral.

Lloyd George was neither a pacifist nor a little-Englander who deplored the British Empire, but he regarded war as a disaster, representing civilisation's failure to settle disputes sensibly. The Boer War was a disgrace. It was not so much that it was unnecessary, but that it was clearly the result of the Colonial Secretary's intransigence, in Prime-Minister Salisbury's words, 'Joe's war', caused by the refusal of Joseph Chamberlain to negotiate a compromise. The problem was that the Dutch/Boer government of the Transvaal had become immensely rich due to the discovery of the Rand gold and diamond mines. President Kruger invited immigrants (uitlanders) to work the mines for generous wages but scant political rights. In 1896, Chamberlain secretly backed an invasion of the Transvaal by the irresponsible adventurer, Dr Leander Starr Jameson. The uitlanders were supposed to rise against Kruger's regime in Jameson's support. But the plot miscarried disastrously. Jameson and his merry band were rounded up. Chamberlain denied any knowledge – 'the lying-in-state', as one wit called it. Kruger responded by purchasing machine guns from Germany in readiness for the next round. 'What do you want them for?' demanded Milner, the British High Commissioner. 'Oh, Kaffirs, Kaffirs' (i.e., blacks) was Kruger's not wholly convincing answer. The British transported a sizeable army to the Cape and refused to withdraw it in response to Kruger's ultimatum. The Boers therefore invaded. The ensuing British defeats were embarrassing enough: if the Boers had headed straight for Capetown, the war would have been over by Christmas 1899. Diplomatic incompetence would have been crowned by military failure on a staggering scale. The British Lion would have been subjected to worldwide ridicule.

Lloyd George was an intuitive military strategist. He distrusted experts, generals in particular, his conflict with the high command reaching its climax in World War I. In the Boer War, however, he was on the side-lines, never visiting South Africa. Yet he felt instinctively that the British had got it wrong. How could it be otherwise when 70,000 Boer troops, soon reduced to 2,000 irregulars, defeated 450,000 British and colonial soldiers of whom 22,000 died? The war had cost around £223 million. Things went from bad to worse when Kitchener decided that the only way to defeat the Boer irregulars was to cut them off from their supplies. Boer farmhouses were burnt down and their wives and children imprisoned in concentration camps where over 20,000 died. The Nazis were right to claim that concentration camps were a British invention. These tactics, objectionable morally, proved to be disastrous militarily. Household names 15 years later – French, Haig, Gough – charged across the empty velt at the head of cavalry units until they were held up by cleverly concealed Boer machine-gunners. Men and horses died like flies. Lessons were not learnt. Meanwhile continental observers led by the German Kaiser laughed uproariously at the humiliation of the unpopular British imperialists whose tails were clearly being twisted with impunity.

Lloyd George was unjustly blamed for joining in the laughter, for he was too good a patriot for that. He needed no expert tuition to appreciate the moral implications of diplomatic and military disgrace. Lloyd George was profoundly influenced by his chapel background even if he was not tightly bound by orthodox Christian belief. Throughout his life in politics he was always on the side of the underdog, like the Welsh. He had total contempt for the bullying tactics of 'Joe's War'. 'Have you the right to be unjust to a man because he is poor and weak and insignificant?', he demanded of the House of Commons. 'Every honest man would say you should treat him with more generosity.'[14] In general, Lloyd George suspected big businesses, especially Jewish, of involvement in the war. More precisely he was convinced that the Birmingham munitions firm Kynoch's was profiting from selling arms to the British army. The Chairman of Kynoch's was Arthur Chamberlain, Joe's brother. This particular scandal was juicier than Lloyd George realised, in that Kynoch's also sold arms to the Boers. Joseph Chamberlain's protestations of innocence did not carry conviction. The hitherto ineffectual leader of the Liberal Party, Sir Henry Campbell-Bannerman, increased his own street-credibility when he described the army's resort to concentration camps as 'methods of barbarism'. Lloyd George was glad to back him. The hands of the British Government, he averred, were 'stained with the blood' of Boer children. The Liberal Party should take its cue from Sir Henry who personified old-fashioned kind-heartedness, a man who used to commiserate with whichever of his walking-sticks he had to leave behind.[15]

No prominent politician divided the nation on the issue of the Boer War more decisively than Lloyd George. As it happened, the Liberal Party was torn between its imperialist wing (Grey, Asquith, Haldane) and its radicals (Campbell-Bannerman, Morley, Lloyd George.) The Tories were unanimous in supporting the war though some were uneasy about the camps. Their new leader, Salisbury's nephew Arthur James Balfour, had a soft spot for Lloyd George, once unhelpfully commending him to Campbell-Bannerman for future cabinet office. The country was bitterly divided, no more so than in the Caernarfon Boroughs. Lloyd George was beaten up, hit on the head and shouted down in public meetings. His family were victimised. Uncle Lloyd and William George were burnt in effigy. Lloyd George's face became lined and his hair turned grey. His elder son Dick was bullied at Dulwich College. In his biography of his father, Dick recalls how bewildered he was: 'I could not put forward my case – look, chaps, this is me, Dick. Dick Wales. You know. What's wrong with you fellows? I'm just the same as I ever was.' They repeatedly stole his cap so that eventually Maggie forced the truth out of her son. 'I won't have it!', she shouted, and insisted on Dick being enrolled at Portmadoc Grammar School where he became the school's most fluent Welsh-speaker.[16]

All this pales before the events of the celebrated meeting in Birmingham Town Hall on 13 December 1901, when a mob of at least 30,000 shouted 'Kill him!', and prevented Lloyd George from speaking. Ironically, Lloyd George intended to discuss Liberal reunification under Sir Henry Campbell-Bannerman. But the mob never discovered this. Chamberlain regretted that a police escort of over 300 frustrated the mob when Lloyd George was smuggled out disguised as a policeman. PC James Stonier, who was told to swap clothes with the little Welshman recalled that Lloyd George was reluctant to go ahead with the disguise, as he thought it would make him look ridiculous, while Stonier himself had the greatest difficulty getting into Lloyd George's clothes. They got away with it, though unfortunately two people were killed and 40 seriously injured. One of the dead was a policeman, the other a rioter. 'Poor fellow', Lloyd George wrote to his brother about the rioter, 'I suppose it was his own fault, but no doubt he was disinterested'.[17] Lloyd George received letters both threatening and appreciative addressed to 'PC Lloyd George'.[18]

It is impossible not to admire Lloyd George's moral and physical courage in standing up for the Boers. There is irony indeed given the subsequent history of white South Africa under Kruger's successors. Apartheid was hardly the ideal legacy for Wales' greatest democrat, and the 13,000 blacks who died in Kitchener's concentration camps were the forerunners of the victims of sad and disgraceful events such as Sharpeville. But this is to abuse hindsight. One can only admire Lloyd George's courage and idealism when he addressed his constituents during the 'khaki' election of October 1900. His Tory opponent, Colonel Platt, had accused him of disloyalty to Her Majesty's troops. Lloyd George replied:

> Five years ago the electors of the Caernarfon Boroughs handed me a strip of blue paper, the certificate of my election, to hand to the Speaker as their accredited representative. If I never again represent the Caernarfon boroughs in the House of Commons, I shall at least have the satisfaction of handing back that blue paper with no stain of human blood upon it.[19]

The result on 6 October 1900: Lloyd George, 2,412; Platt, 2,116.

Lloyd George's opposition to the Boer War was perhaps the most idealistic act of his life in politics. He lost financially, in that his resulting unpopularity drove clients away from Lloyd George and

George. He encountered physical dangers including serious attempts on his life. Members of his family were threatened. Maggie had a worrying few days when her husband accepted the invitation to speak in Birmingham. Maybe the odious racist Paul Kruger was an unusual angel. But all in all Lloyd George was indeed on the side of the angels when he opposed the monstrous waste of blood and money which the Boer War involved: 'Not a lyddite shell exploded but it carried away an old age pension', he told the Liberals of Caermarthen. Lloyd George's career in politics benefited enormously from his courageous stance against the Boer War. He was no longer an obscure backbencher. People disagreed with him over what he had done. But he became an instantly recognisable national figure whose courage, eloquence and humour demanded respect. He was no longer an unknown Welshman: he was a prominent, key-player on the British stage who could look forward to high office in a future Liberal government.

Balfour's Education Act, 1902

Lloyd George's next challenge was directed against the Education Act which the Conservative Leader of the House, A. J. Balfour, introduced in March 1902 and continued to pilot through Parliament after he had succeeded his uncle Lord Salisbury as Prime Minister. It is known as 'Balfour's Act'. While the Boer War had made Lloyd George's reputation nationally, even among Liberals he had remained a divisive figure. Now he was lucky enough to be involved in a row which united Liberals in both England and Wales. The controversy over Balfour's Education Act gave him the leadership of Anglo–Welsh Nonconformity – and therefore a preeminent position in the Liberal Party as a whole.

Whether Lloyd George's assault on the Act was wholly to his credit is a fair question. According to John Grigg: 'The Education controversy of 1902–1905 is an important rather than a glorious episode in Lloyd George's career. It was a pity that he had to take the line he did, because it was largely insincere.'[20] Prompted by Grigg's scepticism as to Lloyd George's honesty and integrity, we have to ask, did Lloyd George have the interests of English and Welsh children at heart, or was he fighting for the Liberal Party's advantage or indeed his own?

Arthur James Balfour seemed a natural target for Lloyd George's acerbic wit – a strange man, very Eton and Trinity, a fastidious bachelor whose school nicknames were 'Clara' and 'Pretty Fanny'.

According to Winston Churchill, 'he was like a powerful and graceful cat walking delicately and unsoiled across a rather muddy street'. He once demolished Asquith by claiming that 'his lucidity is a positive disadvantage when he has nothing to say'.[21] Yet he and Lloyd George admired and respected each other. Balfour referred to Lloyd George behind his back as 'the Little Man' without any wish to belittle. Both realised that there was a lot wrong with British education. There was also a lot wrong with the Department of Education presided over by the uninspiring and lazy Duke of Devonshire. Unfortunately, the chief civil servant, Robert Morant, who really cared about education, could not overrule his political masters. The Vice-President was Sir John Gorst who, when not administering pinpricks to his departmental boss, used to read his speeches to the senior clerk in the department before delivering them in the Commons: 'This will tickle them up', 'them' being his own government, or 'Balfour won't like this; he'll squirm'.[22] No wonder Balfour led from the front.

The Act tried to tidy up the inefficient and wasteful coexistence of Voluntary (i.e., Church) and Board Schools, putting them all under County Council and County Borough Education Committees. The rate-payer now became responsible for funding both Voluntary and Board schools. In return, members of the County Councils were to be involved in the appointment of teachers. Religion was to be taught outside the regular timetable, so that opportunities for pros-elytising by Anglican vicars were limited. Thus, there was something for both sides in the bargain. The Act also addressed the absence of secondary schools in most towns and country districts apart from those in the independent sector. County Councils were encouraged to provide grammar or technical schools, though unfortunately there was no obligation to do so. There was indeed a real problem here: not only did the Boer War reveal the physical decrepitude of British youth when a third of recruits to the army were rejected as unfit – a scandalous state of affairs which the Boy Scout movement founded by Boer War hero General Baden-Powell was supposed to rectify, but the scientific and technological backwardness of British education, and consequently of British industry and Britain's armed forces was there for all to see. For instance, British ship design was flawed, illus-trated by the vulnerability of the Royal Navy's capital ships shortly to be revealed at Jutland (31 May 1916) as Admiral Beatty famously observed.[23] The Kaiser enjoyed pointing out the inadequacy of British locomotive design after Queen Victoria's funeral train only just made it on time to Victoria Station.

The prevalence of the Arts, especially the Classics, over science was self-evident in society as a whole. Not until 1979 did Margaret Thatcher become the first ex-professional scientist to be Prime Minister. By opposing radical advances in technical and scientific education, Lloyd George was definitely not on the side of progress. Nor did he support the features of the bill which tidied up the muddle in British educational administration. John Grigg is right to suggest that Lloyd George displayed cynical opportunism in changing his attitude to Balfour's Bill when he saw on which side his political bread was buttered. Perhaps lack of perception rather than insincerity was his crime, though there was certainly some inconsistency in his attitude. In a letter to Maggie, Lloyd George gave his first impressions:

> Balfour is developing a most revolutionary Education Bill. Sweeps away School Boards – creates the County Council the educational authority for the county and puts the School Boards and the Voluntary Schools under it … Up to the present I rather like the bill. It is quite as much as one would expect from a Tory Government.[24]

But Lloyd George soon changed his mind when the Nonconformist establishments in both England and Wales gave Balfour's Bill the thumbs down. They objected to any financial support for church schools by the rate-payer or the tax-payer. 'Rome on the rates' was their slogan, though in sober truth it was more a case of Canterbury on the rates. What would now be called 'faith schools' were to be supported by County Councils funded by rate-payers, the majority of whom – certainly in Wales – were Nonconformists, or at least non-Anglican. Nothing better illustrates Lloyd George's flexibility (some would say cynicism) than the way he changed his mind on Balfour's Act. When he saw which way the wind was blowing, he swung round to benefit personally from the change. In powerful, offensive speeches he recalled his childhood in Llanystumdwy School when the children were forced to learn the Creed and the Catechism and non-Anglicans were excluded from the teaching profession. 'I am a specimen of what your Church schools turn out', he taunted his Conservative opponents.[25] When Balfour persuaded his Anglican colleagues to agree to Nonconformists entering the lower grades of the profession, that provoked predictable howls of rage – 'why only the lower grades?' In the House of Commons Lloyd George prophesied that 'the clergyman would come down to the school like a roaring lion, seeking what Nonconformists he could devour at the expense of the rate-payer'. While this could be dismissed as knockabout stuff, Lloyd George gave a sober analysis of justifiable Nonconformist grievances, in that special advantages and privileges were to be given to Anglican but not to Nonconformist or Board schools:

> The Church have [*sic*] over 12,000 schools in the country, which are mission rooms to educate the children of the poor in the principles of the Church. In 8,000 parishes there are no other schools. The total expense of the staff in these schools is £3,400,000 yearly, and the State gives £3,600,000 per annum, so that the staff engaged in teaching Church of England principles is wholly paid by the state. Out of 2,000,000 children in Anglican schools, 1,000,000 are Nonconformists. The maintenance of the schools is now to be thrown entirely on the rates; they have simply to keep the schools in repair. They are grumbling even at this. The Duke of Northumberland writes to complain of it.[26]

His old enemy, the London and North Western Railway provided the setting for an unlikely confrontation which miraculously ended in attempted compromise and even friendship. When Lloyd George shared a railway carriage with his erstwhile enemy, A. G. Edwards, the Bishop of St Asaph, from Chester to London (Euston), he displayed one of his most attractive characteristics: the readiness to make concessions and see the best in an opponent. The two men – the Baptist freethinker and the Anglican prelate – got on fine. A few weeks later Lloyd George stayed overnight with the Bishop at his palace, received Holy Communion from him and borrowed an episcopal overcoat in order to play golf in the rain. He also arranged for the Bishop to officiate at his friend Winston Churchill's wedding. In private he became far more tolerant, prompting an archdeacon to ask him why a recent diatribe had been so rude. Lloyd George's reply was a classic: 'That was purely a fighting speech. I had my war paint on then.' On the other hand, he attacked the bill in forthright terms when it came up for its second reading in May 1902:

> You cannot base any good system of education on an injustice to a large section of the community. In Wales, at any rate, the vast majority

of the children are nonconformists, yet they are not allowed to enter the teaching profession except on condition of their becoming members of the Church of England.[27]

When the government allowed nonconformists to enter the lower grades of the teaching profession, Lloyd George indignantly demanded, 'Where does the principle of equality come, I ask?'[28]

Unfortunately, Balfour the Etonian philosopher, his senior civil servant Robert Morant, the Wykhamist intellectual and Lloyd George 'educated privately' by Uncle Lloyd, missed a great opportunity of bringing British primary and secondary schools up to date. As the Classics triumphed over modern languages and the sciences, religious prejudice triumphed over the children's welfare. As Joseph Chamberlain remarked to the Birmingham Liberal Unionists,: 'Believe me, gentlemen, if in this discussion we could hear a little more about the children and a little less about the sects, we should make greater progress.'[29] Such common sense was lost on Lloyd George. His priority was to mobilise the sects in both England and Wales in order to defend Nonconformist principles and thus promote the cause of the Liberal Party – and of himself. One of Lloyd George's parliamentary speeches attacking the Tory Party and the Anglican Church supposedly in favour of non-denominational instruction showed him at his most unctuous:

I have only one word to add. If you are going to teach religion in the true tradition of Christianity, there is only one book from which our children should be taught. It is the Word of God, the Holy Scriptures. We have had enough posturizing by bishops and priests. Let the cry go forth, 'Pray silence for the Master!'[30]

Was this Christian commitment or sanctimonious claptrap? To be fair, Lloyd George attacked the *social* teaching of the Catechism in refreshingly down to earth terms:

I was taught to order myself lowly and reverently to my betters. With an inquisitive instinct I asked, "Who are my betters?" and they said, "The squire" ... What is meant by being lowly? "By being lowly I understand that I must know and keep my true position ... You must cringe to the rich. If you see a wealthy man crawl before him ... Do you call this Christianity? Is this what the carpenter's Son came down for? No, it is not religion. It is snobbery ... Let the children hear for themselves the best friend they ever had, and the most dangerous foe the priest could ever encounter.[31]

Thus was Lloyd George's leadership of both Welsh and English Nonconformity cemented by such contrasting eloquence.

Arguably, Lloyd George aimed at the most obvious and tempting target, namely what he called 'priestcraft', when he should have supported Balfour's campaign for secondary education, especially in science. The 1902 Education Act really was an admirable measure which he should have continued to welcome – his first thoughts on the subject were right. As a consequence of Balfour's Act, 1,123 secondary schools had been established in England and Wales by the outbreak of World War I. Two-hundred thousand pupils attended these schools, one third of them on free places. Unfortunately, not enough science was taught, while the new schools were moulded socially by the ancient public school ethos of Eton and Winchester as represented by Balfour and Morant, that is to say prefects wearing gowns, compulsory uniforms, Latin and Greek as opposed to Italian and German, to say nothing of physics and chemistry. But the schools were actually there for the first time thanks to Balfour, Morant and his allies such as Sidney and Beatrice Webb; Bernard Shaw and R. H. Tawney among the Fabians; and R. B. Haldane from Lloyd George's own party, who especially admired Sidney Webb's efforts on behalf of secondary and tertiary education in London.

Here Lloyd George's record compares badly with Webb the Fabian, a far less charismatic figure who had nevertheless founded the London School of Economics and proved that a local authority could run secondary schools. Webb was a genuine crusader who believed that all British citizens deserved the best, from infant schools to tertiary colleges. Here he is responding to a suggestion that society could not afford to provide secondary education for the many because there would always be a need for 'hewers of wood and drawers of water' for the convenience of the few (in other words, the professional classes):

> I want no class of hewers of wood and drawers of water, no class destined to remain there and forbidden from rising, because we do not provide for it. I cannot believe that we are only to provide the means of instruction for a limited number of people, who we think will rise, while the rest are to toil for our convenience. For our convenience! Our comfort is to stand in the way of enabling these people,

our fellow citizens, to attain anything better than being mere hewers of wood and drawers of water. I must apologise for betraying a little heat, but I do object to the notion that for our convenience, we are to keep people as hewers of wood and drawers of water.[32]

These are great words. Sidney and Beatrice Webb were a formidable partnership who persuaded Balfour 'to use his majority like a gentleman' (Beatrice Webb's diary) in the cause of the entire nation's young people. They battled for what would, half a century later, emerge as the comprehensive ideal – and for the teaching of science and technology.

Lloyd George, by contrast, looked backwards, devoting himself to obstructing the Act, especially in Wales, by rabble-rousing tirades about 'priestcraft' and 'Rome on the rates'. His campaign there providentially coincided with an evangelical revival. The government had to introduce a default bill which denied local authorities who refused to implement the Act state funding. When Chamberlain asked Morant why the state could not simply subsidise state schools, the reply was unanswerable: 'Because of your war, there's no money left.' Typically, Lloyd George at the same time negotiated with the Bishop of St Asaph and with Morant in pursuit of compromise. This attempt failed – it was condemned both by St Asaph's Anglican colleagues and by Welsh Nonconformists. But it illustrates again Lloyd George's willingness to break ranks for the greater good of the Liberal Party and for idealistic causes in which he believed. In England Lloyd George appeared on public platforms with the Baptist Dr John Clifford, in a joint campaign to mobilise English nonconformity as a political movement, opposed to the Act. He also recruited Liberals such as Rosebery, Asquith and Grey.

Lloyd George's humour contrasted with the austere eloquence of 'John the Baptist'. Here he is mocking the way that teachers would be appointed in schools run by Anglican clergy:

How will this Bill work to select a teacher? Three men will come, each having good certificates. Well, the first man comes up. First-rate testimonials, splendid experience, all speak well of him … Then the parson says: 'What are your views about the apostolic succession?' (Laughter) The teacher says: 'I have no views about it.' Then the parson says: 'You can go.' The second man comes up. Very good testimonials – not so good as the first. Still, they are good … The parson says: 'Can you play the organ?'

He says: 'No, but I can play the cornet.' (Laughter) They say: 'No thank you, we don't think that will do.' The third man comes with third class testimonials, third class experience, third-class certificates. The parson says: 'Can you play the harmonium?' He says: 'Yes, like Paderewski.' (Roars of laughter). I am not sure that is the instrument which he plays. However, Paderewski is appointed. The one thing which will dominate the selection of the teacher is the handiness of the man for the purpose of assisting the clergy on Sundays. He is the clerical handiman.[33]

Lloyd George attacked clerical control of schools by pointing out the absurdity of the chaplain in charge of a warship. 'The chaplain on the bridge' became a telling phrase to bandy around. In the House of Commons Lloyd George was tireless in standing up for Nonconformist children in Anglican schools. He spoke over 160 times, earning from Prime Minister Balfour the acknowledgement that 'the Member for Caernarvon Boroughs had played a most distinguished part and had shown himself to be a most eminent Parliamentarian'. It is strange that historians do not quote more of these speeches, though many are very brief and perhaps of ephemeral importance. What comes across is Lloyd George's devotion to detail and determination not to sell the pass to his old enemies, the squire and the parson. Balfour clearly felt that Lloyd George believed in what he was doing – hence the generous compliment. Whereas Lloyd George knew well what a sound education he himself had received from David Evans at the Church of England school in Llanystumdwy, nevertheless he was concerned that other children from Nonconformist homes should not be penalised. In this light, Grigg seems a little harsh in convicting Lloyd George of insincerity. Perhaps his greatest failure was to miss the importance of a continuous education from primary school to university for as many of his fellow citizens as possible, irrespective of class, race and gender. In this context, the Webbs were better democrats.

When the Liberals came to power, their attempts to improve the Act were frustrated not only by the House of Lords but by the real merits of Balfour's vision. Goodness knows, the bill was not perfect, but it worked. The way forward was to improve it, not obstruct it. To be fair to Lloyd George, Hansard proves that this was his aim. Furthermore the next major stage in the establishment of state education for all in Great Britain was Fisher's Act in autumn 1918 when Lloyd George himself was Prime Minister – a process which Balfour, Morant and the Webbs had begun.

In the meantime Lloyd George kept himself in the public eye. He campaigned incessantly not merely in North Wales, but in South Wales as well, in England and Scotland. He became a British politician. On 11 March 1904 he was invited to dine with Lord Tweedsmouth to meet Edward VII who had expressed a wish to be introduced to the fiery radical. 'Do you play Bridge?', asked the King. 'No.' 'That is a pity, for it is a very good game.'[34] That was the end of Lloyd George's intercourse with his sovereign – for the time being, at least. Meanwhile, he supported the Bethesda slate quarrymen in his own constituency who maintained a three-year strike against their tyrannical employer, Lord Penrhyn. He attacked the government's threat to trade-union practice by alleging that the employment of Chinese labourers in the Rand mines could be copied in British mines. He continued to 'go for Joe' by attacking Chamberlain's proposals to introduce Protection. Such measures divided the Tory Party, for Balfour's leadership was flabby and ineffectual. But thanks to Lloyd George's militancy on behalf of Free Trade to say nothing of free trade unions – he had his war-paint on now – the Liberal Party was united and ready for government.

So was Lloyd George. A remarkably prophetic anticipation of the great Welshman's future role on behalf of national efficiency and national welfare was expressed by Lord Milner in April 1903: 'Perhaps a great *Charlatan* – political scallywag, buffoon, liar, stump orator and in other respects popular favourite – may some day arise, who is nevertheless a *statesman* ... and who, having attained power by popular art, may use it for national ends.'[35] Lloyd George had yet to prove his ability to fulfil this not entirely flattering prediction. But in autumn 1905 the prospect of high office could not be ignored. Lloyd George's role as a backbencher had been colourful and entertaining. He had shone as a critic, as an iconoclast, as a wrecker. Success in these contexts had demanded courage and intelligence – and perhaps on occasions a dash of tendentious raillery if not downright dishonesty, as Milner had demanded. Time would tell if Lloyd George possessed the positive qualities necessary in office.

3

Cabinet Minister (1906–1909)

If you can meet with Triumph and Disaster
And treat those two impostors just the same

– R. Kipling, *If*

Triumph

AFTER MONTHS of dithering, on 4 December 1905, Balfour suddenly resigned. Why then? Possibly he believed that the Liberals were divided on free trade amongst other issues, possibly he had got wind of disloyalty among Campbell-Bannerman's colleagues, which might make it hard for him to form a government. Everyone was surprised, not least Lloyd George who was on holiday in Genoa with his brother William. He remarked cynically that the Tories were departing 'with their cheques in their hands', and hurried home so as to be available when the modern loaves and fishes were distributed.

Campbell-Bannerman was, in fact, faced with more acute problems than usual when making the key appointments to his Cabinet, not least with regard to his own position. A plot had been hatched by Asquith, Grey and Haldane whereby Campbell-Bannerman was to be shunted off to the Lords, while Asquith was to represent the Prime Minister in the Commons. The three plotters had met at Relugas, Grey's shooting-lodge in the Highlands. All three agreed not to take office unless 'CB' cooperated. But 'CB' had no intention of cooperating with 'Master Asquith', 'Master Grey' and 'Master Haldane', as he called them behind their backs. He had been tough enough to get the better of Arthur Balfour in a celebrated parliamentary confrontation:

> The Right Honourable Gentleman has asked certain questions which he seemed to think were posers ... I have no direct answer to give to

them. They are utterly futile, nonsensical and misleading. They are invented by the Right Honourable Gentleman for the purpose of occupying time in this debate. I say, enough of this foolery. Move your amendments and let us get to business.[1]

'Enough of this foolery', was a brilliant sally, not quickly forgotten. So when 'CB' accepted the King's commission, it was on his own terms. He remained in the Commons and all three Relugas conspirators fell into line, Asquith being the first to break ranks. Lloyd George knew little about Relugas. He had contempt for his upper-class colleagues whom he dismissed as 'the Eton-Balliol' clique. Campbell-Bannerman had reservations about Lloyd George, whom he had reason to regard as a troublemaker – 'I suppose we ought to include him'.[2] One is reminded of President Johnson's preference for a trouble-maker to be inside the tent rather than outside. But 'CB' recognised in Lloyd George a left-winger who would be a balancing influence against the Relugas brigade, and therefore offered him a place in the Cabinet, either in charge of the Local Government Board or the Board of Trade. There was a rumour that he had been offered the Home Office with the much higher salary of £5,000 per annum, but he did not relish sentencing criminals to be hanged or dispatching troops against strikers – and in any case Herbert Gladstone was appointed. Lloyd George was glad to accept the Presidency of the Board of Trade at £2,000, with guarantees about Wales and education – or so he claimed in a letter to William. Ordinary MPs were unpaid at this stage, so this relatively huge salary was welcome, especially as Lloyd George was £450 overdrawn despite his brother's generosity. It was some promotion for the boy from Llanystumdwy. Uncle Lloyd purred:

Had Welsh Cause guaranteed before undertaking office, granted him unreservedly. Am so proud of this, secured after all his self-spent life of efforts of all kinds on her behalf. Good Providence protect, help and bless my dearest boy, and crown his service to his generation by thy blessing.[3]

Lloyd George's first challenge was the general election of January 1906, which Campbell-Bannerman was happy to call at once, largely because a sizeable Liberal majority was expected. One reason for this was that in retrospect the Boer War had become intensely unpopular, so Lloyd George in particular was bound to benefit. Whereas hitherto Caernarvon Boroughs had been highly marginal, Lloyd George could now be confident of success. His opponent was R. A. Naylor, a non-Welsh-speaking timber merchant whose only distinction was the ability to write hymns. Lloyd George was so confident that he supported other candidates such as Timothy Davies (Mrs Tim's husband), travelling much of the way by car which inspired him to boast that he would puncture his opponent. So it turned out: Lloyd George 3,221; Naylor 1,997.

This was the first general election when Lloyd George's position was totally safe. He was one of 399 Liberal victors, giving them a sizeable majority of 128 over all other parties. Indeed, the collective reaction of the Liberal high command was initially one of astonished bewilderment combined with sloth, personified by their amiable and not especially dynamic chief. Asquith burrowed around in the Exchequer; Grey was absorbed by the Foreign Office where the officials were determined to keep him 'straight' (i.e., pro the Anglo-French Entente engineered in 1904 by the Tory specialist Lord Lansdowne who had had no trouble with Balfour, his fag at Eton); and Haldane went native in the unfamiliar War Office, where he created the Territorial Army and the British Expeditionary Force. Other ministerial colleagues were even less experienced, such as John Burns who, when offered the Local Government Board, exclaimed, 'Sir 'Enry, you never did a more popular thing in your life'. Lloyd George therefore, who exuded ability and initiative, stood out as a positive and self-confident star. This superiority increased during the next two and a half years as the new government went through a rather flat period during which a number of measures such as a licensing act and a new education bill were turned down by the Lords.

This interference with legislation put forward by a democratically elected government provoked indignation from the Board of Trade:

> If the House of Lords persisted in its present policy, it would be a much larger measure than the Education Bill that would come up for consideration. It would come up on this issue, whether the country was to be governed by the King and his peers or by the King and his people.[4]

The King exploded. His secretary Lord Knollys wrote to Campbell-Bannerman: 'His Majesty feels that he has a right and it is one on which he intends to insist, that Mr Lloyd George should not introduce the sovereign's name into those violent tirades of his ...'[5] Campbell-Bannerman, elderly and ailing, with a dying wife to look after, nevertheless supported his minister against his King. Mr Lloyd George, he maintained, was entitled to be offended by the Lords' interference with government policy, he had only mentioned the King because he did not want to imply that it was simply a question of peers versus people, and he could give no undertaking that Mr Lloyd George would not repeat such a sally.[6] And he was right not to. For on 26 June 1907 Lloyd George produced his most celebrated gibe about the House of Lords. To the suggestion that the Lords served as a watchdog, or a mastiff defending the constitution, he replied: 'A mastiff? It is the Right Hon. Gentleman's poodle. It fetches and carries for him. It barks for him. It bites anybody that he sets it on to.'[7] 'Mr Balfour's poodle' was a winner. Lloyd George at his wittiest.

Lloyd George was already in trouble with the King over his plans for a Welsh Assembly, and also with the Welsh people when he discouraged pursuit of disestablishment before the Lords were emasculated. He was certainly a hero in North Wales where his own people were intensely proud of their Cabinet Minister, but he had no intention of following previous Welshmen who had failed when challenged to identify the right tactics. Lloyd George insisted that the true opponent should be pursued, that is to say the power of the House of Lords. The fact was that Wales did not have any chance of fair play from the Lords as matters stood. They hated its radicalism, they despised its Nonconformity and they could indulge their scorn freely because Wales was so small. 'I will say this to my fellow countrymen. If they find the government manoeuvring its artillery into position for leading an attack on the Lords, the Welshmen who worried them into attending to anything else until the citadel had been stormed ought to be put in the guardroom.'[8]

This speech caused resentment in Wales and is a reminder that he was never afraid to preach home truths to his fellow countrymen. He gambled on his self-evident Welshness, enthusiasm for Welsh culture – he seldom missed an Eisteddford – and commitment to Welsh Nonconformity seeing off accusations of disloyalty to Wales. His commitment to his own land and people was emotionally and extravagantly conveyed in his speech to the Nonconformist League in Cardiff on 9 October 1907:

> No man gives his best to a people who distrust him. You have got to trust somebody. Let me say this to you. If you can find a better go to him, but in the meantime don't fire at us from behind. Who said that I was going to sell Wales? Seven years ago there was a little country which I never saw, fighting for freedom, fighting for fair play. I had never been within a thousand miles of it, never knew any of its inhabitants. Pardon me for reminding you. I risked my seat. I risked my livelihood. (A voice: 'You risked your life.' A roar from the meeting. By this time the audience was on its feet, some members were cheering, some including the speaker were sobbing.) Yes I risked my life. Am I going to sell the land I love? (A breathless silence, then in Welsh.) God knows how dear Wales is to me![9]

The guard room speech was forgotten. Lloyd George was again the people's hero: what a performance, in its blubbering hyperbole and shameless exploitation of his audience's emotions, typical of the hwyel of Welsh Nonconformity and prescient of other, more evil, racist, tub-thumping orators of doubtful honesty. Both sides, however, could invoke the highest authority for their measures. Conservative opponents of the government's Licensing Bill (1908) were to retaliate with placards piously proclaiming 'Thou shalt not steal'.[10]

Meanwhile, Lloyd George entered in to his kingdom with zest. His headquarters were in Whitehall Gardens, only a stone's throw from Westminster. His study, he claimed, was as large as the whole of the ground floor of the house which he and Maggie had bought in Routh Road. Among his first visitors were Mair and Olwen who were 'very pleased with the offices'. He quickly established a cordial relationship with his staff. His parliamentary secretary was Hudson Kearly, his permanent secretary was Hubert Llewellyn Smith, his Welsh secretary was John Rowland – all capable and loyal. They were supported by 750 civil servants of varying ranks and a budget of £270,000. Lloyd George was liked for his good humour and courtesy, and respected for his industry and quickness of mind. He mastered the necessary paperwork as though it was a lawyer's brief, though he preferred oral discussion with colleagues or subordinates who really knew their stuff and were prepared to confide in him. He liked to pick the brains of 'experts' outside the normal ranks of the officially qualified. His tendency to leap around from one topic to another earned him the not entirely flattering nickname of the 'Welsh Goat'. He chased out dinosaurs, for instance the head of the electricity board, who was incapable of working the intercom.[11] But on the whole he was a good boss. He did, however, have an eye for lady typists. Indeed, more or less to his dying day, Lloyd George made advances to female employees. There is a letter dated 2 June 1907 to John Rowland in the archives of the National Library of Wales from A. E. Widdows (personnel): 'He was afraid that even if the Lady in whom Mr Lloyd George is interested possesses the necessary qualifications it is impossible to hold out the hope of early employment ...'[12]

Lloyd George soon got down to more professional business. At a speech at the Guildhall in January 1906 he demonstrated his awareness that radical initiatives were necessary:

> Mr Lloyd George then stated that he had received a number of questions containing the following – 'Are you in favour of payment of Members of Parliament; of paying returning officers' fees out of Imperial taxes; of a Bill for settling trade union disputes; of amending the Compensation Act; of the taxation of ground rents; of old-age pensions?' Leaving out the last for a moment, he would say that he was absolutely in favour of all the others ... As to old-age pensions. The money spent on the South African War would have been sufficient to give old-age pensions to every man over 65. They had reckoned it up at the time. Therefore the matter, when taken up, must be taken up gradually. They must first of all put the national finances in spick and span order, and then see that every man too old to pursue his ordinary avocation should be saved from the humiliation of the workhouse or parish charity.[13]

While Lloyd George appreciated the necessity of seeing off the radical challenge of the Labour Party, he was also anxious to promote British trade. 'How can I help British industry?' he demanded. His Merchant Shipping Bill reflected interest in seamen's welfare dating back to Portmadoc days, but also his willingness to accommodate the employers. He risked provoking sailors' hostility by raising the Plimsoll Line, established by W. Plimsoll 30 years before to outlaw 'coffin ships', sent to sea deliberately overloaded so that the owners could collect the insurance money when the ship sank. To some extent, modern steam-driven ships could afford to take on more cargo at the outer limits of their voyages, since the ensuing consumption of coal would drastically raise the ship in the water. However, Lloyd George demonstrated a readiness to distort statistics for his own purpose which was to emerge on several subsequent occasions. 3,000 British seamen were to lose their lives in 1912, when reliable statistics were compiled.[14] The owners who were relieved of the obligation to build new ships were delighted by the minister's willingness to negotiate and by his readiness to penalise foreign competitors by making them comply with British regulations. To conciliate the seamen, Lloyd George introduced new regulations which enhanced the conditions of all sailors trading with Britain. He improved the standards of catering, repatriation, accommodation and medical care. H. Du Parq quotes Commander Cawley's gratitude to Lloyd George: 'In his younger days he had known the salt abomination called meat, and had partaken largely of the insect life existing without concealment in the bread.'[15] Regulations for the administration of the Port of London were tightened up, typically following a visit by the minister to European ports so that he could see how such matters were handled elsewhere. Again, he secured the ship-owners' approval. Indeed, they were amazed how pleasant Lloyd George was to deal with, always good-humouredly listening to their point of view and usually prepared to make concessions. It was a new experience to negotiate with such an accommodating minister who clearly liked businessmen. totally noncontroversial was a Census of Production Bill which was designed to equip the Department with reliable, up-to-date information on which to base its policies. Similarly, no-one could object to a Patents and Designs Bill which would protect British firms from illegal and unfair competition from abroad. A Companies Amendments Bill obliged businesses to provide detailed information for creditors and shareholders. All these clearly admirable measures were passed by the House of Lords, perhaps, as Lloyd George mischievously suggested, because they did not understand them. Despite the cheapness of the jibe, the Board of Trade clearly led the field in positive activity. His stodgy colleagues were jealous, but could hardly complain.

Lloyd George's negotiating skills were even more in evidence in the context of industrial relations. He solved disputes in shipping and in the Port of London, but his greatest triumph was to avert a nationwide railway strike in October 1907. British railways were in a deplorable condition. The land which had given birth to railways in

1825 and witnessed their growth through the middle decades of the nineteenth century was now encumbered with a clumsy, wasteful system with out-of-date rolling-stock and antiquated signalling. Profits were low, shareholders discontented and employees relatively badly paid. The government reversed the Tory Taff Vale Act of 1902 which made trade unions liable for losses incurred during a strike. But the 29 railway companies refused to recognise the two main unions, one the National Union of Railwaymen, representing the footplate men, the other, the Amalgamated Society of Railway Servants, representing everybody else. Deadlock ensued. The unions threatened a nationwide strike. Then Lloyd George intervened, summoning both sides to the Board of Trade. He persuaded the employers to entrust their cause to six railway directors, while the unions were similarly represented. Negotiations lasted several days. Lloyd George hammered out a settlement with one party which he then sold to the other. The unions abandoned their demand for recognition in return for the employers' acceptance of satisfactory negotiating machinery. Lloyd George would emmulate this techniquein subsequent disputes involving employers and unions, the governments of great powers and political parties. This way, he would pull off a number of dazzling settlements of which the rail strike of 1907 was the first.[16]

Lloyd George was the hero of the hour. In general, Campbell-Bannerman proclaimed him the outstanding success of the ministry – as Lloyd George happily reported to brother William. Everyone had dreaded a rail strike which would certainly do untold damage. Arguably the danger was postponed, rather than cancelled, but Lloyd George had pulled off a great coup. He was feted and flattered. As it happened, the German Kaiser was visiting his uncle at Windsor. Lloyd George was summoned and introduced to the 'All-Highest'[17] who spent twice as long chatting with Lloyd George as with anybody else, including the King and the Prime-Minister. Lloyd George preened himself, remarking in a letter to Maggie rather ungraciously that he came away having a low opinion of crowned heads.[18] This was symptomatic of the paradoxical and self-contradictory figure he had become. In public he remained the Welsh radical, the posturing fire-brand, extravagant in language and extreme in self-expression. Yet behind the scenes, in Cabinet, at Court, negotiating settlements with opinionated, arrogant leaders, he was pragmatic, emollient, flexible and willing to compromise. As a result he was enormously admired, a future leader of the nation and the people's hero. He was over the moon, on top of the world, the next Prime Minister or at least the next but one. Triumph!

Disaster

It was then that personal tragedy cruelly struck him down. On 25 November 1907 Lloyd George sauntered into his study to find a message from his secretary that Maggie would not be able to meet him in town because Mair Eluned had been sent home from school in a taxi, feeling unwell. Mair was her father's favourite – Dick, the eldest, was always convinced that he was never forgiven for not being a girl. While Mair was clever (pencilled in to read Maths at Cambridge), well-liked and extremely attractive, Frances Stevenson, her contemporary at school (and later Lloyd George's lover), recalled a certain wistful sadness. Photographs suggest what some cynical historians have suggested, that Mair and Lloyd George were especially devoted to each other. He enjoyed discussing politics with her, though only one letter from him has survived. When he heard of her illness he immediately left his office and hurried home. After some delay a doctor was summoned and then a specialist. Mair had a ruptured appendix. Lloyd George's study was converted into an operating theatre, but it was too late. Five days later, aged 17, Mair was 'alive and dead', as the Anglo-Saxon Chronicle described sudden death.

Her parents were overcome with grief, though in different ways. Maggie was largely the self-controlled, undemonstrative woman who grieved in private. Her emotional husband was nothing if not demonstrative, as his brother William confirms. Having been extracted from court in Criccieth, he arrived later in the day to escort his sorrowing brother from the house of death to the House of Commons, leaving Maggie to supervise the removal of the corpse. Lloyd George stayed for several days at his rooms at Westminster, in his brother's words 'distraught with grief, pacing up and down the corridor in his darkened room at the Board of Trade office'.[19] Well-meaning officials tried in vain to distract their devastated chief. Messages of sympathy from the royal family downwards coincided with heartfelt condolences from lesser folk. The Bishop of St Asaph recommended a short holiday, offering to accompany the sorrowing father to France – an offer Lloyd George turned down, perhaps reflecting what a scandal that would cause with his Nonconformist supporters. Sympathisers greeted the funeral train from Euston to Criccieth, laid on by the LNWR. The blinds were down, though the irrepressible Megan, aged five, managed to wave to the crowds. A huge congregation attended the funeral when the marble statue on the grave by Goscombe John was much admired. The grieving father looked a tragic figure, leaning on his brother's shoulder at the grave side. He took a long time to get over Mair's death, complaining that the grave was not grand enough and weeping when he was made Chancellor because his favourite child was not there to share his triumph. Nor did he derive comfort from religion. Mair's last words, carved on her tombstone, were 'He is just and merciful'; Lloyd George could not have disagreed more. Maggie on the other hand kept her thoughts to herself. She was closer to Mair – they shared the same sense of humour, for one thing, and were often mistaken for sisters. There is no reason to doubt her sense of loss.

Frances Stevenson believed that Mair's death damaged the relationship between husband and wife:

> From what L. G. told me, after Mair's death they had drifted apart. They each had their poignant grief but could not go to each other for sympathy and understanding – there was no sharing of the trouble, both blaming the other, perhaps, for what went wrong, the delay in calling the doctor, the carrying out of an emergency operation without a highly skilled staff and hospital amenities. The gap of incompatibility which had always been there became emphasised and more difficult to bridge.[20]

Lest it be thought that this is an example of Frances playing down her lover's affection for his wife, a letter which Lloyd George wrote to Maggie when their youngest child Megan and now Lloyd George's favourite succumbed to measles is full of unsaid reproach: have we engaged sufficient qualified nurses, is the necessary medical equipment available, would she benefit from country air? Is all this code for: this is how you should have dealt with Mair's illness? Is it furthermore impossible that Lloyd George did not think that Maggie grieved enough while she despised him as a sentimentalist who overacted to conceal his guilty lack of affection? While no two bereavements are the same, possibly only the seriously bereaved can evaluate Lloyd George's grief.

Probably he was genuinely hurt in his self-centred way, though it was typically melodramatic and selfish of him to run away to Westminster, to refuse to go back to Routh Road and indeed from then on to avoid the whole neighbourhood. After all, not only Maggie, but Mair's brothers and sisters had been bereaved and were severely shaken. Little Megan hopped around unconcernedly, but the other three were old enough to grieve. If they needed their father's support, they did not get it. To be fair, some colleagues were sufficiently convinced of the father's grief to suggest to the Prime Minister that Lloyd George could be cheered up by a salary increase from Party funds. They also offered to buy on Lloyd George's behalf the freehold on their London house in Cheyne Place. Maggie was in favour of them accepting this kindness, while Campbell-Bannerman was prepared to go along with this plan. But Lloyd George refused. 'I'm not going to accept the charity of the party, come what may. I have made up my mind not to. Tom Ellis did it and was their doormat ... It's very kind of him but I won't have it. I'll take my chance and I know that I can rely on your help.'[21] Lloyd George took his two sons to the South of France before Christmas and wrote affectionately to Maggie: 'Three weeks without your gentle and soothing influence have been very trying and heart-breaking. I would rather have you – jealous old Maggie as you sometimes are – I would rather see you near me in my trouble – you and Uncle Lloyd. You don't mind me bringing him in, do you?'[22]

Campbell-Bannerman himself was a dying man. In April 1908 his resignation was received by Edward VII who accepted Asquith as Campbell-Bannerman's successor with Lloyd George as chancellor. Asquith travelled to Biarritz in order to kiss hands – an eccentric necessity dictated by his sovereign's love of French high life. No objective observer could doubt that Lloyd George deserved the promotion. But it was typical of his stormy career that this wonderful moment of triumph was sullied by further unpleasantness. 'I am to be Chancellor of the Exchequer, and second in command of the Liberal Host', he boasted to his brother.[23] On 8 April 1908 – three days before the official announcement – Asquith returned to London to find that an accurate list of the new Cabinet had been published in the *Daily Chronicle*. Gossip averred that Lloyd George had been indiscreet. Asquith was furious and ready to believe his wife Margot who eagerly broadcasted Lloyd George's guilt. She suggested to

Lloyd George's friend Winston Churchill that his only hope of salvation was to apologise to the new Prime Minister unreservedly, but Lloyd George refused. Having now received the offer of the Chancellorship he accepted the promotion but indignantly denied that he had been indiscreet, and demanded to know the identity of his accusers: 'Men whose promotion is not sustained by birth or other favourable conditions are always liable to be assailed with suspicions of this sort. I would ask therefore, as a favour, if you would not entertain them without satisfying yourself that they have some basis in truth.'

Asquith accepted the denial, refused to name the accusers and suggested that 'we move on and put it behind us'. Lloyd George's letter suggests a sizeable chip similar to the gracelessness with which he accepted favours from his wealthy friends. Was Lloyd George guilty of indiscretion? Possibly. He was not a truthful man and he had an obvious motive in trying to 'bounce' Asquith who could hardly now go back on his offer. McKenna was more probably the informer, despite his denials on the matter; he loathed Lloyd George and had wanted the job. Thus ended Lloyd George's brilliant tenure of office at the Board of Trade. Lloyd George had indeed met Kipling's famous imposters – triumph in his professional brilliance and disaster in Mair's death and Asquith's suspicions of disloyalty – and tackled both with fervour.

4

The Political Chancellor (1909–1915)

I have got to rob somebody's hen-roost.[1]

– Lloyd George

'To THIS end was I born', could have been Lloyd George's text when he was appointed Chancellor of the Exchequer in April 1908. As he remarked to Charles Masterman, 'All down history nine-tenths of mankind have been grinding the corn for the remaining tenth, and have been paid with the husks and bidden to thank God that they had the husks'.[2] His justification for the pursuit of high office had always been his intention to turn this situation round to the benefit of his fellow countrymen and women. No office would give him greater opportunities for doing this than the Exchequer. This was especially the case because he envisaged his role as chancellor in a completely new light compared to the assumptions of his predecessors. More especially he distanced himself from his great Liberal predecessors such as Gladstone, for whom the chief qualifications for the job were ruthless determination and competence in basic arithmetic; the Chancellor's *raison d'être* was to reconcile the expenses of government with its income. More specifically he had to survey the outgoings with what a later holder of the office, Roy Jenkins, would call 'rigorous scrutiny'; these included the costs of maintaining the armed forces and the salaries of ministers and civil servants, plus the crown's expenses. Income was derived from customs and excise and from other forms of direct and indirect taxation. With luck, income would exceed expenditure. If this was not the case – and there had been a shortfall for much of the nineteenth century – such measures as income tax had to be adopted. This was regarded as regrettable, and Gladstone in particular had always hoped to abolish income tax altogether.

'Peace, retrenchment and reform', or in other words the avoidance of war and the adoption of efficient management of the domestic economy, was therefore the policy advocated by the Chancellor. There was no question of drastically redistributing wealth between rich and poor; the Chancellor's *beau ideal* should be Scrooge, not Robin Hood.

As it happened, Lloyd George needed all his customary high spirits and self-belief when he moved to 11 Downing Street. Soon he was no longer the admired prodigy that he had been at the Board of Trade. His civil servants, headed by the aristocratic Sir George Murray, looked on him with the gravest suspicion, despising his unprofessional ignorance and plebeian background. He was generally regarded as a poor replacement for his distinguished predecessor. Indeed it was widely believed that Murray was Asquith's spy, expected to report dangerous deviations to his orthodox Prime Minister. Lloyd George was disliked and envied by his Cabinet colleagues, of whom certainly Reginald McKenna and John Morley (known as the 'The Grand Old Maid') would have liked the job. His only friends were Charles Masterman and Winston Churchill, another parvenu in snobbish Liberal eyes who 'had discovered the poor' as Masterman sardonically remarked, sharing the widespread cynicism about the aristocratic Churchill's idealism. Really, apart from Churchill, his only other supporter was Asquith. There now was formed one of the most remarkable and fruitful political partnerships of modern times. While it would be stretching the truth to depict the two men as close friends, Asquith and Lloyd George respected and valued each other's merits, and each soon had good reason to be grateful for the other's loyalty. The fact that the partnership ended badly in December 1916 should not be predated; neither should the malice of Margot Asquith who, it will be recalled, believed that Lloyd George could not see a belt without hitting below it, be underestimated.

The two households coexisted happily for eight years, symbolised by friendship between six-year-old Megan and her next door contemporary Anthony 'Puffin' Asquith who once disrupted a meeting by chasing Megan round the glass cupula in the Cabinet room ceiling. Lloyd George now had the support of Maggie, his Welsh staff and his children who all moved in to No. 11. 'I am the maid', the diminutive Megan explained when she opened the front door to a distinguished visitor. Number 11 became an outpost of Criccieth; Welsh was normally spoken by everyone from Lloyd George downwards.

'What am I to do with this lot?' exclaimed the formidable retainer Sarah Jones when she surveyed the cumbersome cooking utensils in the kitchen. With hindsight, Maggie preferred No. 11 to No. 10 which was too much of an office for her liking.

Lloyd George's first challenge was to fund the Old Age Pension of five shillings a week to everyone over 70 whose income was less than £26 per annum. It is ironic that Lloyd George should receive the credit for old age pensions rather than Asquith who had piloted the bill through the Commons and negotiated its details while still chancellor, but such was the case. Old people talked about collecting 'their Lloyd George' and often referred to him as *Lord* George out of misplaced gratitude for their two half crowns. Actually, Lloyd George deplored the bill's unnecessary generosity to the old whom he regarded as less deserving than working men who fell upon hard times through injury, illness or unemployment. He was baffled as to how the pension rights of illiterate Irish applicants could be calculated as their births had seldom been reliably recorded, not least by themselves. But it was the sheer expense of old age pensions which really distressed him because it immediately made his job more difficult. The costs of the handouts to the old – while not being exactly munificent – necessitated a major search for revenue. The problem was exacerbated by wholly admirable funding of free school meals and medical inspections for children in state schools and the wholly regrettable agreement to equip the Admiralty with eight dreadnought battleships over the next two years – as Churchill wittily put it, 'Lloyd George wanted only four, the sailors wanted six, so we compromised on eight'. This added another £6 million to the state's outgoings.

In his quest for the money Lloyd George was determined to innovate by drastically increasing direct taxation. To be fair to his predecessors, income tax had long been a well-established fixture, penalising the wealthy to a limited extent: the great question was, to what extent? In 1894, Sir William Harcourt had raised income tax from 8 pence to 9 pence in the pound, had increased the exemption level from £150 to £160 income per annum and had introduced death duties. It would be very difficult for later Chancellors to go back on such concessions to basic justice. Lloyd George, however, envisaged a tax system which went much further in redressing the flagrant injustices of Edwardian society with which he was emotionally and intellectually preoccupied.

Although never a great reader, he was at least aware of the arguments which the classic Liberal propagandists J. A. Hobson and L. T. Hobhouse had put forward, plus Charles Booth's remarkable work on slum conditions in London[3] and Seebohm Rowntree's horrifying account of working class York, *Poverty: A Study of Town Life.*[4] Lloyd George had himself experienced modest circumstances during his childhood, despite Uncle Lloyd's business acumen which enabled him to employ two assistants and make a profit over the years. He had personally witnessed squalor and deprivation in the London slums. If the poor were to be helped, where was the money to come from? Derek Fraser, in his *The Evolution of the British Welfare State*, quotes *The Times'* judgement that the most significant result of the 1906 'Liberal Landslide' was the election of 53 Labour MPs. Did the future depend on them rather than the Liberal legions? Fraser argues that the unprecedented government majority of 356 gave the Liberals what was probably their last chance of proving that they, and not Labour, could be trusted with the welfare of the poor. This was certainly Lloyd George's perception.

Thus the most self-consciously political Chancellor of the Exchequer in living memory welcomed opposition and criticism, not only from the Tory-Unionist opposition but from his own colleagues and his socialist allies. The 'People's David' shocked the House of Commons on 29 June 1908 when he predicted a widely spread search for money to meet the state's expenses:

> I have no nest eggs at all. I have got to rob somebody's roost next year. I am on the lookout which will be the easiest to get and where I shall be the least punished, and where I shall get the most eggs, and, not only that, but where they can be most easily spared, which is another important qualification.[5]

This declaration of intent shocked conservative opinion on both sides of the House. But the Chancellor was unrepentant and, echoing *The Times*, justified his approach at Swansea a few weeks later: 'I have one word for Liberals. If at the end of an average term of office it were found that the present Parliament had done nothing to cope seriously with the social condition of the people, then a real cry will arise in this land for a new party, and many of us here in this room will join in that cry.'[6] Hence the notorious People's Budget, debated in advance and at some length in 14 acrimonious meetings of the

Cabinet during March and April 1909. Lloyd George's proposals were supported by Asquith and Churchill and opposed in particular by Harcourt, Runciman, McKenna and Burns. John Morley resigned at least once a week.

The People's Budget

The Budget was unveiled to the House of Commons, and hence to the public, on 29 April 1909, in a speech which lasted four and a half hours. With pardonable vanity, the Chancellor arranged for his brother and his elder son, Dick, to be present in the gallery to partake of his triumph. Virtually everyone agreed, however, that it was a terrible performance. Not even the orator himself was happy. This might seem surprising given that this should have been the peak of Lloyd George's political career to date, and there was no doubt that he took his speech-making seriously. The trouble was that his usual technique was not only to rehearse his speech beforehand but also to learn it by heart so that he could deliver it 'spontaneously': in other words, without notes. However, not only was Lloyd George's first budget speech too long, but it was also too complicated and full of indigestible detail to be delivered 'spontaneously'. So the Chancellor had to read from voluminous notes, often losing his place, hesitating and stumbling so much that many of his harsher critics, such as Leverton Harris, the Unionist MP for Stepney, suggested to R. B. Haldane that Lloyd George himself did not understand his own speech. 'Of course he doesn't', Haldane replied, 'Why, we have been trying for weeks to make him understand clause X of the bill, and he *can't*'. After four hours he was audibly and visibly exhausted, and could barely be heard, let alone understood. With typical generosity Balfour signalled to Asquith that a half-hour break might save Lloyd George's vocal chords from permanent harm, to say nothing of the patience of his audience who had had to listen to this tedious effusion and must have been almost as weary.

Fortunately, we do not have to endure the speech in order to grasp the main proposals. Income Tax on earned income up to £2,000 was to be levied at 9 pence in the pound and at 1 shilling on the £2,000 – £3,000 level. Supertax was imposed on incomes over £5,000, payable at 6 pence in the pound on receipts over £3,000. There were duties of £2 million levied on tobacco and £1.8 million on spirits. There was to be an increase of £2 million on liquor licences. The Chancellor penalised the rich by imposing a levy of 3d on a gallon of petrol and he introduced a licence on cars. There was a levy of half a penny in the pound on undeveloped land – a measure dear to the heart of the landlord-hating Chancellor. We can appreciate Lloyd George's claim that this was a war budget, the first great shot in his campaign against injustice and exploitation of the weak. When press and public, to say nothing of MPs, were able to digest the small print, they were shaken if they were reactionary, exhilarated if progressive. To an extent, direct taxation replaced indirect, while the lifestyle of the rich was penalised. Lloyd George's budget was a major step on the road to the Welfare State. Herbert Samuel summed it up in a letter to Herbert Gladstone: 'Not a great speech, this – so think most of our men – but it is a great budget.' Bruce Murray, in his *The People's Budget*,[7] argued that Lloyd George achieved the modernisation of the British system of taxation, the financing of the British social-service state, the defeat of tariff-reformers and the Parliament Act of 1911. This in its turn led to the demise of the House of Lords veto and the plunge towards civil war in Ireland.

Both contemporaries and historians have argued about Lloyd George's motives. Obviously he had to raise money by helping himself to the contents of available nesting boxes, as he had predicted. But did he aim at being both offensive and provocative? Looked at from the perspective of a century later, his taxes appear quite reasonable. So was the *principle* of attacking the privileges of the rich more threatening and significant than the amounts raised? In particular, did Lloyd George deliberately defy the House of Lords to reject the budget? Quite probably he hoped that the Lords would not be so stupid. After all, his immediate priority when he rose to his feet on that memorable 29 April was to force the rich to pay their just contribution to the nation's overall expenditure. While he had spent his whole career threatening to take the aristocracy down a peg, did he really want to do it now, when cash was his most pressing priority?

At first he was apparently unaware of the gross offence he had caused, obsequiously flattering Uncle Lloyd that *he* was the budget's real author. It was only when prominent members of the Upper House threatened to break the unwritten code that the Lords would not attack money bills that 'the people's David' rose to the challenge. In the long term, the figures caused less offence than his justification for them. If indeed Lloyd George's first priority was to raise money, the Budget was successful. There was a more than satisfactory surplus of £6,545,000 in 1911/12. The *Economist* of 20 May 1911 commented: 'Mr Lloyd George may stand on record as the author of the most successful budget, from the revenue producing point of view, which the financial historian of this or perhaps of any other country can recall in times of peace.'[8] If, however, Lord Lansdowne and his friends wanted a fight, they would get it, with dire consequences for the whole aristocracy. After the budget was passed by the Commons by 379 to 149 votes, it was rejected by the Lords by 350 votes to 75. War it was to be, so it seemed.

Lloyd George signalled that he was determined to take on the Tory establishment in a seminal speech which he delivered to a packed audience of 4,000 at The Edinburgh Castle, a pub which had been a mission hall at Limehouse in the East End of London. The date was 30 July – a crucial day in the history of British democracy. The general implication of Lloyd George's speech was class warfare. The particular occasion for the announcement of the campaign was the government's decision to lay down the four additional dreadnoughts raising the naval budget by another £6 million. Lloyd George's argument was that Britain's underprivileged were willing to pay the cost of such national priorities as the four battleships, while the landowning aristocracy on the other hand were too selfish, too irresponsible, too stupid to recognise their obligation to pay their just share; hence their refusal to welcome the budget. A good example was the spectacular profits made by the owners of the Hackney Marshes, rated at £3 per acre and sold for housing development at anything up to £8,000 per acre. Lloyd George had nothing against self-made businessmen such as Mr Gorringe, who had made money by enterprise and hard work. All went well until he was exploited by his landlord the Duke of Westminster who increased Gorringe's ground rent from £400 a year to £4,000. After appropriate comment, Lloyd George then shifted his attack to the owners of coalmines:

> Have you been down in a coalmine? I went down one the other day. We sank down into a pit half a mile deep. The earth seemed to be straining – around us and above us. You could see the pit-props bent and twisted and sundered. Sometimes they give way, and then there is mutilation and death. Often a spark ignites, the whole pit is deluged in fire, the breath of life is scorched out of hundreds of breasts by the consuming flame. In the very next colliery to the one I descended, just a few years ago, 300 people lost their lives in that way; and yet

when the Prime Minister and I knock at the doors of these great land-lords, and say to them: 'Here you know these poor fellows who have been digging up royalties at the risk of their lives, some of them are old, they have survived the perils of their trade, they are broken, they can earn no more. Won't you give us towards keeping them out of the workhouse?' they scowl at us. We say, 'only a ha'penny, just a copper'. They retort: 'you thieves!' And they turn their dogs onto us, and you can hear their bark every morning. If this is an indication of the view taken by these great landlords of their responsibility to the people who, at the risk of their life, create their wealth, then I say that their day of reckoning is at hand. We are putting burdens on the broadest shoulders. Why should I put burdens on the people? I was brought up among them. I know their trials. When the Prime Minister did me the honour of inviting me to take charge of the national Exchequer at a time of great difficulty, I made up my mind in framing the budget which was in front of me, that at any rate no cupboard should be barer, no lot should be harder. By that test, I challenge you to judge the budget.[9]

As entertainment, the contrast between Lloyd George's budget speech and Limehouse could hardly be greater. This was truly an even finer hour – at least if you happen to be a democrat and an idealist. This was great rhetoric, and it caused a storm of protest from the pampered rich, from the King downwards. The King was furious, as he explained to the Prime Minister, because a minister of the crown was preaching class war. Lloyd George wrote to the King defending the budget. Edward replied that he had no quarrel with the budget itself, but strongly objected to the Chancellor's speech at Limehouse. Asquith remonstrated with Lloyd George on behalf of the King, and also on behalf of the more right-wing Liberal grandees who believed that Lloyd George was losing the Party votes with his provocative extremism. Margot Asquith agreed, imploring the Chancellor to think before he spoke. 'If your speeches hurt and alienated lords, it would not matter. But they hurt not only the King and men of high estate, but quite poor men, Liberals of all sorts. They lose us votes.'[10] Lloyd George preferred to be encouraged by letters such as one he received from J. E. C. Bodley, dated 31 July 1909, the day after the Limehouse speech was delivered:

Will you let me thank you for your speech at Limehouse? It is the first utterance by any member of this government of good intentions, which gives a ray of hope that the people will be guided to reject tariff reform. As you have become like me a Brighton resident for part of the year, I hope that one day I may see you. One of my Eton boys would be made very happy if he could see you, as, in spite of the contrary influence of his school, he is a keen self-taught liberal.[11]

Buffeted this way and that, Lloyd George decided to stand by his Limehouse guns and welcomed the arrows which assailed him from the right wing establishment. A *Punch* cartoon depicted him as 'the Saint Sebastian of Limehouse'. On 9 October he made a speech in Newcastle upon Tyne, which was even more provocative than Limehouse. As *The Times* wittily put it, 'it outslimed Slimehouse'. Lloyd George beefed up his attack with ridicule, thus joining the immortal band of political satirists which included Jonathan Swift, the youthful Disraeli and Randolph Churchill. The Newcastle speech is highly offensive, and all the more effective because it is so entertaining. It is the opposite of deference. Lloyd George electrified an audience of 5,000 in the Palace Theatre:

> Only one stock has gone down badly – there has been a great slump in dukes. They used to stand rather high in the market, especially the Tory market, but the Tory press has just discovered that they are of no value. They have been making speeches lately. One especially expensive duke made a speech, and all the Tory press said, 'Well now, really, is that the sort of thing we are spending £250,000 a year upon?' Because a fully-equipped duke costs as much to keep as two dreadnoughts – and they are just as great a terror – and they last longer. As long as they were content to be mere idols on their pedestals, preserving that stately silence which became their rank and intelligence, all went well. But then came the budget. They stepped off their perch. They have been scolding like omnibus drivers purely because the budget cart has knocked a little bit of the gilt off their old stagecoach. Well, we cannot put them back again.

Ridicule now gave place to invective:

> Let them realise what they are doing. They are forcing a revolution, and they will get it. The Lords may decree a revolution, but the people will direct it. If they begin, issues will be raised which they little dream of. Questions are asked which are now whispered in humble voices, and answers will be demanded then with authority. The question will then be asked whether five hundred men, ordinary men chosen accidentally

from the unemployed, with the first of the litter having precedence, should override the judgement – the deliberate judgement of millions of people who are engaged in the industry which makes the wealth of the country. That is one question. Another will be: Who ordained that a few should have the land of Britain as a perquisite? Who made ten thousand people owners of the soil, and the rest of us trespassers in the land of our birth? Who is it who is responsible for the scheme of things whereby one man is engaged through life in grinding labour to win a bare and precarious substance for himself, and another man who does not toil receives every hour of the day, every hour of the night, whilst he slumbers, more than his poor neighbour receives in a whole year of toil? These are the questions which will be asked. The answers are charged with peril for the order of things which the peers represent: but they are fraught with rare and refreshing fruit for the parched lips of the multitude who have been treading the dusty road along which the people have marched through the dark ages which are now emerging into the light.[12]

Lloyd George's speeches in parliament, at Limehouse and Newcastle have always provoked controversy. Did they inspire a Liberal recovery or play in to the hands of Conservative critics? Tempers certainly rose. 'Mr Asquith, I'm afraid that I am going to have to be very rude and vicious during this next session', the new leader of the Conservative Party, Andrew Bonar Law, warned Asquith. The Lords, for the most part, were outraged, and on 30 November rejected the budget by 350 votes to 75 – after it had passed its third reading in the Commons by 379 to 149. The King was apoplectic with rage, and indeed there were those such as Margot Asquith who maintained that Lloyd George was his murderer. His death on 6 May 1910 transformed the political situation, bringing to the throne the inexperienced and diffident George V. In the meantime, Asquith's appeal to the country (January 1910) on the mistaken supposition that the King would create enough Liberal peers to implement the swamping of the Lords proved ineffectual. The result was disappointing in that the massive Liberal majority of January 1906 was wiped out. Now 275 Liberal MPs would require the support of 40 Labour and 82 Irish members, so as to outvote 273 Conservatives.

The King's Speech with which Asquith welcomed the new House was disastrously ineffectual. He had to admit that the King had refused to play the game, insisting on a *second* Liberal victory before he would agree to such a spectacular innovation as the mass-creation of new Liberal peers. Deadlock therefore prevailed, until the King's death seemed to justify a conference between the two parties charged with the mission of a compromise, which would get the young monarch off the hook. Always a man for negotiation, Lloyd George welcomed the idea of a conference, gladly agreeing to serve in the Liberal team (Asquith, Lloyd George, Crewe and Birrell against Balfour, Lansdowne, Austen Chamberlain and Cawdor). Lansdowne rebuffed an invitation from Crewe to meet at his country house: 'Will not criticism at the hands of our friends be much more severe if it can be said that we had been "softened" by the excellence of Crewe's champagne and the other attractions of a hospitable and luxurious country house?' It was not to be a success. Fourteen meetings of this admirably idealistic experiment got nowhere. All proposals for constitutional revision foundered on the rock of Irish Home Rule. Now, however, Lloyd George shone. While others were plunged in gloom, he was exhilarated. This was his hour. The answer was a coalition. He had always been a coalitionist, ever since his conflicts with the Anglicans over Welsh disestablishment in 1894. Lloyd George rushed around producing schemes for membership, procedures and agenda. He conferred with likeminded colleagues such as Churchill and sympathetic enemies such as F. E. Smith. Balfour was disposed to be flippant: 'Now, isn't that like Lloyd George? Principles mean nothing to him – never have. His mind doesn't work that way. It is both his strength and weakness.' Lloyd George got excited, but his time had not yet come. Only the threat of defeat in a great war brought about coalitions, first in May 1915 and then in December 1916. Now the key players in the Tory Party, Lansdowne and Bonar Law, would not cooperate, while the leading Liberals were unconvinced. Asquith, like Balfour, just laughed at the little Welshman's 'missionary activities', believing that there was no realistic prospect of success. Yet coalitionists such as Smith, Churchill and above all, Lloyd George, believed that it was in the interests of the country to eliminate party issues in order to carry such comprehensive measures as national insurance and Welsh disestablishment. But it was not to be – yet.[13]

So, what next? Now that George V had agreed to create the necessary peers if the electorate agreed – Asquith had even nominated his first batch consisting of Bertrand Russell, Thomas Hardy, Gilbert Murray and J. M. Barrie[14] – another general election was called. If the country declared for major change, the King would conform. Though the result was once again inconclusive, the revelation that the King would indeed create as many as 500 peers brought the Lords to their knees. A cartoon showing a coronet-topped peer with '499' on his back encouraged the 'hedgers' to defeat the 'ditchers' by 131 votes to 113. Lloyd George could congratulate himself on this result: the Lords could only delay measures which had passed the Commons on three occasions; the automatic passage of finance bills was confirmed; and there was now to be a general election every five years at most. MPs were to be paid £400 per annum – a sop to Labour for supporting the government, and acceptable to Lloyd George himself who had been unpaid for his 15 and a half years as a backbencher. George Barnes (Labour), echoing Lloyd George, opined that there would be no difficulty in finding 'plenty of unemployed who would be glad of the job'.[15] There was now a green light for Home Rule, Welsh disestablishment and for Lloyd George's social reforms.

National Insurance

When piloting old age pensions through Parliament, Lloyd George, as we have seen, had made it clear that he rated the protection of the poor against unemployment and sickness as even more important. Although Winston Churchill had established labour exchanges throughout the country, insurance against unemployment was still necessary. Similarly the motley array of friendly societies, clubs and local deals with the medical establishment ensured that remaining healthy was a hazardous occupation, given the vested interests competing for the worker's hard-earned savings. Lloyd George's reforms also threatened the providers of the gruesome paraphernalia associated with death which working class (and not just working class) convention demanded. The moral blackmail to spend lavishly exercised by undertakers' men – glass hearses, brass-bedecked coffins and horses with nodding plumes – left many financial loopholes through which the poor could be exploited. Taking on and defeating the combined racket perpetrated by employers, doctors, 'the Men from the Pru' and funeral directors was indeed a creditable episode in Lloyd George's career.

Lloyd George's Insurance Act was founded on the achievement of Winston Churchill's labour exchanges. The scheme which Lloyd

George eventually sold to the Cabinet and which finally became law tackled two ominous problems for working class people – unemployment and ill-health – both exacerbated by sheer poverty. His act established the Ministry of Labour's responsibility for unemployed people in specified trades, mainly engineering, building and ship-building. Two and a half million workers were thus protected. The employer, the worker and the state each contributed two pence half penny a week, so that if he was unemployed the worker would receive seven shillings a week for a maximum of 15 weeks in the year. The cost to the Exchequer was £20 million. The presumption was that, in due course, the scheme would be extended to other trades. Compulsory health insurance for workers over 16 who earned less than £160 per annum was financed by 4 pence from a man, 3 pence from a woman, 3 pence from the employer and 2 pence from the state. Thus was made possible free medical treatment and sick-pay of 10 shillings a week for a maximum period of six months. Funeral expenses were to be defrayed. His assistants in this creditable endeavour were several gifted civil servants, notably J. S. Bradbury, R. C. Hawtrey and W. J. Braithwaite. The last named was a typically unorthodox source; he was sent to research German insurance and report to his boss relaxing on the pier in Nice. Lloyd George bought everybody drinks and released Braithwaite: 'Now then, tell us all about it.' Thus was the National Health Service born. Incidentally there is no pier in Nice, though perhaps there was then.

The opposition which Lloyd George encountered was formidable; his struggle to place his act on the statute book must command our admiration. He had to defy the Labour Party, Beatrice and Sidney Webb and legions of journalists. He had to grapple with the British Medical Association and the voluntary societies. He had to make concessions against his preferred judgement, such as abandoning funeral benefits. He had to recognise the formidable political clout of the 70,000 collectors who had access to thousands of homes. He out-trumped the BMA by establishing fees which were higher than those which the BMA had negotiated, to the delight of junior doctors who were glad to join the panels set up by Lloyd George. Two weeks before the new arrangements came into force, the Northcliffe press (*The Times* and the *Daily News* in particular) encouraged employers to refuse to buy the insurance stamps. Many aristocratic letters predicted the dismissal of domestic servants because the stamps were so expensive. The Chancellor was delighted to resume the offensive at Woodford in July 1912:

> They write letters to the papers threatening to reduce the wages of their servants, threatening to lengthen their hours – I should have thought that almost impossible – and in the end threatening to dismiss them. They are always dismissing servants. Whenever any Liberal Act of Parliament is passed they dismiss them. I wonder that they have any servants left. Sir William Harcourt imposed death duties: they dismissed servants. I put on a super-tax: they dismissed more. Now the Insurance Act comes, and the last of them will have to go. You will be having on the swell West End houses notices like, 'Not at home – her ladyship's washing day'.[16]

Roy Hattersley states that the People's Budget, the defeat of the House of Lords and the National Insurance Act made Lloyd George 'the greatest radical in British history'. This verdict, coming from an ex-Shadow Chancellor, has to be respected.[17]

Frances Stevenson

The summer of 1912 was something of a zenith in the Chancellor's career. Thereafter – and during the last few months before his great Liberal reforms were endangered by the outbreak of World War I – problems personal and professional would afflict him. Most importantly, his marriage, which had jogged along for several months in London, was a source of decreasing happiness to both Lloyd George and Maggie, the latter spending more and more time at Criccieth. Lloyd George now formed a new relationship with a young woman half his age (born in 1888), which blossomed during a two-year period from 1911. According to John Grigg, their relationship was 'secretly formalised' on 23 January 1913, and lasted until Lloyd George's death, 32 years later. This gross act of betrayal and disloyalty to Maggie affected their relationship until her death in 1941. The young woman was Frances Louise Stevenson, a clever and attractive school-mistress, who had been at school with Mair and whom Lloyd George had recruited to tutor Megan during the school holidays. Her father was a company secretary, her mother a mildly bohemian artist. They were highly respectable. Frances tells how she fell in love with her employer after a Welsh-speaking colleague took her to hear him preach at the Baptist chapel in Castle Street near Oxford

Circus. Through Frances had no Welsh and so could not understand a word, she was bowled over. When it came to her notice that the Chancellor was advertising for a tutor for his daughter, she applied and was interviewed by Lloyd George at 11 Downing Street. She tells us how his eyes had a unique penetrative quality which seemed to lay bare her soul.[18] There is no reason to doubt that the attraction was mutual. Frances got the job. There followed several months of distant courtship. Frances was invited along to Criccieth to begin her duties. A visitor, Charles Masterman, wrote: 'I could not work out who Miss Stevenson was.' Lloyd George was excited and rejuvenated by this marvellous apparition and enjoyed showing off, climbing trees, paddling in the Dwyfor when he displayed his scarlet underpants and behaving like a 14-year-old. Clearly he was in love, though Ffion Hague suggests that he was also excited by the prospect of presiding over the investiture of Edward as Prince of Wales: George V had commissioned Lloyd George to teach his son a little Welsh. (Incidentally, he remained on good terms with Edward until after the abdication crisis of 1936.)

The relationship with Frances climaxed in 1913 when Lloyd George opened his heart to her. He offered her a very peculiar job which could be described as a glorified personal assistant, making it clear that they would also become lovers and sleep together. There was no question of marriage while Maggie was alive. Frances certainly possessed appropriate skills – she spoke French fluently, she typed and had shorthand, her sharp mind was demonstrated in a number of interesting books which she wrote – all serving as a blind to the truth.[19]

When Frances told her parents about the Chancellor's offer, her mother was furious. Frances' parents wanted their daughter to marry well, but not *that* well, and in any case they insisted on a proper marriage. Lloyd George tried to improve the family atmosphere and cheer up his lover by inviting her parents to lunch at No. 11. This was an astonishing episode, illustrating Lloyd George's breathtaking insensitivity and arrogance. If Mr and Mrs Stevenson were meant to be reconciled to their daughter's immorality and dazzled by her lover's compensating brilliance, the plan did not work. Frances was more or less cut off from her home, to her immense distress. There were occasional gestures of friendship: her father once sent Lloyd George a present of some high quality cigars. Lloyd George was considerate and sympathetic when the Stevensons' only son was killed on the Western Front. But Frances' parents never ceased to hope that she would leave Lloyd George and marry a nice middle class schoolmaster, businessman or vicar.

In the meantime, Lloyd George maintained two homes, one in London (or at Walton Heath near a convenient golf course or, later, at Churt in Surrey) and the other in Criccieth. The truth could not be kept from Maggie, though in the past many liaisons had indeed been concealed. She was angry and hurt, and refused to welcome Frances at Criccieth or tolerate her in Lloyd George's London homes. The four children, in their different ways, sided with Maggie and loathed Frances, whom they dismissively referred to as 'Flossie'. Lloyd George called her 'Pussie', her school nickname. Actually Lloyd George was unfaithful to 'Pussie' right up to his death – and she to him – though he reluctantly kept his promise to marry her when Maggie died in 1941.

Is this louche tale of concern to the historian? Some would argue that it is irrelevant and can therefore be ignored. Still less is it the historian's job to make a moral judgement, many would argue. Frances Stevenson, however, was influential in political affairs now and again, while Lloyd George's betrayal of Maggie throws significant – though hardly flattering – light on his character. It is fascinating that he got away with virtual bigamy. Perhaps in those days journalists were less judgemental than nowadays, or less well-equipped to make discoveries, or too aware of their own immoral private lives to throw stones at others. Or perhaps they worked for disreputable proprietors such as Beaverbrook, Northcliffe and Riddell.

Marconi

Frances was finally summoned permanently to her lover's side when he was in trouble over an equally damaging though very different fall from grace. In April 1912 he was seriously involved in financial corruption, hardly an appropriate scenario for the Chancellor of the Exchequer. He needed the support and sympathy of a quick-thinking PA who was very much more than a PA. We have seen in Chapter 2 that Lloyd George was vulnerable to the temptation to make improper profits on the side. In his days as a backbencher, he might be forgiven for financial impropriety, given that his salary was zero. Now, however, as chancellor he earned £5,000 per annum and might be thought to be above skulduggery. Alas, not so.

When shares in the American Marconi Telecommunications Company went on sale at £2 each, Lloyd George was told that they would rocket in value. They were much in the news after the murderer Crippen had been arrested in New York due to a tip-off conveyed by Marconi. Lloyd George bought 1,000 shares; so did the Attorney-General Rufus Isaacs; so did Alexander Murray, the Liberal Chief Whip, who then proceeded to buy 3,000 shares on behalf of the Party. Soon the shares had doubled. Unfortunately, the British Marconi Company had obtained a government contract. Had the ministers known about this in advance and used the knowledge for their own gain? Several weekly journals broadcast the story, especially Leo Maxse's *National Review* and Cecil Chesterton's *Eye Witness*. Maxse's motive was political, Chesterton's anti-Semitic, Isaacs being Jewish. The politicians, including Lloyd George, denied that they had bought shares in the company which the government had backed – this was, strictly speaking, true – but they did not divulge their purchases in the American firm until this admission was extracted from them by a select committee. Calls for Lloyd George's resignation were fended off to a great extent by Asquith's loyal support; the latter nevertheless permitted himself the smug comment that 'the idol's wings have been clipped'. Lloyd George was frightened and needed his clever mistress at his side. Kipling's nasty anti-Semitic masterpiece *Gehazi* was inspired by the Marconi scandal:

> Thou mirror of uprightness,
> What ails thee at thy vows?
> What means the risen whiteness
> Of the skin beneath thy brows?
> The boils that shine and burrow,
> The sores that slough and bleed–
> The leprosy of Naaman
> On thee and all thy seed?
> Stand up, stand up, Gehazi,
> Draw close thy robe and go.
> Gehazi, Judge in Israel,
> A leper white as snow.[20]

'The judge in Israel' was obviously the Jew Rufus Isaacs, the Attorney General whose conduct especially provoked Kipling's contempt. But the mud stuck to his friend and fellow-conspirator, the Chancellor.

There had been no actual crime, but at best Lloyd George's conduct had been injudicious, at worst economical with the truth.

Votes for Women

Lloyd George's unease over Marconi may have prevented him from coming out with his moral armoury blazing on behalf of another issue where he felt strongly but acted feebly. The issue was women's suffrage. J. Graham Jones reinforces the opinion of several historians when he writes: 'It is difficult to resist the conclusion that the failure of the pre-war Liberal governments to enfranchise women was one of the worst blots on their record.'[21] The case for giving women the vote was unanswerable. Gradually men had been enfranchised as Britain lurched towards true democracy. Lloyd George himself, to his credit, had spoken in favour of women's suffrage in the 1890s. He eventually piloted through the first great breakthrough for half the British population when, on his watch, the Representation of the People Act (1918) gave women above the age of 30 the vote – but sadly not during the Liberal 'Great Reform Ministry'. As its most prominent radical, Lloyd George is necessarily in the dock for this omission. Perhaps the distraction of Marconi is an alibi of sorts; so too was the discreditable, surprising and absurd prejudice of the Prime Minister who purported to believe that the enfranchisement of women would benefit the Tories. True, France, the birthplace of political freedom, did not enfranchise women until 1945, for the very reason that, under the influence of a conservative Church, women would obey their priests and vote right, but Britain was not France. As Lloyd George frequently pointed out, the answer was to give both working class men and women the vote.

A further excuse for the Liberal regime's feebleness was the conduct of the suffragettes themselves. Whereas Emily Fawcett's suffragists campaigned with restraint, the Pankhursts, led by Emeline and her daughters Christobel and Isobel, led an injudicious assault on Parliament and public opinion which alienated more people than it attracted.[22] Lloyd George reflected the opinion of many who were, in fact, sympathetic to women's demand for full democratic rights, but put off by extremist violence. Not only were windows smashed, letter-boxes set on fire and meetings interrupted, but prominent politicians who opposed votes for women such as Asquith were assaulted, and stunts performed such as interference with the Derby when Emily

Wilding Davison was killed rugby-tackling the King's horse. Lloyd George himself, despite expressing sympathy for the cause, was physically assaulted, interrupted at meetings and endangered when part of his house at Walton Heath was burnt down before it was completed. He apologised to his landlord, Sir George Riddell, for being 'such a troublesome and expensive tenant.'[23] A high-profile protest was violently broken up at Llanystumdwy on the occasion of the opening of a new village hall, financed by libel damages, which Lloyd George had won against newspapers alleging sexual misconduct. Lloyd George refused to dance to the tune of 'Queen Christabe' by cancelling the meeting. It was war almost literally to the death, in that several local rowdies clearly intended to rough up any women who interrupted the proceedings. 'Votes for women', shouted the suffragettes when Lloyd George tried to speak. 'Throw them in the river', shouted the heavy mob who now beat up the protesters and sexually abused the women. 'They are in Wales now, they are among Ancient Britons, and we will show them how to deal with suffragettes.' Just how serious these assaults were is hard to establish. Clearly Lloyd George's appeals for restraint fell on deaf ears. Questions were asked in Parliament, letters written to the press. Lloyd George never admitted responsibility or expressed regret, but he tried to mend his fences with the suffragettes with an emollient speech at Swindon (23 October 1913):

> Here we men have been governing the country for thousands of years, and we find wretchedness and misery, poverty and slums everywhere, and we seem somehow to have made a mess of it. When one sex has rather conspicuously failed in some of the essentials of good government, I think we might try a partnership of the two.[24]

The Land

Marconi, bigamy, betrayal of democracy – these were sad lapses which impeded Lloyd George's continuing campaigns for social justice. The government as a whole was frustrated in its plans for Welsh disestablishment and for Home Rule, despite the Parliament Act, while Asquith was slowly losing his zest for adventure and initiative. So it fell to Lloyd George to find a crusade to raise the morale of his colleagues. We should not be surprised that his answer was the land. From the earliest days of his career he had campaigned for better use of the nation's land and for better conditions for those who worked there. Assisted by a committee of experts, including Seebohm Rowntree and C. P. Scott, financed by W. H. Lever and Joseph Rowntree, Lloyd George issued a Rural Report in October 1913 and an Urban Report in April 1914. Minimum wages for agricultural workers, land courts to fix fair rents, a ministry of lands and forests to revolutionise the standards of housing in the countryside, a drastic enquiry into land values which, as Lloyd George averred, amounted to a revival of Domesday Book – all admirable ideas which were, alas, aborted by the outbreak of war. The government's opponents were not, in fact, unsympathetic, apart from a juvenile campaign mocking Lloyd George's allegation that landlords' pheasants devoured mangel-worzels destined for cattle. It turned out that Lloyd George was, in fact, right.[25]

Lloyd George launched his land campaign with two speeches at Bedford on 11 October 1913. This was quintessential Lloyd George at his best – provocative, colourful, analytical:

> The cradle is rocked on the land, and the grave is sunk in the land. The land enters into everything … the food the people eat, the water they drink, the houses they dwell in, the industries upon which their livelihood depends. Yet most of the land is in the hands of the few. The landowners exercise gigantic powers, terrible powers … A landowner can devastate the countryside; he can sweep every cottage away and convert it into a wilderness. Agricultural labourers work longer hours than any industrial employee, and yet are paid lower wages.

These conditions Lloyd George contrasted with the magnificent parks and houses of the landowners nearby:

> Their response to the grievances of their tenants and employees is to triple the number of gamekeepers who are employed to implement the outrageously punitive game laws against poachers and trespassers.[26]

Lloyd George broadened his assault on greedy landowners by exco-riating the exploitation of urban tenant-holders, bringing in the Labour Party to beef up his campaign. Sadly, it is probably true that Lloyd George's land campaign fell flat. Few of his colleagues shared his visceral loathing for landlords – Asquith the product of Balliol and the Inns of Court; Churchill born at Blenheim Palace; Grey the Northumbrian landowner. Still, it was worth a try – to this end was the Welsh attorney from Llanystumdwy born. The party, however, was more inclined to applaud his 1914 budget. An additional £9.8m was to be raised by increases in death duties and supertax, and by a graduated income tax – but then came war.

So what about the question, did Lloyd George deserve his reputation as 'the people's David'? His response to his mission to save the poor from destitution and misery was uneven. It is easy to carp, agreeing with Haldane that 'Lloyd George had boundless energy and quick intelligence and a really remarkable gift for sensing the drift of public opinion, but he was really an illiterate with an unbalanced mind'.[27] He did, however, display wonderful qualities – courage, vision, flexibility, the capacity to win over opponents with his charm and willingness to listen. A. J. P. Taylor called Lloyd George 'the most dynamic figure in British politics during the first half of the twentieth century'.[28] His achievements were flawed, but as he admitted when his National Insurance Act was criticised, 'we live in an imperfect world'. In a speech at Birmingham, 12 June 1911, Lloyd George claimed to have joined the Red Cross. 'I am in the ambulance corps. I am engaged to drive a wagon through the twistings and turnings and ruts of the Parliamentary road . . . Now there are some who say I am in a great hurry. I am rather in a hurry, for I can hear the moanings of the wounded, and I want to carry relief to them.'[29] The relief he provided could perhaps have been more substantial.

Nevertheless, if Britain in 1914 is compared with Britain in 1905, the contrast is indisputable.[30] Though there was still much for Attlee's great administration to do (1945–1951), the Welfare State had been founded. Others, as well as Lloyd George can justly claim some of the credit. But Lloyd George's role as chancellor was pivotal. Churchill's daughter, Mary, thanked her father for giving her and her fellow citizens liberty by defying Nazism. Mary Soames can justly be compared with Olwen Carey-Evans who always muttered 'thank-you, Father' whenever she drew her old age pension.

5

The Improbable Warlord (1915–1917)

I am the butcher's boy, leading animals to the slaughter.

– Lloyd George

A Militant Chancellor

'To THIS end was I *not* born', could well have been Lloyd
George's claim when he became closely involved in the
direction of Britain's war effort, first as chancellor (August
1914–May 1915), then as Minister of Munitions (May 1915–June
1916), next as War Minister (June 1916–December 1916) and finally
as Prime Minister, from 7 December 1916. For two torrid years he
headed the government which helped to bring Germany and her
allies to their knees and to the negotiating table. Unlike his friend
and colleague Winston Churchill, who made exactly the opposite
claim when he became Prime Minister in May 1940 ('I felt that I was
walking with destiny'), Lloyd George hated war: 'All wars are so hor-
rible in their incidence, and so uncertain in their event, that sensible
statesmen recognise that as soon as you can secure the main object
of a war and bring it to an end the better it is even for the victor.'
Unlike Churchill he had never been a professional soldier. He never
wore military uniforms such as those which adorned Churchill, Stalin
and Hitler. He was always, in appearance and attitude, a civilian. His
admirers do not carry conviction when they quote Lloyd George's
'war experience' in the local militia when he played at soldiers in the
woods above Llanystumdwy, hiding his uniform after parade from
Uncle Lloyd's censorious gaze.

On the other hand, Lloyd George was not a pacifist. His
opposition to the Boer War must not be misunderstood: he was never

a conscientious objector, nor, as mentioned, a little Englander who disapproved of war. His attitude to war was completely consistent. Both in 1899 and in 1914 he regarded war as a tragedy and a disaster – 'organised cruelty', he called it. He summed up his attitude, writing in 1918:

> I hate war ... But you either make war or you don't. It is the business of statesmen to strain every nerve to keep a nation out of war, but once they are in it, it is also their business to wage it with all their might ... I want this to be the last, and it won't be unless this war is effectively managed by us. A badly conducted war means a bad peace, and a bad peace means no peace at all. That is why I urge that this war be conducted with determination.[1]

World War I was a tragedy indeed for all concerned, but especially for Lloyd George when, from the outbreak of war, he became a key participant. For almost nine years he had exhausted himself making the British people better fed, better paid, better insured, healthier in the here and now, with better prospects of stress-free retirement and dignified burial. Now it was his fate to lead the very same people whom he had saved into the mouth of hell, the men to death and mutilation on the Western Front and elsewhere, their families condemned to bombardment, starvation, drowning and above all, bereavement. Lloyd George never shook off his grief that he, of all people, had been involved in the causes and conduct of this mass-slaughter. How had this happened? How had he allowed himself to become involved in this massacre of the innocents? How did he become the supreme warlord trying and often failing to protect the people for whom he had created, if not quite the welfare state, at least the contributory state? No wonder his excuse was to blame others. First, however, we must ask how he became a prominent member of a team of warriors.

Part of the explanation is that Lloyd George had always been interested in the foreign policy of the Liberal government which eventually took Great Britain to war. His personal interventions were certainly few, largely because he was so preoccupied with his work at the Board of Trade or at the Exchequer, but when they came, they were decisive. For instance, he was crucially involved in keeping the state's expenditure down to a level which could be afforded. The funding of the old age pensions which Asquith had bequeathed him was a major preoccupation, but so was the payment for the ridiculously extravagant and apparently unnecessary dreadnoughts. What on earth was the point of these clumsy floating weapons of mass destruction, capable of inflicting mayhem and death at a distance of twelve miles and more? Unfortunately, Germany was constructing equally lethal sea-monsters, and could not be allowed to overtake the British navy: as an island, Britain was uniquely vulnerable at sea.

Actually, Lloyd George was, like most Liberals, naturally pro-Germany. Trading links complemented the close ties between the royal families; Queen Victoria had died in the Kaiser's arms. The music of Bach, Beethoven and Mendelssohn, the last introduced by the Prince Consort, had become increasingly popular. Lloyd George felt an affinity with a modern, enlightened Protestant state which pioneered social reforms such as health insurance. He himself visited Germany in 1908 to see how a welfare state was run. Together with Haldane and Churchill he was glad to respond to German gestures of friendship. He enjoyed meeting the Kaiser, though he did not think much of him. He regarded the naval rivalry as unnecessary and deplorable, so when he made a defiant, anti-German speech at the Mansion House on 21 July 1911, the result was sensational.

Asquith hit the nail on the head when he wrote to Lloyd George in September 1910: 'There is always the possibility of some fresh outburst from the *enfant terrible* in the Imperial nursery.' The Kaiser was indeed a menace. He was the mouthpiece for both the militarist Prussian Junkers and for the excitable middle-class German nationalism which gloried in the Navy League. Ironically, the German Navy was the Kaiser's way of expressing his admiration for all things British; yet it was the single greatest cause of Britain's entry into the Great War. Armageddon came a step closer when, in the summer of 1911, German troublemakers led by the 'All-Highest' made a bid for a German naval presence in Morocco by sending the gunboat *Panther* to the Atlantic port of Agadir. This step was anti-French in that Morocco was being colonised by the French. It was also anti-British as German warships would be able to menace British trade from Agadir if a naval base were to be established there. The coal carried by Germany's latest battle-cruisers enabled them to challenge the Grand Fleet in the North Sea but not further afield. The ultimate German objective, however, was to smash the Anglo-French Entente, initially established by Lansdowne in 1904 and maintained with paranoid emphasis by Grey since 1905. Clearly the German game was to isolate France, in the hope that Britain would abandon her in the face of

German aggression. What would the British government do? Would perfidious Albion rat on the French as usual?

Lloyd George had followed the Agadir crisis with concern. Whatever his natural sympathy for 'our German cousins', he had a low opinion of the Kaiser and his warlords. 'The policy of the jack-boot won't do for us, I am all for peace, but am not going to be jack-booted by anybody',[2] he protested to Sir George Riddell. And he was determined to take his protest further. As it happened, he was due to speak at the annual bankers' dinner at the Mansion House – an excellent opportunity for firing a warning salvo at the German bully. What if Lloyd George of all people, the ultra-civilian man of peace, were to threaten war if the Germans did not back down? This would be a sensational development. Lloyd George was game. He first cleared his speech with both Asquith and Grey:

> I believe it essential in the interests not merely this country, but of the world, that Britain should at all hazards maintain her place and prestige among the great powers of the world. Her potent influence has been many times in the past, and may yet be in the future, invaluable to the cause of human liberty. It has more than once in the past redeemed continental nations who are sometimes too apt to forget that service from overwhelming disaster and even from national extinction. I would make great sacrifices to preserve peace. I conceive that nothing could justify a disturbance of international goodwill except questions of the gravest international moment. But if a situation were to be forced upon us in which peace could only be preserved by the surrender of the great and beneficent position Britain has won by centuries of heroism and achievement, by allowing Britain to be treated where her interests were vitally affected, as if she were of no account in the Cabinet of nations, then I say, emphatically, that peace at that price would be intolerable for a great country like ours to endure. National honour is no party question. The security of our great international trade is no party question. The peace of the world is much more likely to be secured if all nations realise fully what the condition of peace must be.[3]

Is it fair to blame Lloyd George for bringing war nearer? Certainly the Kaiser was furious, and abused the British ambassador 'like a pickpocket'. He announced an increase in naval rearmament 'so that no one can dispute our place in the sun'. But Germany climbed down over Morocco. Lloyd George told Masterman: 'People think that because I am pro-Boer I am anti-war in general and that I should faint at the mention of a cannon. I am not against war a bit. I like the Germans but I hate the Junker caste.' For the next few months he was too busy piloting national insurance through Parliament and settling rail strikes to be involved directly in foreign policy. But he was usually invited to the Committee of Imperial Defence and made an influential and sadly unperceptive speech in July 1914 in which he opined that the sky had never been bluer in the international hemisphere.

When the storm clouds threatened at the end of July, Asquith expressed his appreciation of the Chancellor's moderation: 'Lloyd George, all for peace, is more sensible and statesmanlike for keeping the position still open.' He can be compared to the dog in the Sherlock Holmes story which did *not* bark in the night. Lloyd George pointedly refused to lead the pacifist, anti-war clique headed by Burns, Harcourt and Morley; had he done so, there might well have been a stampede of left-wing Liberal MPs against a declaration of war. On the other hand, Lloyd George avoided the noisy belligerence of Churchill and Haldane. 'Loulou' Harcourt's diary records Asquith's exasperation with Churchill; he told the Colonial Secretary that 'one half of the whole [cabinet time] was taken up by one man.' Harcourt was infuriated by Lloyd George's unreliability, in particular his distinction between Germany's invasion of Belgium and its occupation. Lloyd George supported Asquith and Grey, who bent over backwards to avoid provoking Germany. For Lloyd George the safety of Belgium was paramount, not for any sentimental regard for small countries but out of consideration for British security. No hostile power should control the Channel. Similarly, he regarded the security of France as a vital British interest.[4]

Further questions should be posed here. Was Lloyd George justified in blaming Grey for concealing from the cabinet British commitments to France? And could war have been prevented if Grey had made Britain's intentions clearer to Germany? Lloyd George and Grey were never especially close, though their correspondence was cordial enough in 1913–1914. They respected each other's expertise. But they were very different – Grey the aristocratic Northumbrian landowner, Lloyd George the Welsh adventurer. It was only later, however, when he wrote his *War Memoirs* in the 1930s – when Grey was old and blind – that Lloyd George criticised him for keeping his colleagues in the dark, in particular with regard to commitments to France, when Grey glibly protested, 'they've got nothing in writing'.

> There is no more conspicuous example of this kind of suppression of vital information than the way in which the military arrangements we entered into with France were kept from the Cabinet for six years. They came to my knowledge, first of all, in 1911, during the Agadir crisis, but the Cabinet as a whole were not acquainted with them before the following year. There is abundant evidence that both the French and the Russians regarded these military arrangements as practically tantamount to a commitment on our part to come to the aid of France in the event of her being attacked by Germany ... When in 1912 (six years after they had been entered into) Sir Edward Grey communicated these negotiations and arrangements to the Cabinet the majority of its members were aghast. Sir Edward Grey allayed the apprehensions of his colleagues to a certain extent by emphatic assurances that these military arrangements left us quite free, in the event of war, to decide whether we should or should not participate in the conflict. The Prime Minister also exercised his great authority with the Cabinet in the same direction. In spite of these assurances a number of Cabinet Ministers were not reconciled to the action taken by the Foreign Office, the War Office and the Admiralty.[5]

Lloyd George argued that it was even more remiss of Grey not to make Britain's obligations clear to the Germans:

> Had he warned Germany in time of the point at which Britain would declare war – and wage it with her whole strength – the issue would have been different ... he could have intimated to the German government that if they put into operation their plan of marching through Belgium they would encounter the active hostility of the British Empire. And he could have uttered this warning in sufficient time to leave the German military authorities without any excuse for not changing their dust-laden plans.[6]

Here we have one of the great might-have-beens. No-one can prove Lloyd George right or wrong, but it is hard not to agree with the judgement pronounced on Grey by Sir Hugh Bell, a fellow director of the North Eastern Railway, quoted with approval by Lloyd George: 'Grey is a good colleague because he never takes any risks: and he is a thoroughly bad colleague for the same reason.' Insular, remote, out of touch with the common man, Grey was, in Lloyd George's opinion, a disastrous Foreign Secretary. He himself would have loved the job. Interestingly his brother William tried to get Lloyd George to tone down his criticism of Grey, but Lloyd George was unrepentant, claiming that 'his reputation is not based on any achievement'. What sort of a Foreign Secretary Lloyd George would have made, is a question which was never put to the test.[7]

No war is inevitable, but Professor Margaret Macmillan[8] is only the latest of several historians who have depicted the shocking irresponsibility of the handful of European politicians and soldiers who blithely took the decisions which condemned Europe to a lemming-like stampede into catastrophe. Their only excuse is that they did not know what war would be like, though they should surely have had a pretty good idea. But it is probably unfair to blame Grey for not restraining the Kaiser, Tsar Nicholas, Count Berchtold, Field Marshal von Moltke, Field Marshal Conrad and others. Ironically, the only prominent personage who realised what a catastrophe war would be was the Archduke Franz Ferdinand. Could Grey have made any difference whatever he did, given the Kaiser's notorious contempt for the British army? Could Lloyd George, if he had had the authority? Writing to the Editor of *The Times* on 1 August 2014, Professor John CG Röhl reiterated the arguments advanced by Fritz Fischer, which have caused outrage in right-wing German circles, establishing the guilt of Germany's leaders for the outbreak of the Great War:

> It is to be hoped that the enthusiasm generated by recent works proclaiming the "innocence" of the Kaiser and his advisers for the catastrophe of July 1914 subsides again before any damage is done to the Federal Republic's admirable reputation for dealing frankly with a difficult history.[9]

Lloyd George certainly served his country well as chancellor by preventing panic among 'the flapping penguins of the Treasury' when war broke out. The bank holiday of Monday 3 August was extended by three days. £1 and 10/- notes were issued and the bank-rate stabilised at 5 per cent. A vote of credit from Parliament of £100 million was supplemented by increased income tax and supertax. The Chancellor deservedly received a letter of thanks from the Prime Minister for his determination and quick thinking, though some might blame him for fuelling inflation by irresponsible borrowing and issuing paper money.

The Chancellor at War

Lloyd George was soon deeply disturbed by the conduct of the war. Forward planning was not in evidence. The eventual Commander-in-Chief (hereafter C. in C.) of the British Expeditionary Force, Sir John French, sent Riddell, Lloyd George's benefactor and golfing-partner, a revealing note on the evening of 2 August: 'Can you tell me, old chap, whether we are going to be in this war? If so, are we going to put an army on the Continent, and, if we are, who is going to command it?'[10] French was told to report to Downing Street next morning, when he was duly appointed.[11] In his *1914: Fight the Good Fight*, Allan Mallinson criticises the War Office for assuming that the French army would be simultaneously mobilised with the British Expeditionary Force's deployment in France: 'The War Office failed both the army and the country.'[12] Mallinson's view commands respect as he was a professional soldier for 35 years, total chaos prevailed. The failure was political as well as military as the secretary of state for war was a member of the cabinet. Lloyd George was of a similar opinion we shall examine critically his own attempt to square this particular circle when he himself became prime minister in December 1916. In August 1914, the politicians blundered in step with the generals, as the director of operations, General Sir Henry Wilson, predicted when a staff college student could not believe that statesmen would display such inconceivable stupidity: 'Haw! Haw!! Haw!!! Inconceivable stupidity is just what you're going to get.'[13]

This disturbing state of affairs was by no means remedied by the appointment of Lord Kitchener as Secretary of State for War. Asquith made a shrewd appointment politically when Kitchener was hijacked off the ship to Egypt where he was the British representative and brought back to London to take over the War Office. The Conservative Party was impressed by the recruitment of the Empire's greatest soldier and the general public responded to the most famous recruiting poster of all time. But was Kitchener more than 'The Great Poster' (Margot Asquith)?[14] Warming his backside in front of his office fire a few weeks later, he told a visitor that this would be the first Christmas he had spent at home for 30 years. He really was that far out of touch. Furthermore, he was full of prejudices, for instance against Sir John French, whom he loathed, and against Haldane's admirable Territorial Army. So it should have been no surprise to Lloyd George that Kitchener opposed the creation of Welsh divisions and the commissioning of Nonconformist chaplains. These relatively trivial quarrels were soon resolved, though only after almighty rows in Cabinet in which Field-marshall Earl Kitchener of Khartoum KG KCVO, etc. was reminded by the little Welshman that he was just one member of the government, and had to accept criticism like everyone else. 'You are not an autocrat but only one out of a body of equals.'[15] Very worrying was the performance of the British army under Kitchener's 'administration'. Before long he was known as 'Lord K of Chaos'.

Given the questionable condition of the armed forces, there was a considerable amount of wishful thinking, even downright dishonesty, in Lloyd George's tirade at the Queen's Hall on 16 September 1914, as discussed in the Introduction. After dismissing the Prussian Junker as 'the road hog of Europe, hurling small nations to the roadside', he raised jingoism to an art-form.

What some might regard as sentimentality was certainly effective, and is arguably no worse than the moral blackmail preached by Anglican bishops or the self-deceiving poetry of, say, Rupert Brooke. Lloyd George excelled when war rhetoric was demanded. To be fair, somebody had to do it, and it is hard to think of anyone who could have done it better – Churchill, maybe, but he was becoming more unpopular by the day. Robert Graves, poet and essayist, was impressed when his father took him to hear Lloyd George speak to the Honourable Cymmroddorion Society:

> Lloyd George was up in the air on one of his 'glory of the Welsh hills' speeches. The power of his rhetoric amazed me. The substance of the speech might be commonplace, idle and false, but I had to fight hard against abandoning myself with the rest of his audience. He sucked power from his listeners and spurted it back at them.[16]

Surely the opening sentence of Lloyd George's speech at the Queen's Hall is the give-away – 'How I envy you young people …' The truth was that among the political leaders of the English nation Lloyd George was the least inclined to go anywhere near the front if he could help it. He did not like coming under fire – and this applied also to Zeppelin raids over London which reduced him to an abject state of terror. He was shaken by his visit to Dieppe and the Western Front on 17 October 1914. He was uncomfortable when he came within a mile of the frontline. And he well knew that the young idealists to whom he preached would join a mismanaged crusade, hence his crafty dispatch of his own two sons to safe staff appointments.

To be fair to Lloyd George, however, he was openly and noisily disturbed by the self-evident cluelessness of the generals. He was quick to grasp that this was a new form of warfare posed by the uninterrupted line of trenches running from the North Sea to the Alps, protected by the mass-produced marvels of modern science such as barbed wire, machine-guns, poison gas, grenades, mortars, artillery and trenches. The Anglo-French generals were convinced that the only way to win the war was to attack. But it was increasingly clear to Lloyd George that the offensive was suicidal. As long as the experts of the General Staff failed to grasp this inconvenient fact, Lloyd George was convinced that he knew more than the professionals. Here was a new form of warfare which soldiers and civilians alike faced with equal inexperience and ignorance. The question was, who was the quicker on the uptake when it came to working out how to avoid the holocaust of the nation's youth, condemned to die in a nightmare from which there was no escape. Max Hastings describes the horror of a French soldier who watched enormous rats fleeing from under the greatcoat of a dead soldier: 'out of his gaping mouth a foul animal jumped'.[17] A representative anecdote, as Lloyd George would have recognised.

It soon became apparent what was happening. In various sanguinary engagements on the Western Front, British soldiers were sent to certain death armed with whatever puny weapons they could manhandle – that is to say, rifles, bayonets and grenades, the platoon commander giving away his identity with a futile revolver. The attacks were invariably frontal because there was no flank to turn. Surprise was non-existent as the attacks were preceded by artillery bombardments too ineffectual to demolish the enemy's defences but sufficiently protracted to give away the time and the place of the coming attack by the PBI (Poor Bloody Infantry). General Sir Horace Smith-Dorrien, Haig's opposite number as commander of II Corps, ('Smith-Dorris', as Haig generously dubbed him) refused to order his men to go over the top, on the grounds that soldiers should never be told to attempt the impossible. He was instantly sacked ('Orace, yer for ome',[18] in the words of French's Chief of Staff, the demotic Sir William Robertson.) French, as C. in C., badly needed an alibi and so blamed shortage of artillery shells. *The Times* correspondent,

Colonel Repington, published this alarming message, and so it became common knowledge that our boys had failed because the artillery bombardment was inadequate. Asquith's Liberal government was replaced in May 1915 by a coalition still headed by Asquith but which included Bonar Law, Balfour and Lansdowne. As the war at sea had been equally unsuccessful, Churchill, whom in any case the Tories loathed, was sacked from the Admiralty. Lloyd George earned Asquith's gratitude by remaining loyal and by accepting the newly created Ministry of Munitions. Self-effacing and patriotic, he was replaced at the Treasury by Reginald McKenna.

Lloyd George at the Ministry of Munitions

Lloyd George can be seen at his most impressive at Munitions. It is impossible not to admire his cheerful refusal to be dismayed by opposition or lack of the necessary materials. From day one, his style was apparent: the hotel which had been requisitioned for him contained a table, two chairs, several mirrors and no civil servants. Soon, a couple of workmen arrived to confiscate the chairs – just the scenario Lloyd George loved. His parliamentary secretary was Dr Christopher Addison, once saving lives as a professor of anatomy, now devoting his time to blowing people up. Lloyd George was in his element recruiting technicians, businessmen and railwaymen such as Eric Geddes who had managed the North Eastern Railway. The Minister's office was run by J. T. Davies, Frances Stevenson and William Sutherland whose specialism was bamboozling the press. Significant by their absence were professional soldiers. 'Delighted to hear you are coming to help me',[19] wrote Kitchener, under the mistaken impression that Lloyd George was his subordinate and that the new department would be part of the War Office: one of Lloyd George's first achievements was to exclude the War Office completely. He ignored military 'experts', having a low opinion of most 'experts', but military ones in particular. He never acknowledged the real if limited progress already made by the War Office.

Soon he had divided Britain into twelve self-supporting districts which he visited and galvanised as only he knew how. New factories were established, new targets agreed. The results were astonishing. Monthly output of shells when he took office was 70,000; when he left it was over a million. Production of machine-guns averaged 6,000 in 1915, 33,000 in 1916. He overruled the War Office by insisting on new designs for mortars and machine-guns, in some instances borrowing ideas from the French. Because US industry was already stretched when it came to the mass-production of guns, Lloyd George innovated by commissioning Canadian enterprises to fill the gap, thus procuring the ordinance and giving Canadian industry a boost. The War Office opposed Lloyd George's orders as being excessive and unnecessary, but the Cabinet supported Lloyd George who was proved right. He cooperated with Churchill in the early stages of the tank's development. He welcomed local initiatives in bypassing War Office bottlenecks. The unfortunate General von Donop, the War Office's master general of ordnance, did not know what had hit him when he complacently assured a planning group that enough machinery had been ordered 'to meet all possible requirements'. He was supported by Kitchener, but demolished by Lloyd George with Asquith's approval.

Did Lloyd George always succeed? Certainly not. He had a hard time solving the problem of labour: there were not enough skilled workmen available. He had great difficulty squaring the unions when it came to the necessary dilution of skilled workers as a result of the recruitment of unskilled men – and women. Skilled men reluctantly tolerated these new recruits, fearing for their own jobs after the war. Lloyd George found that his eloquence and charm did not always disarm suspicion. For instance, he suffered a humiliating failure at Glasgow on Christmas Day 1915, when he assured a hostile crowd of workers that the lot of a minister of the Crown was not easy. 'The money's good', shouted a heckler, provoking ribald laughter.[20] Lloyd George sat down visibly shaken. His hair fell across his forehead. 'Get your hair cut!' bellowed the crowd.[21] The hall was packed in more senses than one. Lloyd George was sufficiently affronted to have Gallagher and Kirkwood, the chief Communist agitators, temporarily imprisoned.

Truth told, Lloyd George deserved to be challenged. Take his sentimental rubbish at Bristol in September 1915: 'I know the workman, and the tenderness I received from an old workman's household made me a friend of labour.' He assured his audience that he got a letter from that same workman every day to which he always replied. Of course, Uncle Lloyd was not a typical British workman, but a highly religious and self-educated man of letters and a prosperous employer of labour: never mind, it was good rabblerousing stuff.[22]

A remarkable story was the mass recruitment of women.[23] Lloyd George's allies were none other than Christobel Pankhurst and her redoubtable mother. Lloyd George cooperated with the Pankhursts in organising a huge demonstration on Saturday 17 July 1915 on the Embankment in favour of the employment of women. His Ministry helped to fund the occasion and he addressed the demonstrators, promising them a fair deal. He was as good as his word. Eventually, 1.25 million women were recruited into war industries. Lloyd George ensured that they were paid as much as the men; he looked after their health and hygiene and provided cafeterias at which suitable food was served. The significance of this story went beyond war-work. The Minister of National Service, Neville Chamberlain, remarked that 'the nation has been surprised and delighted by our women's contribution to the war effort'. However patronising, Chamberlain correctly celebrated the victory over prejudice against women. It was a great argument for 'votes for women'. Lloyd George gave women their reward in the Parliament Act of March 1918.[24]

One of Lloyd George's most eccentric measures was his attempt to outlaw alcohol. 'We are fighting Germany, Austria and drink, and so far as I can see the greatest of these deadly foes is drink', he argued with melodramatic oversimplification. Beer was diluted as well as the labour force. He even persuaded the long-suffering King to ban drink from Court, though 'Squiffy' Asquith and the rest of the Cabinet did not fall into line. Nor did Lloyd George's campaign go down well with the workers.

Lloyd George cut himself off from his left-wing roots in many ways, not merely by attacking working class drinking habits. His dragooning of workers on the factory floor made him trade union enemies just as his advocacy of conscription into both the armed forces and armament factories was considered deeply illiberal. Lloyd George defended himself, for example on 6 May 1916 to his constituents in Conway: 'I have no shame in declaring for compulsory enlistment ... I hate war. But you either make war or you don't.' His very job alienated his Nonconformist supporters. The irony was not lost on Lloyd George that he, the great moral crusader, should end up making ammunition with which human lives would be torn to pieces. Uncle Lloyd was not the only Welsh Nonconformist who deplored his dear boy's move from the exchequer to munitions. Nevertheless, there was a war on which necessitated blowing up the enemy. If he really was the man who won the war, there is a case for basing this claim on his work as minister of munitions, rather than, as is usually assumed, on his achievements as prime minister which were certainly remarkable but, as we shall see, flawed.[25]

War Minister

Two dramatic events dispatched Lloyd George to the War Office. The first was his involvement in Ireland. During the Easter celebrations of 1916, extreme nationalists staged a rebellion in Dublin. The coup was a miserable failure. The British government however very unwisely executed many of the coup's leaders. Lloyd George earned his leader's gratitude by deploying his flexibility and realism in negotiating a settlement: the 26 nationalist counties were given Home Rule, while the six unionist counties were excluded. But unfortunately this was a fudged solution, as it was not made clear whether it was temporary or permanent. Lloyd George had not heard the last of Ireland.[26]

The second cataclysmic event was the mining of the cruiser HMS *Hampshire* off the Orkneys on 6 June 1916. Among the dead was the War Minister, Kitchener, who was on his way to Russia. Was Lloyd George the right man to succeed him? It was either Lloyd George or Bonar Law – who in the end did not want the job.

Lloyd George was becoming critical of Asquith's lethargic management of the war, for example reiterating the words 'too late' in a much-quoted and tactlessly offensive speech to the House of Commons: 'Too late in moving here, too late in coming to this decision, too late in starting with enterprises, too late in preparing!'[27] So why not send Lloyd George to the War Office, which was notorious for delays and postponement of necessary reforms? Actually, Asquith had hoped to send him to Russia with Kitchener, but Ireland intervened. Otherwise, as Grigg felicitously puts it, they would have gone together, and Asquith would have shed two inconvenient colleagues.[28] This option void, he decided to risk Lloyd George as Kitchener's successor. The Tories were less than happy, as they wanted a safe man as secretary of state, but were partially appeased by the appointment of the reliable Lord Derby as Lloyd George's parliamentary undersecretary – in other words as his 'minder'.

Lloyd George's stint there was unhappy for several reasons. First, he inherited powers which had been reduced, so that Kitchener could be controlled by the Chief of the Imperial General Staff, Sir William 'Wully' Robertson. ('The bugger's agreed!' crowed Wully when Kitchener accepted the limitations.) Lloyd George tried and failed to get the original powers restored. Secondly, Lloyd George now disagreed with the Prime Minister. Everyone liked Asquith, but by mid-1916 no-one respected his leadership. He was a rotten chairman of the War Committee and the Cabinet, indecisive, badly informed and inattentive. 'Mr Asquith, do you take an interest in the War?'[29] asked a society lady. His habit of writing letters to his mistress, Venetia Stanley, justified Kitchener's complaint that several ministers wrote injudiciously to their wives while some wrote to other men's wives. Lloyd George, for his part, did not rate the soldiers at the War Office, least of all Wully, who detested politicians, especially Lloyd George.

The fact that the war was going badly poisoned his relations with the new C. in C., Field Marshal Sir Douglas Haig. They were oil and water. Whereas Lloyd George and Wully really should have got on, both having risen through the ranks (Wully had been in domestic service before entering the army as a private), Haig was emphatically out of the top draw – educated at Clifton, Brasenose College, Oxford and Sandhurst. He was Haig's whisky, a cavalryman and, having married a lady-in-waiting, a personal friend of George V. 'Tyde what may whate'er betyde, Haig shall be Haig of Bemersyde'[30] was the family motto. While he was not quite so ungenerous towards Lloyd George as Wully who considered him 'an ill-bred swine',[31] Haig of Bemerside dismissed Lloyd George of Highgate with perfunctory and patronising comments in a letter to his wife: 'Quite a pleasant little man when one has him alone, but I should think most unreliable.'[32]

The poor chemistry between Lloyd George and Haig is captured in a brilliant photograph, taken when Lloyd George visited the Western Front in September 1916. According to Haig, the Minister turned this visit into a joy-ride involving 'breakfasts with newspapermen, and posings for the cinema shows'.[33] Lloyd George had been puzzled by some mounted cavalrymen who jingled past behind the line. 'What are they for?' asked our intrepid 'expert'. He recounts in his memoirs how Haig and his French opposite number, General Joffre, fell on him with ecstatic enthusiasm. A photographer chanced to snap this high pressure tutorial. Haig is, as ever, immaculate in the uniform of a cavalry officer: gleaming boots, 'Sam Browne' and general's insignia. Lloyd George is the complete civilian; a good caption would indeed be, 'get a hair-cut'. Haig's obvious exasperation with his dim pupil is equalled by Lloyd George's undeferential scepticism. He was surely correct to question the case for cavalry on the Western Front. Haig's defenders argue that cavalry amounted to a mere 3 per cent of the total British Expeditionary Force; Still 3 per cent of the total comes to approximately 60,000 men, plus fodder, plus accommodation, etc.[34]

While struggling with recalcitrant generals at the War Office, Lloyd George must have harked back nostalgically to his happy time at Munitions. On 19 July 1916 he warned Montagu, his successor, against being uncooperative, prompting the delightful, hand-written reply: 'My dear Creator and Creator of my Office, Surely you know that everybody in this office, civilian or soldier, male or female from the Minister to the latest joined youngest and most dewy messenger-girl are at your service (properly speaking)...'[35]

Shortly after Lloyd George's arrival at the War Office, the Somme Offensive began. At 7 am on 1 July 1916, the British army implemented General Haig's disastrous plan – that is to say, frontal attacks by infantry across no-man's land against virtually intact, scientifically prepared German defences. As there had been a week-long artillery bombardment of the German frontline there was no element of surprise. On the other hand, enough machine-gunners had survived the bombardment to exact horrific massacre of the British PBI, extending uninterrupted for miles. Nineteen thousand British soldiers died on the first day. The campaign was continued with bull-headed obstinacy until mid-November. Six-hundred thousand casualties resulted. What emphatically did not result was the decisive break-through predicted by Haig – to be exploited by the cavalry straining at their leashes. It never happened, and as the Germans retreated to previously prepared positions, Haig came up with a new justification for this mass murder – 'attrition'. The theory was that the Germans would be 'worn away' by non-stop British aggression. Perhaps they were, but unfortunately so were the British. Lloyd George was totally unconvinced; In fact, he was appalled.

But Lloyd George was similarly frustrated by his inability to influence the deployment of forces on a broader front. For instance, to his rage and distress, Romania was overwhelmed due to the allies' inability to dispatch forces to her rescue (two divisions were earmarked, but too tardily to make any difference). Meanwhile, Lloyd George's ill-concealed indignation earned him threats from the generals' tame press lord, Northcliffe of *The Times*, who promised to 'break' him if he persisted, and from Wully Robertson, who protested that strategy should be left to the generals. Lloyd George replied:

> It ought to be decided whether I have the same right – although I am War Secretary – to express an independent view on the War in the discussions which take place as any other members of the War Council – or whether, as long as I am War Secretary, I must choose between the position of a dummy or a pure advocate of all opinions expressed by my military advisers. You must not ask me to play the part of a mere dummy – I am not in the least suited for the part.[36]

So the suicidal offensives on the front favoured by the generals ground on relentlessly. Lloyd George was decidedly underwhelmed. Contrary to his wishes, tanks were committed piecemeal in September 1916, with initially encouraging results – but there were too few of them for success to be followed up. The War Minister did not visit the troops enough, partly because he was ashamed of what was happening, partly out of sheer funk, partly because he was squeamish about blood and suffering. On one visit to the Front he was asked to comfort the horribly wounded son of John Hinds, a Welsh MP. Half the young man's scalp had been shot away and Lloyd George's procurement of the best medics could not save him. When he got home, Lloyd George wailed to Frances, imploring her to distract him:

> I wish I had not seen him. I ought not to have seen him. I feel that I cannot go on with my work, now that the grim horror of the reality has been brought home to me so terribly. I was not made to deal with things of war. I am too sensitive to pain and suffering, and this visit has almost broken me down.[37]

In a way his horrified grief does him credit, indeed he was right to be appalled; perhaps more politicians and generals should have been more cognisant with the facts of death. But his blubbering self-pity was rightly criticised by Lloyd George's elder son, Major Dick, when he came home on leave:

I'll make him understand. Why must he be protected? Why should we all baby him? Sickness, misery, death – these were the things he feared. He could never look on the face of death. But now he would have to. I'd see to it that he did know what was happening.

Lloyd George got in first: 'All right, Dick. You must tell me what it's been like.' But one look at his father's face told Dick that he already knew.[38]

When Lloyd George shuddered at his obligation to drive men to the slaughterhouse like the butcher's boy, he knew very well what their fate would be. Indeed, while his horror is to his credit as a humanitarian, it is also a reason for despising his indecisiveness when faced with the appalling repetition of young Hinds' fate literally thousands of times over, now, and still more in the months ahead when he had become prime minister.

One sin which we might think should have been on Lloyd George's conscience was brought home to him from an inconvenient voice from the past. Julia Henry was one of his many mistresses before Frances arrived. Lloyd George had sent her packing in 1911, provoking tearful hysterics. Now, her only son Cyril went missing on the Western Front. Before his death was confirmed, Julia wrote reproachfully to Lloyd George accusing him of finding safe billets for Dick and Gwilym. There was just enough truth in this unkind suggestion for Lloyd George to have a case to answer.[39] As we have seen there was an unwholesome contrast between his gung-ho recruitment speeches and his sly dispatch of his two boys to risk-free staff appointments.[40] Now Raymond Asquith was killed on the Somme, and the unfortunate Prime Minister was filled not only with sorrow but with remorse, because he had hardly ever written to his eldest son, while writing to his mistress every day. He was, indeed a broken old man by now, no longer a convincing leader of warriors.

The Fall of Asquith

When Asquith was replaced by Lloyd George, was he the victim of a palace coup? Historians used to think so – Roy Jenkins, Donald McCormick, Trevor Wilson, for example. The American historian, George H. Cassar, claims that 'Lloyd George elbowed Asquith out of the premiership'.[41] When Lloyd George went to the War Office, Margot Asquith exclaimed prophetically: 'We're out.' She loathed

Lloyd George, regarding him as unscrupulous, deceitful and Satanic, as opposed to her saintly husband who was indeed betrayed by the subordinate whom he had befriended, promoted and defended. On the other hand, recent historians such as Lord Kenneth Morgan, John Grigg and J. Graham Jones reject the conspiracy myth. According to John Turner, 'It is a mistake to see the December Crisis as an encapsulated palace revolution'. Actually, Asquith could look after himself, if only the war was going well. But it was not.

Defeat in Mesopotamia, as well as in Picardy, was mirrored by a depressing picture at sea. On 31 May 1916, the great battle fleets met at last. But Jutland was not Trafalgar any more than Jellicoe was Nelson. Although the High Seas Fleet turned for home, leaving the Grand Fleet in occupation of the North Sea, more British ships and more British sailors were lost than German. Worst of all, the Germans got home first and broadcast their version of the battle to the world. When Beatty's battle-cruisers limped into Rossyth – some of them towed – their crews were booed as they came ashore. The U-boat menace, threatening British trade, was even more worrying. 'Squiffy' Asquith, now visibly dependent on drink, was out of his depth, too old, too depressed and utterly hopeless. Constance Battersea, a family friend, found him 'red and bloated, quite different from what he used to be'.[42] When Bonar Law visited Asquith on a Sunday morning at the Wharf, his home near Oxford, he found the Prime Minister playing bridge with three young ladies. Bonar Law was himself a bridge enthusiast, nor despite being a 'PK' (American: 'Preacher's Kid') would his sabbatarian prejudices have been offended, but he was concerned by this scene of irresponsible frivolity.

There were, in fact, two things wrong, as Asquith's increasingly worried critics realised. One was the leader; the other was the system – an oversized Cabinet failing to control an unrepresentative War Committee. Asquith was a disastrous chairman. 'Well, I think we're all agreed', he would say glancing happily round the table. 'Can anyone tell me what precisely we are all agreed about?', boomed Sir Edward Carson. Nobody could. Asquith survived as long as he did because there was no agreement about his successor. Lloyd George stood head and shoulders above the alternatives, but not only was he unpopular and mistrusted, he did not particularly want the job – not, at any rate, when things were going so badly. It would be naïve to pretend that Lloyd George lacked ambition, but he needed a decent chance of success to realise his goals. The only other obvious possibility for the role was the Tory leader Bonar Law – low-key, diffident, by no means assured of his own party's support. Asquith consistently under-estimated him, but Lloyd George liked and admired him, disagreeing with most Liberals. In fact, it was Bonar Law who broke the deadlock.

On 5 December 1916 Lloyd George had what should have been a constructive meeting with his chief. After smoking a cigar at the War Office with his press-lord supporter, Lord Riddell, he walked over to Downing Street where, in an affable discussion, he persuaded Asquith to agree to a streamlined war cabinet of three, to be chaired by Lloyd George but which the Prime Minister could attend when he had the time. Later, Asquith withdrew his consent after *The Times* published details of Lloyd George's scheme which he presumed had been leaked by its author. Even more wounding was *The Times* gloss on the scheme, stressing the inevitable supersession of the Prime Minister. 'I have not seen *The Times*' article', Lloyd George protested somewhat disingen-uously. Asquith was far from convinced and refused to co-operate, asking, 'What is the proposal that I who have held first place for eight years should be asked to take a secondary position?'[43] His disavowal of *amour propre* does not ring true. Either way, Lloyd George, now aware that Asquith would not cooperate, promptly resigned.

George V tried to break the deadlock by convening an informal conference. When invited to form a government, Bonar Law agreed, provided that Asquith would serve under him. When Asquith indig-nantly refused, Bonar Law suggested Lloyd George, under whom he professed himself glad to serve. Asquith did not think Lloyd George would be capable of attracting enough support. With all his admirable qualities, Asquith was too vain, too complacent, too ill-advised to see the truth. 'The noblest Roman' as they called him,[44] fell on his sword when he made way for Lloyd George, confident that his rival would not be able to form a government. He rejected Lloyd George's offer of the Lord Chancellorship. He was right in his presumption that his Liberal colleagues, McKenna, Grey and Runciman, would also refuse to serve under Lloyd George, but wrong, terribly wrong, in expecting his Tory allies to remain faithful. Not only Bonar Law, but Curzon who cared primarily about his own career, Austen Chamberlain who had always admired Lloyd George, Carson and Long all fell into line. The greatest disappointment for Asquith, who was indeed bewildered by the turn of events, was Balfour, who was offered the

Foreign Office and accepted with the memorable words, 'You hold a pistol at my head'.[45] In actual fact, he and Lloyd George had always got on well. Austen Chamberlain continued at the India Office, F. E. Smith became Attorney General and Sir Robert Finlay became Lord Chancellor. Riddell thought Finlay a good choice – 'He is an honest old boy and a great lawyer'. Lloyd George burst out laughing: 'Well he looks honest anyway. That is a great asset for a lawyer.' The only prominent Tory not to join Lloyd George was Lansdowne, who told Bonar Law that 'the proceedings left a nasty taste in my mouth'.

Was Lansdowne right to be disgusted? He was no fool, and had had a long and distinguished career – Governor-General of Canada, Viceroy of India, Secretary of State for War. As Foreign Secretary he engineered the alliance with Japan (1902) and the entente cordiale with France (1904), subsequently supporting France during the Morocco crisis of 1905. He had led the Conservative and Unionist Party in the Lords during the constitutional crisis, 1909–1912. He had presented a paper to the Cabinet in November 1916 advocating a negotiated peace with the Central Powers, his conviction that the war was both evil and futile no doubt reinforced by his own son's death on the Western Front. His antipathy towards Lloyd George was complemented by sympathy for Asquith and Grey. In a letter to the Duchess of Devonshire, Lansdowne reported that he had taken Grey down to Bowood 'for a rough shoot, which I think he thoroughly enjoyed'. The aristocrats of both main parties were on friendlier terms with each other than with their own plebeian subordinates – Bonar Law, Lloyd George, Henderson et al. Lansdowne obviously identified with the aristocratic Grey and with an honorary aristocrat like Asquith – described by Haig's Chief of Intelligence Brigadier Charteris as a 'sahib'.[46] Lansdowne informed the Duchess:

> While we were fraternising in the country, a red-hot conspiracy was coming to a head in London … I am not too well pleased at the manner in which the business was handled, and I am afraid old Asquith thinks he has been badly treated, which, so far as Lloyd George is concerned, is probably true.

Lansdowne was sure that Balfour would refuse to join when 'L. G. would then have to try his hand and like Jezebel face the question: "Who is on my side, who?"'. Lansdowne not only misquoted 2 Kings 9, but like Asquith wrongly anticipated Balfour's response; but he was correct about his own future when he was not invited to join Lloyd George's administration, though he wrongly thought that 'this is not the kind of last act to which I looked forward for my poor play'. In a year's time Lansdowne's letter to the *Daily Telegraph* would make him the most hated figure in Britain; in other words, his last act was still to come.

Oceans of ink have been consumed in debate about Lloyd George's conduct, especially his treatment of Asquith. Did he cynically and brutally torpedo his old chief? What are we to make of the letter which Lloyd George wrote to Asquith on 5 December 1916? 'As you yourself said on Sunday, we have acted together for ten years and never had a quarrel. You have treated me with great courtesy and kindness ...'[47] Years later, Lucy Masterman was surprised to see a signed photograph of Asquith on Lloyd George's piano. 'Yes, there he is, the dear old boy,' exclaimed Lloyd George.[48] Hypocrisy? Barely concealed treachery? Robert Cecil implored Asquith to offer to serve under Lloyd George, but Asquith was too proud, too certain that Lloyd George would fail. Historians opposed to Lloyd George do not believe his proclaimed reluctance to take the job, preferring to attribute to him devious and disloyal ambition. But Lloyd George kept repeating, 'I'm not sure that I can do it'.[49]

Some fascinating evidence on this subject has been lodged in the National Library of Wales, consisting of letters written by Lloyd George to his brother William: 'In the melting pot so far. Nothing has been decided. I have refused to become Prime Minister myself. Bonar wishes me to become PM' (6 December 1916). 'Nothing has been decided as yet. God help us' (7 December 1916). Then: 'Presided over my first War Cabinet ... Tell Uncle Lloyd that he is responsible for putting me in this awful job.'[50] Lloyd George would hardly try to deceive William, who knew him too well, though maybe he was deceiving himself like the holders of top jobs who claim that they are there 'for their sins'. One observer was in no doubt. Uncle Lloyd crowned a half century of adulation: 'The man is greater than the office.' Ten weeks later he died, contented.[51] Churchill, however, doubted what had really happened.[52]

And so should we. As ever Lloyd George is a man of elusive mystery and paradox. Do we go with David Thompson, who argues that 'Asquith was ousted from power by a complex intrigue conducted by Lloyd George with ruthless skill',[53] and with George H. Cassar who refers to 'the blatant disloyalty of Lloyd George who undermined him whenever it suited his purpose?'[54] Or do we prefer Cameron Hazlehurst's total rejection of the 'conspiracy myth'?[55] Or somewhere between?[56] The editors of *British Liberal Leaders*[57] claim that Lloyd George became Prime Minister 'effectively through a parliamentary coup against Asquith organised with the help of leading Conservatives'.[58] Surely there was collusion between Lloyd George, his Conservative allies and press lords such as Beaverbrook and Riddell. But the truth is that if anyone betrayed Asquith, he betrayed himself by becoming a womanising drunk and rejecting a realistic escape clause by refusing to serve under Bonar Law or Lloyd George. He was further let down by Margot flitting around in the background at 10 Downing Street, badgering her husband for not standing up to Lloyd George and imploring the senior Liberals to 'remain faithful to Henry' while she watered his whisky.

Asquith was literally hopeless, both having lost hope and failing to inspire hope. Lloyd George personified hope, hence his advocacy of the knockout blow and his forthright rejection of Lansdowne's memorandum advocating a compromise peace.[59] Those who supported Lloyd George put loyalty to their country ahead of loyalty to Asquith. This was patriotism, not intrigue. In his way, Lloyd George was a patriot too. For all his awareness of the difficulties ahead, in Cassar's words: 'much as he wanted to be Prime Minister, he was not certain that he could command the necessary votes in Parliament'. Like Pitt the Younger, however, he was convinced that he alone could save his country.[60]

6

The Passchendaele Butcher (1917)

He did for them both with his plan of attack.
— Siegfried Sassoon, *The General*

DAVID LLOYD George was perceived by his many admirers, and not least by himself, as 'the man who won the war.' But others, both contemporaries and historians, have been less impressed. The dirge sung in the trenches to Sir Arthur Sullivan's tune 'St Gertrude' – the endless 'Lloyd George knew my father, My father knew Lloyd George' – can be seen not only as a comment on the boredom and pointlessness of trench warfare but also as a somewhat jaundiced view of the great war-leader 'whose rule was dynamic and sordid at the same time'.[1] How many soldiers attributed the responsibility for the horrors of war and the bereavements in so many families to the mistakes and miscalculations made by the new Prime Minister?

Lloyd George was determined to distance himself from Asquith's regime. He formed a War Cabinet of five: himself in the chair, Milner, Curzon, Bonar Law, who alone had other direct responsibilities – he was Chancellor of the Exchequer and Leader of the House, and Henderson, who informally represented the support, not only of the Labour Party, but of organised labour as a whole. This last vital recruitment set the seal on Lloyd George's solution. Frances Stevenson describes her lover's brilliance when he addressed the National Executive of the Labour Party: he warned them that the allies were losing the war and that only a united nation, particularly including Labour, could turn the situation round. According to Frances they arrived at the meeting in a surly, uncooperative frame of mind but were overwhelmed by Lloyd George's charm and good humour. He told the party leader, the conscientious objector Ramsay McDonald, that if he had to lock him up, he hoped that on the day that he was released he would breakfast with him in Downing Street. 'Well, you've courage, George! You've courage!' was Bonar Law's assessment.[2]

On the night of 7 December 1916 Lloyd George went to Buckingham Palace to assure the King that he could form a government which would command majority support in Parliament. He kissed hands. Maggie thoughtfully assured Margot Asquith that she need not hurry in moving out of No. 10. Actually, the Asquiths were indeed in no hurry since they were sure that they would soon be back. Lloyd George himself was still in a sombre mood, not so much about his chances of political survival but rather over the enormity of the task. 'I'm not sure that I can do it', he again confided to Frances. Was this, as some historians have claimed, false modesty? Not necessarily. He was well aware what he was up against, though perhaps he had slightly overdramatised his problems when he told his brother to blame Uncle Lloyd 'for getting me into this dreadful position'.

There is, however, an excellent case for arguing that Lloyd George had a harder task than Churchill in May 1940. The Churchill myth, promulgated by his admirers including himself, is that Great Britain had virtually no chance against the Fascist dictators. But Britain and her Empire were guarded by a navy that was five times the size of the Third Reich's fleet, while the British economy was much healthier than Germany's – as convincingly demonstrated by David Edgerton in his *Britain's War Machine*.[3] Britain in December 1916 had had a terrible year of defeat and frustration, especially on the Western Front. Not even Haig's tame publicist Lord Northcliffe could conceal the non-stop arrival of those forlorn telegrams to thousands of grieving homes. The situation was dire in Mesopotamia and Romania. Russia was on the verge of total collapse. America was weeks away even from diplomatic intervention and it would take a year for her contribution to be any more substantial. The war at sea was about to enter a massive crisis as the German U-boat arm was increasingly successful. The First Sea Lord, Admiral Jellicoe, professed complete bafflement and lugubriously predicting total defeat.

Lloyd George addressed these problems with his customary determination. He dominated his war cabinet of five, which resembled the Committee of Public Safety spawned by the French revolution. Once, when he found the Archbishop of Canterbury there having been invited by Lord Curzon to attend as a Trustee of the British

Museum, he threw him out. Efficient notes were taken of discussions, leading to clearly recorded resolutions. The presiding genius here was Lieutenant Colonel Maurice Hankey of the Royal Marines, and therefore both a soldier and a sailor. Carson was First Lord of the Admiralty; Derby, War Minister; Balfour, Foreign Secretary. One prominent politician who was not recruited was Winston Churchill; the Conservatives refused to join if he sat alongside them. 'You don't care for my personal reputation', Churchill blubbered to his old friend. 'No', he replied 'I don't care for my own at the present moment. The only thing I care about now is that we win this war'.[4] Lloyd George created some new departments, such as National Service under Neville Chamberlain (Lloyd George's worst appointment – 'When I saw that pin-head, I said to myself he won't be any use')[5]; Shipping (Sir Joseph Maclay, a brilliant success); Food (Lord Devonport); the Admiralty (Eric Geddes, after Carson had failed); and Transport (Lord Rhondda, already experienced as a wartime administrator). An Imperial Cabinet involved the Dominions, despite Bonar Law's prediction that 'you will soon want to get rid of them'.[6] A government-secretariat was established in the Downing Street garden – the 'Garden Suburb'.[7] As part of his agreement with the Tories, the high command of the army was left untouched: Robertson remained chief of the Imperial General Staff; Haig continued as commander in chief in France (whom George V made a field-marshal on New Year's Day – a blatant anti-Lloyd George gesture). This raised an unavoidable issue in who exactly was in charge of strategy; nevertheless Lloyd George had made it. His administration was in place.

The Campaign Against the U-boats

The first challenge which the new government had to face was starvation. The ocean-going German U-boat of World War I was frighteningly efficient. Indeed it is hard to distinguish it from the Class Seven U-boats of Admiral Doenitz's *Kriegsmarine* which almost won the Battle of the Atlantic in 1941–1943. During the nightmare summer and autumn of 1916, the U-boats sent millions of tons to the bottom. Food, weapons and equipment such as machine tools – all lost. The problem was magnified when, on 1 February 1917, Germany declared unrestricted submarine warfare by which all merchant ships sailing to and from Britain would be sunk without warning, irrespective of nationality. This was a calculated risk on Germany's part; such tactics would almost certainly bring the United States into the war, but Britain would surely be starved into surrender before American assistance kicked in. The impact was terrifying. Over 840,000 tons were sunk in April 1917 alone. Lloyd George's government adopted four solutions: the first was food-rationing; the second was to grow more food at home in allotments, gardens and fields; the third was to build more merchant ships and passenger liners; the fourth was to defeat and destroy the U-boats.

This fourth solution was more easily said than done. There is a myth that Lloyd George had to march down to the admiralty in order to impose convoys on obstinate admirals. Jellicoe, the first sea lord, protected by Carson the first lord, was indeed a problem. He was fanatically opposed to convoys. He even produced a deputation of hand-picked merchant seamen who professed their own incompetence; they proved that convoys were impossible because they would not be able to keep station and avoid collisions at night or in fog, nor could they zigzag effectively. Furthermore, convoys were excessively slow in reaching harbour, limited by the speed of the slowest ship. Jellicoe's tame captains rejected dawdling safely in escorted convoys instead of speeding independently to the bottom of the ocean. But convoys had worked in the past, for instance against Napoleon. Several admirals such as Beatty and Wemyss disagreed with Jellicoe. The admiralty's argument that there were too few destroyers to protect too many sailings was based on faulty statistics; while Jellicoe claimed that nearly 5,000 ships reached British ports every week, the correct figure for ocean-going vessels was about 150. In the context of trade protection, the 5,000 figure was therefore bogus. The hero of this dreadful, unnecessarily prolonged tragedy, was the War Committee's secretary, Colonel Hankey. Lloyd George dithered culpably for six weeks, maintaining that Hankey made too much fuss – 'Oh well, I have never regarded that matter as seriously as you have'. But Hankey at last convinced Lloyd George, after those six disgraceful weeks of delay, that drastic action was necessary. The truth is that Lloyd George certainly did exert pressure where and when it was needed though Hankey and the more intelligent and progressive admirals had already seen the light. By autumn 1917 the crisis had been surmounted, though losses continued to be high.[8]

If Lloyd George was not quite so perceptive or decisive as he liked to maintain, there is a passage in his memoirs which does him credit:

One of the most lamentable effects of the new submarine campaign was the marked increase in the casualty list amongst our sailors. When a ship was sunk by gunfire the sailors had to take to the boats whatever the weather. Even when the disaster occurred within a few miles of the coast the risks were considerable, but when the ship was sunk in the Bay of Biscay or out in the Atlantic, scores of leagues from any shore, the chances of escape were precarious, and in bad weather few lived to tell the tale. It was one of the new cruelties which this conflict added to the practice of war. The old piratical plank was more humane. The agony was not so prolonged. The German plea in defence of their action was to point to their children starved by our blockade. War is a cruel business.[9]

Lloyd George's prophetic remark about new cruelties was only too relevant to the Battle of the Atlantic, 1939–1945. Whereas approximately 14,879 sailors perished on Lloyd George's watch, over 32,000 died under Churchill – and nowhere in his memoirs does he express regret or sympathy with suffering sailors, nor were the necessary measures taken to protect them soon enough. Decorations for gallantry on the Arctic run were not finally awarded until February 2013.

Lloyd George could not afford to be proud of those disgraceful six weeks when he refused to listen to Hankey. This new horror was demonstrated by the fate of the crew and passengers of the liner *Alnwick Castle* torpedoed in the Atlantic 320 miles from the coast of Spain on 19 March 1917. The ship's chief officer Mr A. H. Blackman reported to the Company that of the 31 people in his lifeboat, the storekeeper went mad, a cattle-man committed suicide by jumping into the sea, and the deck-boy expired one evening having 'been quietly dying all day'. When they finally reached land, two of the crew were insane and another died as he was being lifted out of the boat.[10]

The War in France

The government's record with regard to the war on land was far from impressive, for which Lloyd George must accept a great deal of the blame. Haig's admirers and defenders, then and ever since, have claimed that the Somme (July–November 1916) was a victory and have accepted his claim that the German army had been beaten to its knees even if a decisive breakthrough had eluded the allies. All that was required for success in 1917 was another massive offensive, and the Germans would break and run. Despite Lloyd George's doubts, the cavalry would roll up the enemy line. There had been, perhaps, a few basic errors up to now: for instance, the preliminary bombardment would obviously have to be lengthened – a week was too short. Haig was sure that the ideal place for his break-through was Flanders where further substantial gains could deliver the U-boat bases into allied hands.

Lloyd George countered Haig's ambitions by producing, like a conjuror fishing a rabbit out of a hat, the French General Robert Nivelle. This plausible talker spoke English, much to Lloyd George's relief – more fluently than Haig or Robertson – and he had the right shaped head, conforming to the Prime Minister's belief in the pseudo-science of phrenology. (Poor Neville Chamberlain, it will be remembered, had failed this test.) More to the point, Nivelle had backed up his eloquence – and his skull – by several impressive local victories at Verdun. His technique had been to dispense with a long artillery bombardment and thus achieve maximum surprise by sudden assault. Now he proposed to exploit these tactics on a grand scale in Picardy and Champagne. Lloyd George was enraptured. Nivelle, having succeeded Joffre as C. in C., proposed to launch this lightning strike in April and win the war within 48 hours. The British Army was to be subordinated to Nivelle so that maximum success could be achieved. When these proposals were conveyed to Wully Robertson, he hit the roof. According to an eye-witness, the liaison officer Lt-Colonel Spears: 'Wully's face went the colour of mahogany, his eyes became perfectly round, his eyebrows slanted outwards like a forest of bayonets held at the charge – in fact he showed every sign of having a fit.'[11] Turning to his aid-de-camp he bellowed, 'Get 'Aig!' The two generals then shouted at Lloyd George, who at first refused to compromise and launched a tirade of intemperate abuse at Haig. It now turned out that the War Cabinet had not been consulted. When Lloyd George gave a highly tendentious account to his colleagues of his row with the generals, Robertson remarked to Haig, 'He really is such an awful liar'.[12] The generals appealed to George V who had, it will be recalled, recently promoted Haig to field-marshal and now assured Lloyd George that British troops would refuse to be subordinated to a French general. Lloyd George replied that in that case he would appeal to the British people for their support. Democracy would triumph over both monarch and soldiers.

In the event, Lloyd George modified his proposals. Nivelle would not have operational control of the British and Haig was allowed to appeal to his government if he felt that his army was at risk. Haig and Plumer mounted a successful though rather expensive diversion on Vimy Ridge (120,000 Canadian casualties) in April, but Nivelle's offensive was a catastrophe. The French army, having lost 110,000 men in a week, made sheep-like bleating noises when marched to the front and then mutinied. Nivelle resigned. Lloyd George was humiliated, his self-confidence shattered. He had lost the credibility to prohibit Haig's summer offensive, and was too cowardly even to try.

So the new field-marshal went ahead with his preparations for the Third Battle of Ypres, otherwise known as Passchendaele. Throughout the summer, horses, guns, mortars and above all soldiers floundered through the muddy quagmires of Flanders towards the front. Siegfried Sassoon's poem, 'The General' is spot on: 'He did for them both with his plan of attack.'[13]

Whether or not it was Haig that Sassoon had in mind, the field-marshal certainly did for the British Army again. His plan of attack was a repeat of the Somme, that is to say a massive artillery bombardment followed by frontal attack by the PBI. The cavalry were on hand 'to roll up the enemy line'. A colleague of Haig's once remarked, 'If I was the enemy, I would always know exactly what Douglas was going to do'. Now German reconnaissance planes droned overhead in the summer sky as the unending columns trudged up to the frontline. 'Good old Duggie', exclaimed a cynical soldier, 'sending a postcard to Berlin as usual'. As 'Duggie' had promised, the preliminary bombardment lasted a fortnight, not a week – thereby churning up the already saturated Flanders terrain, soaked by the usual late summer downpours. Now tanks were to be committed en masse, despite the tank specialists' pleas that they should not be expended in such unsuitable circumstances. Haig's only concession to the apprehensive War Committee was to promise to call off the attack if satisfactory progress was not being made – as it turned out, a worthless undertaking: first because it was always possible to maintain that all was going well, second because it was not easy to halt an attack in twentieth century warfare once it had begun.

General Sir Ian Hamilton, who had commanded at Gallipoli, later remarked that 'Passchendaele was the most damnable battle in history and should never have been fought'.[14] One of Haig's staff wept when driven through the battlezone: 'Good God, did we send men to fight in that?' 'It's worse further on', grunted the driver.[15] Foch asked Henry Wilson, 'Who was the fool who persuaded Haig to go on his duck's march through Flanders?' and a poet castigated the generals: 'There is a hell, they call it Passchendaele.'[16] From August to November 1917 the nightmare lasted. Men and horses drowned as well as being blown to bits, soldiers went mad though there was little evidence of desertion in the highly disciplined British army, and court-marshals for cowardice were hushed up.[17] Both Wully Robertson and Haig's army commanders implored him to call a halt, but he was convinced that his intelligence chief Brigadier Charteris, who anticipated the faith-based predictions of George W. Bush, confidently identified symptoms of German collapse, dismissing Macdonnagh's reports from the War Office that German morale was undented as influenced by Roman Catholic sources – and therefore unreliable. Tanks were useless, floundering in the mud, until at last they were deployed as their generals demanded on firm ground and in fine weather. Thus was achieved the tank victory of Cambrai, November 1917. The War Office ordered church bells to be rung. But Haig had used up all his reserves, so the breakthrough could not be exploited – indeed the Germans counterattacked and recovered their lost ground.

During that dreadful autumn about 300,000 British casualties were inflicted, to little real purpose. In January 1918, Lloyd George asked Petain how casualties could be reduced. 'By appointing better generals', was Petain's blunt reply. However, this was easier said than done.

Can any excuse be made for Passchendaele? None really, according to a recent study by Robin Prior and Trevor Wilson, an adverse verdict confirmed by David French.[18] Interestingly, while pilloring Haig's generalship, they are equally critical of the political feebleness of the British management of the War. According to Lloyd George, 'We have won great victories. When I look at the appalling casualty lists I sometimes wish it had not been necessary to win so many'.[19]

In an attempt to control Haig, Lloyd George developed an idea which he had advanced more or less as soon as he became prime minister. He now agreed with the French and the Italians to set up the Supreme War Council (SWC) at Versailles, consisting of Foch, Cadorna and Sir Henry Wilson. Robertson insisted on doubling as both chief of the Imperial General Staff and British member of the

SWC. When Haig, who had been infuriated by Robertson's belief that Passchendaele would not succeed, told Robertson that he could not have both, he resigned from both. Sir Henry Wilson replaced him as CIGS – an intriguer and a liar. But he was a gentleman, having been to Marlborough and so was acceptable to Haig. Lloyd George got on with Wilson: 'I like criminals. I could so easily have been one myself.'[20] General Rawlinson went to Versailles, vacating his army command. Wilson tentatively asked Haig if he would support Robertson as Rawlinson's successor as General Officer Commanding Fourth Army. Haig who was consistently disloyal to men who had loyally supported him replied that Wully 'was quite unfitted to command troops'.[21]

One feels sorry for Robertson. His failure to be straight with the War Committee about his expectations of disaster at Passchendaele was downright dereliction of duty, in which he was excessively motivated by his bias in favour of soldiers versus politicians, or 'brasshats versus frocks' as Wilson put it.[22] But he was let down by Haig and mocked by Lloyd George, who enjoyed imitating his lumbering walk and his snorts and grunts expressing contempt and disbelief ('I've 'eard different').[23] Robertson could not bear Lloyd George's prolonged working breakfasts which interfered with his regular bowel-movements. He preferred Asquith's lifestyle, once pointing out some enormous women's bloomers on a washing-line and exclaiming, 'There are some pants for you, Prime Minister!'[24] The generals were fond of Asquith, for he was indeed their ideal 'frock' – deferential to military experts, amiable and often half-cut. Lloyd George was none of these. Under his aegis, mutual dislike and contempt between politicians and soldiers (and sailors) sank to rock bottom. There was a real problem here which Robertson summarised admirably:

> Where the politician goes wrong is in wanting to know the why and the wherefore of the soldier's proposals, and of making the latter the subject of debate across a table. You then have the man who knows but who cannot talk discussing important questions with the man who can talk but does not know, with the result that the man who knows usually gets defeated in argument and things are done which his instinct tells him are bad.[25]

All that has to be added is that the politician – who can talk but does not know – nevertheless is not necessarily wrong, as we have seen with Lloyd George on the folly of Passchendaele. Furthermore, as Dick testified after looking into his father's eyes, Lloyd George *did* know – but lacked the moral courage to back his own judgement. He let his soldiers down and was the real Passchendaele butcher. This is a dreadful story, out of which Lloyd George emerges with no credit. His awareness of young Hinds' agony was multiplied thousands of times. Lloyd George should have somehow called a halt. To suggest that a more nuanced description of Passchendaele is justified flies in the face of facts.

Backs to the Wall

In a curious way, 1918 was to be Haig's year, though Lloyd George would never admit it. Initially Haig got it wrong, failing to predict where the expected German offensive would fall. The unfortunate Fifth Army, which had borne the brunt of the Passchendaele offensive and had been transferred to a supposedly quiet sector, found itself in the firing line of a brief but violent preliminary bombardment. In Churchill's words: 'Exactly as a pianist runs his hands across the keyboard from treble to bass, there rose in less than one minute the most tremendous cannonade I shall ever hear.'[26] It now transpired that the German Quartermaster-General, Eric Ludendorff, had solved the problem which had baffled the Entente generals: how to break clean through the enemy line on the first day. He achieved tactical success through the element of surprise, combining a short, though violent, bombardment; the exploitation of fog, early morning mist and artificial smoke; the infiltration of the enemy front line by highly trained storm troopers; and the entrusting of isolated pockets of resistance to second-class infantry following up the storm troopers. These tactics worked during the course of three massive assaults – 21 March and 9 April 1918 against the British, and 14 May against the French.

Tactics aside, strategic success eluded the Germans. The contrast is marked between Ludendorff in spring and early summer 1918 and von Manstein 22 years later, when Hitler's legions split the allied armies by racing across Northern France to the Channel. Ludendorff failed to separate the British and French, failed to take Paris, failed to reach the coast. All he could deliver was a series of brilliant and totally terrifying raids into allied territory, capturing hundreds of square miles, thousands of prisoners and masses of stores which demoralised his soldiers, rallied as they were on propaganda that the allies were starving. For the first time in the history of the Western Front, the Germans suffered more casualties than the British and French. Even so, the scenario was alarming. Lloyd George was worried. So was Petain, who wanted to conform to German pressure by abandoning contact with his allies. When Haig explained to Wilson that he would be saved by Petain's charity, he was warned that he would find to his cost that Petain's was cold charity. This was perceptive; Petain was all for retiring on Paris and abandoning the British. So who saved the day?

First was Clemenceau, who displayed considerably more resolution in beleaguered Paris than did Lloyd George, viewing the catastrophic Western Front from the safety of Criccieth. Second was Foch, who overruled Petain's timidity in favour of close cooperation with the British. And third was Haig, who manoeuvred Foch into the supreme command in order to counteract Petain's defeatism. When Milner, the British war minister, proposed that Foch should co-ordinate the Anglo-French forces defending Amiens, Haig rejected this as inadequate and proposed that Foch should have command 'from the Alps to the North Sea'.[27] In these bizarre and desperate circumstances, Lloyd George's goal of allied unified command was achieved thanks to Haig, of all people, although there was scant recognition of this from Lloyd George himself. After all, it was he who had remained cheerful during the dark days of the Ludendorff offensives, as Hankey emphatically records.

To a great extent it was now an old-fashioned soldier's war, in which generalship played only a limited part. Countless isolated demonstrations of British and colonial grit took their toll on Ludendorff's storm troopers. On 12 April 1918, Haig set the tone by issuing his celebrated 'backs to the wall' order – for which he has been criticised for melodramatic despair. Let the reader judge:

> There is no other course open to us but to fight it out. Every position must be held to the last man. There must be no retirement. With our backs to the wall and believing in the justice of our cause, each one of us must fight on to the end.[28]

It worked: the Germans had had enough. Further assaults on the French line in July were abortive. The time would soon be ripe for Anglo-French counterattacks. In the meantime Lloyd George tried to associate his colleagues with campaigns in the Balkans. But the Chief of the Imperial General Staff continued to favour the Western

Front in a rambling memorandum (25 July) which Lloyd George dismissed angrily as 'Wully redividus' ('Wully brought back to life').

The Maurice Debate

Actually, Lloyd George was in trouble – not on the plains of Flanders and Picardy but in the House of Commons. On 7 May 1918, General Sir Frederick Maurice, formerly Wully Robertson's Director of Military Operations, committed professional suicide by writing to the press. He accused Lloyd George and Bonar Law of misleading Parliament by knowingly giving inaccurate figures with regard to the strengths of the British Expeditionary Force in France, on 1 January 1917 and 1 January 1918. The issue at stake was the cause of Ludendorff's victories which had so nearly destroyed the British army, the charge, that Lloyd George had been guilty of starving Haig's army commanders of necessary reinforcements. Lloyd George had claimed that there were more soldiers in France in January 1918 than a year before – despite Passchendaele and despite the lengthening of the British line to accommodate the French, which Bonar Law was accused of misrepresenting. Bonar Law was furious that his own truthfulness was being questioned; as Lloyd George put it, 'Bonar hates being called a liar, though it doesn't bother me, as I've been called a liar all my life. Now I've been caught telling the truth!'[29]

Lloyd George shrewdly sidestepped Asquith's demand for a judicial enquiry by appealing for a vote of confidence. In the ensuing debate, Asquith made a wretched speech in which he was heckled and hassled. Lloyd George spoke brilliantly for more than an hour in which he appealed for unity. He won his vote of confidence by 293 votes to 106. Asquith was humiliated.

We now know that Lloyd George indeed played tricks with the statistics, which he claimed Maurice himself had supplied – but which he chose not to admit had been revised. One cannot improve on Haig's letter to his wife: 'Poor Maurice! How terrible to see the House of Commons so easily taken in by a clap-trap speech by Lloyd George. The House is really losing its reputation as an assembly of no-nonsense Britishers.'[30] Perhaps Haig's disgust was especially justified by Lloyd George's appeal to all sections of the House: 'These controversies are distracting, they are paralysing, they are rending and I beg that they should come to an end.'[31] Such comments, while apparently unifying, also had the effect of making his critics appear unpatriotic and irresponsible. Maurice had to resign: Lloyd George had won. But colleagues such as Milner and Hankey knew that he had cheated in order to win a tawdry victory. The correct figures were consigned to the fire by J. T. Davies, Lloyd George's Welsh secretary, and Frances Stevenson, his Anglo-French Personal Assistant.

The Turn of the Tide

And now at last the tide of battle turned. On 8 August 1918 occurred the battle of Amiens, or what Ludendorff called 'the black day of the German army'.[32] Under Haig's overall direction, General Rawlinson's Fourth Army delivered a copy-book attack in which the Germans were sent reeling by a combination of tanks, armoured cars, aircraft and infantry who, at last, were not required to achieve the impossible. According to the operational commander of the Australian troops, General John Monash:

> I had formed the theory that the true role of the infantry was not to expend itself upon heroic physical effort, not to wither away under merciless machine-gun fire, not to impale itself on hostile bayonets, nor to tear itself to pieces in hostile entanglements, but on the contrary to advance under the maximum possible protection of the maximum possible array of mechanical resources, in the form of guns, machine-guns, tanks, mortars and aeroplanes, to advance with as little impediment as possible; to be relieved as far as possible of the obliga-tion to fight their way forward; to march resolutely, regardless of the din and tumult of battle, to the appointed goal, and there to defend and hold the territory gained; and to gather in the form of prisoners, guns and stores, the fruits of victory.[33]

'At last! Sense from a general!', Lloyd George might be forgiven for exclaiming. And, to be fair, he was still the prime minister who employed Haig as Commander in Chief, Rawlinson as Army Commander and Monash in immediate command. Haig now proved himself right and Lloyd George wrong in keeping the German army on the run for the next three exhilarating months, sweeping aside all resistance including the renowned Hindenburg Line, until the Germans sued for an armistice on 11 November 1918. In other words, victory was achieved in 1918 as Haig, ever the optimist but for once a justified optimist, had predicted, and not in 1919 or 1920 as Lloyd George gloomily expected.

It is true that Lloyd George's belief in defeating Germany's allies had paid off, as Turkey and Austria-Hungary also sued for peace. It is also true that Foch was in supreme control and that French, American, colonial and Belgian troops were all involved. However, it is no exaggeration to claim that Haig's British army was the largest and most formidable element in these astonishing 'Hundred Days'. Alas, Lloyd George was shamefully reluctant to acknowledge the British achievement, and Haig's in particular, both at the time and in his *War Memoirs*.[34] What did Haig get from his masters in London? A 'personal note' from Sir Henry Wilson:

> Just a word of caution in regard to incurring heavy losses in attacks on Hindenburg Line as opposed to losses when driving the enemy back to the line. I do not mean to say that you have incurred such losses, but I know the war cabinet would become anxious if we received heavy punishment while attacking the Hindenburg Line without success.[35]

Haig exploded in his diary:

> It is impossible for a C.I.G.S. [chief of Imperial General Staff] to send a telegram of this nature to a C-in-C [commander in chief] as a 'personal' one. The Cabinet are ready to meddle and interfere with my plans in an underhand way, but do not dare openly say that they mean me to take the responsibility for any failure though ready to take credit for any success.[36]

Who Won the War?

As is well known, Lloyd George was happy to campaign in the forthcoming general election under the slogan, 'the man who won the war'. Both contemporaries and sympathetic historians have supported his claim. Of these, the most impressive is Hankey, who emphatically and explicitly awards Lloyd George this accolade. He quotes Lloyd George's contribution to victory at sea, his control of British shipping, his mobilisation of British agriculture, his introduction of rationing, his persistent cheerfulness and good humour. Lloyd George won the battle of the blockade which so contributed to Germany's defeat. Hankey personally witnessed the creation of an efficient executive machine, the garden suburb secretariat, the recruitment of talented outsiders to the government, the smooth working relationship with both big business and Labour and the recruitment of women.

He witnessed Lloyd George's outstanding rhetorical skills. Lloyd George did not achieve these victories on his own, but he established, not so much a dictatorship, as a presidential form of government to which he contributed his own particular brand of vigour and excitement. He was fun to work for, and attracted admiration from wide sectors of society.[37] During the crisis of Spring 1918, Hankey awards Lloyd George the highest marks for leadership. He remained up-beat when others despaired.

With regard to strategy the picture is more varied and controversial. Lloyd George's policy of kicking away the props of the German colossus probably made little difference, though one has to note that Germany's allies did indeed collapse in the autumn of 1918, seemingly causing Germany herself to sink in a cesspool of chaos and revolution. Allenby's victorious campaign against the Turks in Lloyd George's eyes vindicated 'the way round', though Italy proved as much an expensive distraction as it did in World War II. The only true way to achieve victory was to defeat the German army – and the German army was in France, hence the significance of Haig's Hundred Days. If ever an army was beaten, the German army was by November 1918. When the Kaiser envisaged turning his troops on his domestic opponents, Ludendorff had run away in disguise and Hindenburg told his master that the army would not fight for him. So the Kaiser too had no resource left but abdication and exile. There was never a greater lie than the 'stab in the back' myth – the allegation that the German army was 'stabbed in the back' by Jews and Socialists – so beloved and exploited by the right-wing enemies of the Weimar Republic, especially Hitler.[38]

So what was Lloyd George's contribution, if any, to victory on the Western Front? If this was, indeed, the crucial theatre, Haig emerged as 'the man who won the war'. But there was a strong case against Haig, given the immense loss of life on the Somme and at Passchendaele, and failure to follow up Cambrai. Lloyd George's contribution therefore should have been to save lives by dismissing him. Admittedly there were difficulties here, notably Haig's mobilisation of influential supporters from the monarchy downwards, and there was also the problem of finding a replacement. Still, neither consideration would have proved decisive if Lloyd George had had the will and the courage. Haig was fully entitled to say, as Montgomery did to Churchill, 'Back me or sack me'. Lloyd George did neither. In Chapter 8 we shall evaluate Lloyd George's magna opera, his *War Memoirs* and his book on the Peace Treaties. Here we are concerned with Lloyd George's patent uneasiness in his account of the War. He is paranoid about Haig, and rightly so. Lloyd George was responsible for a great many unnecessary deaths because he fought shy of getting rid of Haig. He was therefore as much the butcher of Passchendaele as Haig.

If it is right to admire Lloyd George for his defence of the ultimate superiority of the politician over the soldier, it is also right to hold him to account for not implementing this principle. Yet, together Haig and Lloyd George eventually presided over the allied victory, however much they detested each other and tried to tarnish each other's reputation. Millions paid with their lives – too many millions – before victory was achieved in November 1918. The millions who fought, suffered and, in far too many cases, died were therefore the true victors, the real heroes, as Lloyd George admitted during his visit to the United States and Canada.

There is a further charge which Lloyd George has to answer. In his diary entry for 3 August 1918, Lord Riddell writes: 'The expense of the war never seems to enter into his calculations. He rejoices in the sacrifices and efforts which he induces his countrymen to make.'[39] David French tells us that 'by 1920 the National Debt stood at £7,685 million, a twelvefold increase since 1914'.[40] The Royal Navy's tally of ships rose from 685 in 1914 to 5,018 in September 1918, manned by 408,997 officers and men compared to 145,318 previously. While sailors suffered and died, so did Britain's soldiers who made 'the effot *du sang*' which Lloyd George and his colleagues reckoned necessary to keep France and the other allies in the war.[41] How convincing, how consoling an argument would this have been to the PBI, bleeding and drowning and going insane in Flanders? To reiterate, Lloyd George did not *have* to approve Passchendaele.

Just how *bad* was Haig? How many lives would Lloyd George have saved if he had dismissed the Commander in Chief in, for instance, September 1917, when the Passchendaele strategy was clearly running into sand – or mud? It is impossible to be sure. Haig was a poor defendant, an ineffectual self-propagandist. He was shy, tongue-tied and maladroit in his choice of words; he once congratulated officer cadets on their cross-country running, hoping that 'you run as well in the presence of the enemy'. His own diaries were published after his death – 'the only example in history of a man who committed suicide after he had died',[42] but Haig was neither stupid nor ignorant.[43] Plenty of writers have ridiculed his rigidity and conformity to ideas, including war poets[44] and, more recently, Joan Littlewood, Alan Clark and Ben Elton,[45] but a number of military historians, such as Cyril Falls, John Terraine, Brian Bond and Gary Sheffield, have defended Haig. Without indulging in foolish 'haigiography', they have established his qualities and nailed the more unkind and unjustifiable travesties of truth. Haig was efficient, well-informed and industrious. His chief defects were his willingness to believe Charteris' uncritical optimism and his failure as commander in chief to restrain and correct his Army Commanders' deficiencies. Surely Haig would have made at least an adequate Army Commander under a firm C-in-C, who would have applied a brake to his more unrealistic ambitions?[46]

However, it seems equally unlikely that Lloyd George was quite as *good* a leader as he thought himself, nor as good as his admirers, from Uncle Lloyd onwards, have claimed. It is these admirers who have inspired the opinions of sympathetic historians today, some but by no means all, Lloyd George's compatriots.[47] His most impressive contemporary admirers were not Welsh: John Grigg whose magisterial four volume biography sadly ended in 1918 due to the author's untimely death, and Colonel Sir Maurice Hankey who worked as Lloyd George's chief of staff for four hectic years. As we have seen, Hankey records and celebrates Lloyd George's cheerfulness in the darkest days of 1917 and 1918, and his successful campaigns for convoys and the Supreme War Council. Unbowed by disasters, resourceful in pursuit of victory, Lloyd George, in Hankey's judgement was indeed 'the man who won the war'. It was an informed opinion which must be respected. Likewise, Adam Tooze attributes the eventual victory by the Entente to the resilience of democracy in Britain and France, inspired and led by Clemenceau and Lloyd George.[48] However, Lloyd George was handicapped by the lack of a Chiefs of Staff Committee, which more or less kept Churchill on the rails in World War II – although not without a fair amount of blood, sweat and tears. The Welshman never recognised his ignorance as an amateur, and therefore his need for professional guidance. One is reminded of Hitler: 'This little matter of operational command is something anybody could do.'[49] Nevertheless, Lloyd George's determination to be true to himself was commendable. In August 1916 he defied critics by travelling to Aberystwyth to give the presidential address at the National Eisteddfod:

> Why should we not sing during war? I know that war means suffering, war means sorrow. Darkness has fallen on many a devoted household but it has been ordained that the best singer among the hills of Britain should give its song in the night and according to legend that sweet song is one of triumph over pain. Hundreds of wars have swept over these hills, but the harp of Wales has never been silenced by one of them, and I should be proud if I contributed to keep it in tune during the war by the holding of this Eisteddfod. But I have another and more urgent reason for keeping this Eisteddfod alive during the War. When this terrible conflict is over, a wave of materialism will sweep over the land. Nothing will count but machinery and output. I am all for output. But that is not all. I make no apology for advocating the holding of the Eisteddfod in the middle of this great conflict. Why should we not sing? I am glad that I have come down from the cares and labour of war to listen and join with you in singing the old songs which our brave countrymen on the battlefield are singing in defiance of the enemies of human rights.[50]

While Lloyd George enjoyed romanticising about 'the glory of the Welsh hills',[51] he was always a hard-headed politician who realised the importance in a democracy of the political arm's superiority over the military. Yet he failed to live up to this principle.[52] The excuses his admirers profess do not stand up: the simple truth is that if Lloyd George had sacked Haig, there would certainly have been a political crisis, which might have destroyed Lloyd George's premiership. It will not do to claim that there was no alternative – there is always an alternative, for example, when Churchill's first choice, General 'Strafer' Gott, was killed in an air-crash on his way to take over the Eighth Army, and was thereafter replaced by Montgomery. If Haig had been unavoidably eliminated by a similar mishap (his staff-car might have crashed or he could have fallen off his horse), Plumer, Rawlinson, Allenby or Jacob would have *had* to step in. Lloyd George might even have brought back the great and good Sir Horace Smith-Dorrien, Haig's fellow corps-commander back in 1915, the general who disobeyed crazy orders.[53]

Nothing, however, illustrates Lloyd George's political skill – some would say ruthlessness – better than his decision to call a general election as soon as Germany capitulated. Given the Tory preponderance in the coalition, he could not go to the country without Bonar Law's agreement. Bonar Law, in his turn, had to convince his party that Lloyd George's leadership guaranteed success. Both, with clever cynicism, jointly issued a letter of approval to select candidates, provoking Asquith's witticism that this amounted to a 'coupon', food rationing being in full spate.[54] The coupon was bestowed on most Tory candidates and on Liberals who had voted for Lloyd George in the Maurice debate.

Lloyd George marketed himself as the war-winner and also the social reformer who would guarantee a country 'fit for heroes to live in.' He responded to the Northcliffe press' demands for vengeance on the Hun by promising that the Kaiser would be hanged and that the Germans would pay to the uttermost farthing ('We will search their pockets for it').[55] This combination was irresistible to the enlarged electorate after the 1918 Parliament Act had enfranchised all men over the age of 21 and all women over 30. The necessary steps were taken to enable the armed forces to vote, whom Lloyd George promised to demobilise as soon as possible. The result was a landslide: Coalition, 526 seats; Tories without the coupon, 75; Asquithian Liberals, 120; Labour, 65. As Bonar Law observed, 'Lloyd George can be prime minister for life if he wants'.[56]

Perhaps it would be wrong to question the emphatic democratic endorsement given to Lloyd George by the electorate. He was certainly greeted as a hero by the crowd in Downing Street on his way to the Commons on 11 November 1918, and indeed by both Houses of Parliament when he arrived there. Maybe he did win the war, if any single person did. But at what cost? Literally hundreds of thousands had been killed and maimed, there were so many bereaved homes, war memorials in towns and villages throughout the land, pitifully truncated beggars sitting on the pavements as this author remembers from his own childhood in Barnsley in the late thirties. 'O valiant hearts ...'[57]

7

The Peacefinder General (1918–1922)

Voila!

– Clemenceau to Lloyd George when the Germans
signed the Treaty of Versailles, 1919

' I DON'T think it can be done', muttered David Lloyd George, as
he cast a troubled eye over a map of Europe before the peace
conferences convened in the spring of 1919. He had good
reason to be worried. As well as being the man who won the war, Lloyd
George hoped to be the man who made the peace. For seven and a half
months after the German surrender, he partnered President Woodrow
Wilson of the United States and the prime minister of France, Georges
Clemenceau, in drawing up the treaty which Germany eventually
signed on 28 June 1919, and the treaties with Germany's allies. It was
demanding work. Truly, the map was a problem. Four great empires
had been demolished by the Great War: the Russian, the Ottoman,
the German and the Austro-Hungarian. These empires had contained
peoples longing to be free, driven by nationalism to shake off
centuries-old shackles. President Wilson had promised to free these
nationalities in his celebrated Fourteen Points, but the briefest glance
at the map showed how mixed up these nationalities were, what a
Herculean task it would be to give them self-government, how their
ethnic boundaries conflicted with rivers, railways, roads, mountains
and forests. How could the peace-makers unravel this convoluted
jumble to make the new or 'successor' states militarily and economically viable, notably Austria, Hungary, Czechoslovakia, Yugoslavia,
Romania and Poland? How could they survive against a Germany
sooner or later bent on revenge?

For here was an even greater problem: when the victorious Allies granted Germany an armistice, they implicitly committed themselves to prolonging that country's existence as a great power, dominating central Europe. They might detach territories here and there such as Alsace-Lorraine, a Polish corridor to the Baltic, part of Silesia and Schleswig. But the vast bulk of Wilhelmine Germany still sprawled across Europe, menacing France and Belgium in the west and the successor-states in the east, especially Poland, Austria and Czechoslovakia. The Allies had passed up the opportunity of cancelling Bismarck's work, by not invading Germany and splitting her up in November 1918 – as they would in May 1945. The Allies in 1918 thus made World War II, if not inevitable, at least probable.[1] If the Germany's problem in November 1918 was weakness – she was starving, in resentful chaos and ripe for a Bolshevik takeover – some day the problem would once again be Germany's strength. The only questions were when and how. No wonder Marshal Foch directed that, when he died, he was to be buried upright and facing east. With tragic accuracy he predicted not peace but a 20-year truce.[2]

Clearly the Allies could do their best to solve this difficulty, at least in the short term, by disarming Germany, handicapping her economy, removing her colonies and policing a punitive peace. Lloyd George had no problem with these limited and justifiable goals – within reason, but they were not enough for the French. Proportionately, France had lost more men than any other combatant power (Great Britain and her Empire 950,000,[3] Germany 2.4 million,[4] Russia 2.6 million, France 1.4 million[5]) while her population was a mere 40 million[6] compared to Germany's 68 million[7] and rising. The French pointed to the Treaty of Brest-Litovsk, imposed on defeated Russia, as an indication of German treatment of the losing side. *Vae victis* ('woe to the conquered') had a hallowed Teuton background. French generals and politicians were united in wishing to establish a separate Rhineland, self-governing and independent, guaranteed by Britain and France. This was, above all, Clemenceau's solution. If this was vetoed, and if he had to agree that the eastern bank of the Rhine would still be German, he would accept as a compromise the west bank of the river to be French, as in the days of Louis XIV (1643–1715). President Woodrow Wilson and Lloyd George would have none of it. Lloyd George regarded such a proposal as on a par with the removal of Alsace-Lorraine from France in 1870, bound to perpetuate

German resentment and desire for revenge. Wilson agreed. Lloyd George was prepared to consider a demilitarised Rhineland for a limited period, say 15 years. He and Wilson offered, in addition, an Anglo-American military guarantee, promising immediate assistance if France were to be invaded again by Germany. But the French doubted whether Anglo-American forces would arrive in time, even through a promised channel tunnel, to save France from defeat at German hands. Certainly the Kaiser, the Junkers and the generals had gone, replaced by the democratic, reassuringly plebeian President Ebert and the Weimar Republic. Indeed Weimar was the hope of the peace-loving, civilised world: but for how long?

Such were some of the outstanding problems facing the allied statesmen who gathered in Paris – the venue insisted upon by Clemenceau, against the preferences of Wilson and Lloyd George. They would have preferred a neutral capital such as Geneva, where the prejudices and wounds of war-torn France would have been less influential. When Clemenceau vetoed the presence in France's capital of Communist Russian delegates whom Lloyd George desired, the Prime Minister was furious: 'I never wanted the conferences to take place in his bloody capital in the first place!'[8] In the event, the British settled down to make themselves comfortable, as Frances Stevenson recounts in her *Lloyd George: A Diary.*[9] Lloyd George lived in a capacious flat on the Rue Nitot, attended by Hankey, Lord Riddell, Kerr, his favourite daughter Megan and Miss Stevenson. Frances chaperoned Megan – or possibly the other way round. There is an affectionate letter from this period which Megan wrote to 'Dear Puss' which confirms that she had not yet rumbled the true relationship between Frances and her father.[10] Lord Balfour, the Foreign Secretary, lived on the floor above. George V irritated Lloyd George by pressing for Asquith's attendance – which Lloyd George correctly interpreted as a slur on his own capacity. He interviewed Asquith, who suggested that his knowledge of international law and finance could be useful. Lloyd George looked confused, consulted his watch and picked up some books from the floor. This signalled the end of the interview.[11] There was, however, plenty of room for the 200 or so members of the British Empire delegation who lived nearby at the Hotel Majestic. Drinks had to be paid for. Telephone calls were discouraged for fear of eavesdropping by spies – French, not German. But on the whole, conditions were civilised.

At first a Council of Ten, consisting of the prime ministers and foreign ministers of the five victorious powers, began to draft a treaty. This proved too cumbersome a group. Before long the Japanese withdrew, since they failed to understand a great deal, then the Italians went home because their demands were ignored; Orlando, their premier, was amiable enough, but Sonnino their far from amiable foreign minister, was a grim, unsociable Protestant in a Catholic country who enjoyed solitary walks, wallowing in rage and self-pity. Frances Stevenson watched Orlando burst into tears on the balcony of Wilson's flat.[12] Only Wilson showed any sympathy; Clemenceau displayed contempt – it took a lot to make him cry.

Now 'the Big Three', Wilson, Clemenceau and Lloyd George, decided that they could get on without their foreign ministers, who could be summoned when they were needed. 'The Big Three' got into their stride in March 1919, four months after the Armistice, and were ready with a completed treaty to present to the Germans by the middle of May. They met in comfort at the French War Ministry, where Clemenceau presided, and where, on occasion, the three statesmen could be found lying on their stomachs, pouring over vast maps on the carpet. 'The Slovaks are also a difficulty ... Where are they? I don't seem to place them', confessed Lloyd George, geography never having been his best subject.[13] Sometimes they met in Wilson's austere flat, where he conducted proceedings like a university don taking a seminar. Every now and again, the President would deliver one of his moralistic soliloquies, which would prompt Clemenceau to sigh audibly or catch Lloyd George's eye as if to say, 'he's off again'. On the whole the three men got on and respected each other, though at least once Lloyd George and Clemenceau almost came to blows and had to be parted by Wilson, after Clemenceau had offered Lloyd George swords or pistols, in both of which he was proficient. Lloyd George was becoming disturbingly pro-German and unsympathetic to the French as he became converted to appeasement, but he was aware that working with Clemenceau was infinitely preferable to compromising with the French president, Poincaré. After one of many rows, 'You are a bad boy', Clemenceau rebuked Lloyd George: they had much in common.[14] Once, when a pretty girl came into the room, Clemenceau muttered to Lloyd George, 'Oh to be seventy again!'[15] As well as their native tongues, Clemenceau and Lloyd George spoke fluent English, Wilson fluent American but only very poor French.

So they stuck to English, which gave Clemenceau a strong position. Fundamentally all three aimed at a compromise between, on the one hand, hitting Germany so hard that she would never threaten the peace of Europe again but would seethe with resentment, and on the other, being too soft so that the hawks in Paris and London would be furious. Lord Northcliffe in particular attacked Lloyd George in *The Times* and the *Daily Mail*, both of which he owned. The Prime Minister more than once questioned Northcliffe's accuracy and absurd posturing. When starvation threatened Germany, the *Daily Mail* headline read: 'Hun Food Snivel'.[16] Lloyd George frequently rebuked the ailing press-lord.[17]

In April 1919, Lloyd George returned briefly to England in order to face his critics in the Commons. He gave a masterly performance, comparable to his triumph a year previously in the Maurice debate. This time his opponent was the mighty newspaper proprietor himself, who had not only demanded a seat in the cabinet but also membership of the government's party chosesn to negotiate the peace treaties. Northcliffe was angry and astonished to be turned down in both instances. He had leaked details of the forthcoming treaties in *The Times* which, according to Lloyd George, foreigners took far too seriously, not realising that it was merely an expensive version of the *Daily Mail*.[18] Ridicule is always hard for a vain man to counter, and now Lloyd George implied that Northcliffe was mad by tapping his head. The House laughed. He returned to Paris with his position strengthened.

Lloyd George was now able to see off an even more vitriolic opponent than Northcliffe, the Australian prime minister Billy Hughes, who had already stood up to Wilson. When the President demanded whether he seriously intended to defy the conscience of civilisation by retaining his hold on the Solomon Islands, Hughes replied, 'That's about the size of it, President Wilson'. When Clemenceau asked Hughes if it was true that he was a cannibal, Hughes retorted that it was an exaggeration.[19] Lloyd George won Hughes' support by appointing him to the Empire's delegation on reparations where his no-nonsense approach terrified the Germans. Lloyd George added British hardliners, Lord Cunliffe, a governor of the Bank of England, and Judge Sumner; the 'heavenly twins', Keynes called them.[20] The delegates' hand was strengthened by Article 231, the War Guilt Clause:

> The Allies and Associated Governments affirm and Germany accepts
> the responsibility of Germany and her allies for causing all the loss
> and damage which the Allied and Associated Governments and their
> nationals have been subjected to as a consequence of the war imposed
> upon them by the aggression of Germany and her allies.[21]

Hence the justification for reparations ultimately fixed at £660
milliard.[22] Meanwhile, Lloyd George contented himself with the
German Crown Prince's field-glasses – his personal share of the reparations.
He was, however, beginning to have doubts. A relaxing weekend
at Fontainebleau in March 1919, with Hankey, Kerr, Montagu and
Henry Wilson, produced a memorandum reflecting the British Prime
Minister's increasing sympathy with Germany. Indeed it is a straight
road from Fontainebleau to Lloyd George's notorious visit to Hitler
at Berchtesgaden in September 1936, a road described in Chapter 11
and analysed by Antony Lentin and by Stella Rudman.[23] This was the
gospel of Fontainebleau: 'You may strip Germany of her colonies,
reduce her armaments to a mere police force and her navy to that
of a fifth rate power; all the same in the end if she feels that she
has been unjustly treated in the peace of 1919 she will find means
of extracting retribution from her conquerors.'[24] So what was to be
done? Genuine disarmament must be implemented by Germany's
conquerors as well as by Germany. The Rhineland, demilitarised for
15 years, must nevertheless stay with Germany, with France to be
compensated by a joint military guarantee from the United States and
Britain. Reparations should be wound up by the generation which
had fought during the war. Germany should be admitted forthwith
to the League of Nations.

Adam Tooze nevertheless pinpoints several grievances which the
Germans retained, especially with regard to their relationship with
Poland.[25] While the 3 million or so Germans in the Sudetenland
were treated with generosity and common sense by Masaryk and
Benes, the Poles were 'hopeless' (Lloyd George), 'Kaffirs' (Smuts)[26] or
'orientalised Irish' (Cecil).[27] At Fontainebleau Lloyd George saw the
2.1 million Germans entombed in Poland as a new Alsace-Lorraine:

> I cannot conceive of any greater cause of a future war than that the
> German people, who have certainly proved themselves one of the most
> vigorous and powerful races in the world, should be surrounded by a
> number of small states, many of them consisting of people who have

never previously set up a stable government for themselves, but each of them containing large masses of Germans clamouring for reunion with their native land.[28]

Clemenceau was equally pessimistic, despairing of the League's capacity to police trouble-spots such as Danzig, and putting his faith in the trilateral transatlantic alliance of France, the United States and Great Britain somewhat disingenuously marketed by Lloyd George. As for President Wilson, he displayed his lack of sympathy for France by refusing to visit the areas of devastation perpetrated in northern France by the retreating Germans so as 'not to upset his emotional equilibrium'.[29]

Lloyd George's mature reflections, so different from his election hysteria, were sold to Wilson and Clemenceau and embodied in the territorial, financial and disarmament clauses presented to the Germans on 8 May 1919. Their delegation was headed by a stiff, unsmiling diplomat, Count Brockdorff-Rantzau, who made a long, tactless speech sitting down, causing much resentment – though it subsequently emerged that the unfortunate man was too nervous to stand. To their shame, the Allied statesmen refused to converse with the German delegates, while only the British guard of honour saluted them. It was meant to be a humiliation. After studying the draft, the German government rejected it. Faced with Allied intransigence, however, they eventually signed on 28 June. 'Voila!', Clemenceau exclaimed to Lloyd George who, to his great irritation, had to send a handwritten report to the King. The first draft was actually typed by Philip Kerr and J. C. C. Davidson, though the slovenly handwriting and ink-blots of the final version were genuine Lloyd George.

Terms were agreed with Austria on 10 September at St Germain, and with Bulgaria on 27 November at Neuilly. Lloyd George had received a letter of thanks from the Bulgarians on 4 June 1913, hoping that 'England will remain true to the great traditions of Mr Gladstone'.[30] But there was little that he could do for them in 1919, after they had chosen the wrong side. The successor states – Czechoslovakia, Poland, Romania, Hungary, Austria, Albania – were neither militarily nor economically viable. The old empires, especially Austria-Hungary, had been created by not particularly admirable regimes, but they had been realistically built for future survival, based on rationally developed railways and roads. The successor-states were vulnerable and anomalous. Provisional terms were agreed with Turkey at Sèvres – but these were substantially revised in 1923 at Lausanne on the back of Kemel Atatürk's smashing victories, a story to which we shall return.

Lloyd George relished his stay in Paris. Churchill, when asked which was the worst moment of World War II, replied, 'My dear, I enjoyed every minute of it'.[31] Lloyd George would never have made such a claim about World War I. The anxieties and traumas of leadership visibly aged and traumatised him; his hair turned white and he put on weight. But if he was not a 'natural' as a warlord, he was in his element as a peacemaker, seeking to bring opponents together. When he left Paris in August 1919 he exclaimed to Riddell, 'It has been a wonderful time. We do not quite appreciate the importance and magnitude of the events in which we have been taking part'.[32] Truly he had had the time of his life. He enjoyed the delightful experiences of a rejuvenated Paris. Much like Balfour, who was taken round the Parisian nightspots by a foreign office aide whom he thanked 'for the most degrading and delightful experience of my life' as well as living it up with his mistress, Miss Stevenson. He even invited Maggie over for a brief visit – after which she escorted him home. But as Richard Lloyd George remarked in his affectionate biography of his mother, 'to her the decisions of the Criccieth Urban District Council were more vital and lasting'.[33]

Lloyd George acquired a taste for international conferences, spending the rest of his premiership rushing from one such meeting to another – two dozen in all, from St Remo to Boulogne to Spa to Cannes, on 9 January 1922, where an event of real political significance occurred. Lloyd George tried to teach the French prime minister, Aristide Briand, how to play golf, unfortunately photographed by an attendant pressman, to the discomforture of Briand who had to resign next day.[34] Puffing and panting, no French premier could afford to look a buffoon at the behest of an English prime minister. The climax to these conferences was supposed to be reached at Genoa in April 1922, where the world's remaining problems were to be solved. Lloyd George found this gallivanting around Europe much more fun than drab old London and the tiresome House of Commons, to which he returned reluctantly and infrequently. He had discovered the joys of what later came to be known as 'summit diplomacy'.

Did Lloyd George and his colleagues do a good job in Paris, in 1919 and in the subsequent conferences? He and Maggie were welcomed on their return at Victoria Station by the King. Lloyd George was decorated with the Order of Merit for his services in the cause of peace. When a bay wreath was tossed into the carriage, George V gave it to Lloyd George with the words, 'This is for you'.[35] However, Lloyd George had already indicated to Wilson and Clemenceau that he thought that they had been too hard on Germany: 'We shall have to do the whole thing over again in 25 years at three times the cost.'[36] He countered criticism by Charles Hardinge, the recently retired British ambassador in Paris, by admitting, 'If I had to go to Paris again I would conclude quite a different treaty'.[37] A cartoon by Will Dyson in the *Daily Herald* showed the 'Big Three' and a naked toddler labelled 'class of 1940' (that is, men liable for military service in 1940) sobbing in the background. The Tiger[38] exclaims, 'Curious! I seem to hear a child weeping'.[39]

However we measure the Treaty of Versailles, it certainly provided a catalyst for Hitler's rallying call. Possibly its salient defect was that it represented the unpalatable truth that Germany had been defeated in the Great War: this is what really stuck in the gullets of Hitler and like-minded German chauvinists. That apart, Germany could be considered to have been somewhat let off the hook. John Maynard Keynes in his *The Economic Consequences of the Peace* blamed the Big Three for contravening Wilson's Fourteen Points and imposing debts on Germany which she could not possibly pay.[40] So financially Germany had not got off lightly. Furthermore, the vulnerable economy of Europe as a whole was thereby destabilised. With hindsight it is clear that reparations were a disaster: Germany paid money to Britain and France, who paid money to the United States, who lent money to Germany. If only President Wilson could have responded to Lloyd George's appeal to set a good example by foregoing his country's war-debts, but it was not to be. Lloyd George blamed France's finance minister, Louis-Lucien Klotz, for French greed – 'the only Jew who knows nothing about money', according to Clemenceau.[41] Even Wilson made tasteless and heavy jokes ('Klotz on the brain'[42]), while it was never necessary to scratch Lloyd George hard for his latent anti-Semitism to surface. Reparations were finally cancelled in 1932, by which time irreparable harm had been done. The same goes for the War Guilt Clause which the 'Big Three' incorporated into the Treaty to justify reparations. Article 231 which, as we have seen, blamed Germany and her allies for the war was intensely resented by the Germans who regarded it as debateable and tendentious. What good did it do? It was a pity that the German request for it to be dropped was not granted.

In his massive *The Truth About the Peace Treaties*, Lloyd George puts up a better case on behalf of the disarmament clauses which were supposed to reassure the French and prevent German revenge on the French and the British. Although he was furious when the German fleet made monkeys out of the Royal Navy by scuttling itself at Scapa Flow, in truth the Germans did the British a favour, leaving the Grand Fleet supreme, certainly in European waters. A major British objective had been secured. Further afield, the Washington Naval Treaty (1922), skilfully negotiated by A. J. Balfour, regularised the ratios between the British, the American and the Japanese fleets. Lloyd George was quite jealous of his elderly colleague's success. As for the army, Germany's 100,000 strong Reichswehr, without planes, tanks and a General Staff, was no threat to France, whose victorious army of millions was now the largest in the world. The Rhineland duly remained demilitarised for 15 years according to the terms of the treaty. Hitler then sent the German army back into it in 1936 which the French accepted without military countermeasures and the British, represented by Anthony Eden, culpably ignored. On Germany's eastern frontiers, the Polish and Czechoslovak armies flourished healthily, supplied in the latter case by the Skoda munitions works. But they would be no match for the burgeoning might of the Third Reich.

So what went wrong? Lloyd George had no doubt. The successors to the Big Three were pygmies.[43] Even Wilson's successors were, relatively speaking, men of straw. In France, Prime Minister Clemenceau was upstaged by the contemptible President Raymond Poincaré, who combined the maximum provocation of Germany with the minimum effectiveness. ('Can't you lend me your George V?', Clemenceau, the old republican, asked Lloyd George.[44]) The occupation of the Ruhr in 1923 with 'nigger troops'[45] was Poincaré's finest hour. As for Great Britain, Macdonald, Baldwin and Neville Chamberlain threw away the top cards which Lloyd George had bequeathed. Writing in 1938, Lloyd George recorded in sorrow and anger the dismal procession of concessions to the dictators, especially Mussolini. In other words, there was nothing wrong with the treaties if only they were properly enforced. Alas, everyone knew that Germany got away with clandestine rearmament. Beer-hall audiences laughed in their tankards about the man who in all innocence acquired the parts for a pram – but try as he might – 'and I know that I'm not very bright' – it repeatedly came out as a machine-gun. German tank specialists trained the Red Army under Tukhachevsky in the correct use of tanks, while the visitors acquired on the ground experience. Guderian was the beneficiary. Luftwaffe aces like Captain Goering practiced on Swedish airliners. Pocket battleships with the latest diesel engines and 11.9 guns could outpace and outgun the equivalent warships in the Royal Navy. The *Lutzow* was launched in 1929: it was supposed to be only 10,000 tons but was clearly a lot more.

As for the territorial clauses, Lloyd George was unhappily aware that he and his colleagues had treated Germany badly, from November 1918 onwards when the victorious allies inflicted mass starvation contrary to promises included in the Armistice. There was no way that the Fourteen Points had been observed, so far as the rights of nationalities were concerned. The separation of East Prussia from the rest of Germany was asking for trouble. A plebiscite in Northern Silesia eventually undid a wrong there, as did similar measures in the Saar coalfield. But there were 3 million Germans in the Sudetenland whom Hitler was to exploit – and why should Austria not unite with the Fatherland if her people so desired? Lloyd George always preferred the Germans to the French, despite his respect for Clemenceau. The tragedy was that more was not done to bolster the Weimar Republic before Hitler came to power on 31 January 1933. Why could reparations not be abolished long before Hitler cashed in? Why could German rearmament not be accepted instead of guiltily winked at? Lloyd George was out of office from October 1922 onwards and so cannot justly be blamed for the feebleness of Baldwin, Austen Chamberlain and Ramsay MacDonald – to say nothing of Neville Chamberlain and Lord Halifax – but in due course he was to display a culpable blind spot with regard to Hitler. Suffice now to say that his sympathy for German indignation and self-pity was based on his own guilty conscience. Here, he personified British appeasement.

Even with regard to the punishment of German war criminals, Lloyd George was feeble. To his credit, he was always aware of the sufferings of British merchant seamen at the hands of the Kaiser's submarine pirates[46] – and for these crimes Lloyd George was sure that Wilhelm was personally responsible. Furthermore he argued cogently that it was wrong to prosecute the lesser fry while the Kaiser read P. G. Wodehouse to his bemused courtiers in his Dutch manor house. In the frenetic election campaign of December 1918, Lloyd George eventually toned down his demand for the Kaiser to be hanged – though in private he favoured shooting him in order to deter his successors – but in retrospect he regretted the War Guilt clause. Noel Coward's celebrated 'Don't let's be beastly to the Germans'[47] was a satirical attack on Lloyd George and those who agreed with him. At Versailles, Lloyd George displayed the slippery evasiveness which enabled him to broker deals between trade unions and management, and subsequently between warring factions in Ireland. He only succeeded in pacifying Germany and her conquerors by betraying the French: here he compounded his dishonesty by being unjustifiably pleased with himself.

As well as being less beastly to the Germans by helping and not hindering her economy, Lloyd George was anxious to welcome Bolshevik Russia into the European family of nations. Several attempts were made to establish trade agreements despite the opposition of senior Conservatives and temporary Liberals such as Churchill. In January 1922 at the Supreme Allied Council in Cannes, Lloyd George persuaded the French and the Germans to agree to an economic and financial conference at Genoa, to which Russian delegates would be invited. This was a desperate attempt to rescue Lloyd George's reputation for constructive statesmanship. However, the attempt at Genoa – intended by Lloyd George to be a second Versailles – to welcome Russia into the respectable Western democratic club foundered when the two outcasts, Germany and Russia, did a deal on their own, cancelling war debts at nearby Rapallo without informing Lloyd George. This 'treaty' was a catastrophe for Lloyd George, who needed the two outcasts to remain helpless and dependent on his patronage: no wonder they had gone behind his back.

To be fair, repeated attempts by Germany's foreign minister, Walter Rathenau, to speak with Lloyd George had been rebuffed, or simply referred to Lloyd George's German specialist E. F. Wise. Russia's commissar for foreign affairs, Georgi Chicherin, subsequently boasted that he had 'raped' Rathenau, his German opposite number.

Indeed the intelligent, idealistic Jew Walter Rathenau was a reluctant bedfellow, so far as the Communist was concerned. His car was ticking over when an official ran out of the hotel to inform him that Lloyd George was on the telephone. Rathenau paused for a moment, sighed sadly and climbed into his car with the words, '*le vin est tire, il faut le boire*' ('the wine has been de-corked, we've got to drink it'[48]). When an indignant Lloyd George was told by the German delegates that they had been fobbed off, he blandly and disingenuously replied, 'Who is Mr Wise?' A few days later Rathenau was gunned down by fascist thugs, outraged that Germany should be represented by a Jewish Foreign Minister.[49]

Lloyd George's international escapades were not finished yet, but Genoa was his last conference. He had been humiliated by the Russians and the Germans. The French were impossible, controlled by Poincaré. His companions, Maggie and Megan, did little to cheer him. He wrote self-pityingly to Frances, who had to stay at home in order to steer clear of Dame Margaret:

> Had to sacrifice my Sunday rest to smooth over another French crisis. I am so glad, dearest, you are not *all* French otherwise you would be so difficult to handle. The Conference is still labouring heavily & without a boast I am the only man who can pull it through. *I do so want you here.* I passionately long for you & yet I know it would not be wise. The feeling is getting very bitter amongst the enemies of the Conference ...'[50]

Furthermore, Lloyd George's own enemies were closing in for the kill. Perhaps the best that can be said for the treaties, clumsy and maladroit in so many respects, is that Europe was, at least, pacified quickly.

1918–1922

Bonar Law's prediction, after the coupon election of December 1918, that Lloyd George could be prime minister for life proved to be inaccurate. In the event, he lasted for just under four years, and they were four highly fraught, contentious years in which the domestic scene was as controversial as the foreign. Lloyd George, it turned out, was born unto trouble, just like Job,[51] and the sparks did indeed fly upwards. His dictatorial, or at least presidential, style which had worked well in wartime, proved less appropriate for postwar, peace-time Britain. Britain at war needed an authoritarian at the helm. When he was once accused of bullying his colleagues, Lloyd George denied the charge – 'except for Curzon' because he was so pompous.[52] Curzon certainly was on occasions reduced to tears by his Prime Minister. When Lloyd George claimed that the Turks were in full flight for Mecca, 'Ankara', Curzon corrected him: 'Lord Curzon is good enough to admonish me on a triviality', crushingly retorted the Prime Minister.[53] However, he also wrote appallingly rude letters to Churchill, mocking him for his obsession with Russia (Churchill had accused him of 'grasping the hairy paw of the baboon'). Lloyd George drove Milner out of office by publicly reprimanding him in front of his civil servants. He betrayed faithful assistants such as Montagu and Addison. During his peacetime premiership, Lloyd George alienated all his colleagues, if not by bullying then certainly by his selfish unpredictability. A classic example occurred when he disappeared on holiday into the Scottish Highlands between August and October 1921, dragging the government after him.[54] The cabinet was required to meet in Inverness Town Hall, while a deputation of Labour mayors waited four days for an interview. At one stage, Government civil servants had to make do with one car, no telephone and a railway thirty miles away. Then the Prime Minister went sick with toothache which no local dentist dared treat, so that he was *hors de combat* until reinforcements arrived from London. 'Not good enough' was the verdict of his Tory colleagues. No wonder the coalition began to unravel.

Unfortunately there were insoluble problems at home and abroad. India seethed with nationalistic discontent. The Montagu-Chelmsford reforms were wrecked by Gandhi's opposition. At Amritsar in April 1919 General Dyer ordered his troops to fire into a mob of protesters; nearly 400 were shot or trampled to death in the ensuing stampede. When Dyer was dismissed, 129 Tory MPs voted against the government and the readers of the *Daily Telegraph* subscribed over £10,000 for a gift to the General. Lloyd George conspicuously failed to support Montagu, his Secretary of State.

There were problems, too, in Palestine where Britain simultane-ously protected a nascent Arab state and encouraged the influx of Jews in accordance with the Balfour Declaration. Both Balfour and Lloyd George, in their markedly contrasting schooldays, had been brought up on the Old Testament. So when Lloyd George talked expansively of settling Jews in Palestine 'from Dan to Beersheba',[55] he knew what he was talking about. It had been all very well for 'H. M. Government to view with favour the establishment of a National Home for the Jewish People', but Curzon's question was spot on: 'What is to become of the people of the country?'[56] Lloyd George and Balfour believed that Curzon's was a non-question. 'There was to be a land without people for a people without land.'[57] The problem was that, in fact, it was by no means a land without people. When the existence of the indigenous Palestinians was pointed out to Lloyd George, he showed little sympathy with Arabs who refused to acknowledge the benefits which Jewish immigrants would bring to the Holy Land. Still, there was no clear answer to the unresolved question: Were the Jews to be offered merely the opportunity to settle in a 'National Home' or were they to be free to establish their own politico-military Jewish state? Whereas Balfour received a rapturous welcome from the recently arrived Jewish settlers in Palestine which he visited for the first time in 1925, he was taken aback by Arab hostility, which he found curious. In truth, for the British, Palestine became a hot potato long before Hitler created world-wide sympathy for a Jewish state by implementing the Holocaust.

Where Tory backbenchers did appreciate their leader's skill as a peacemaker was in labour relations. After a brief postwar boom, the British economy nose-dived. Unemployment soared, so did inflation, so did industrial discontent. Lloyd George headed off a miners' strike by continuing government subsidies and promising to implement the Sankey Report, which recommended a 2s./a shift rise in wages and ultimate nationalisation. Then, typically, Lloyd George had second thoughts. 'I think we had better have that strike', he commented grimly.[58] The miners had already been let down on Black Friday, 15 April 1921, when the transport and railway unions refused to join their Triple Alliance partners. Conditions in the mines now deteriorated until the 1926 General Strike.

The Prime Minister also reneged on promises to nationalise Britain's railways. The furthest he would go was to amalgamate the 27 railway companies, which had grown up in a thoroughly uncoordinated way, into four main lines (London, Midland and Scottish; London and North Eastern; Great Western; and Southern). This negotiation brought about a head-to-head row between Lloyd

George and one of the Directors of the LNER, Tory MP Sir Frederick Banbury. They had already quarrelled over the Corn Production Bill of April 1917, prompting Lloyd George to write in his *War Memoirs* that Sir Frederick was 'the only perfect specimen of the prehistoric man left in the economic world'.[59] When the act making women eligible as Members of Parliament was debated in October 1918, the Tellers for the 25 Noes against the 274 Ayes were Mr Peto and Sir F. Banbury.[60] One of the companies forming the LNER was the Great Central Railway, which had named a class of express locomotives after war heroes. One was named *Lloyd George*. Banbury, as a Director of the new LNER had the nameplates removed.[61] Furthermore he ordered that one of the 'Flying Scotsman' class of LNER Pacifics inherited from the Great Northern Railway should be named *Sir Frederick Banbury*. This may seem trivial, but such attacks on the political leadership would not have been tolerated by Lloyd George's opposite numbers in the USSR, for example, who liked to see cities and tanks named after them, and no one else. Lloyd George on the other hand had to survive in the iconoclastic atmosphere of a true democracy.

While having an engine named after you was one way of achieving public recognition, more common was the acquisition of an honour such as a peerage, a knighthood or one of the numerous Orders which now proliferated (e.g., OBE which allegedly stood for 'Other Buggers' Efforts'[62]). Nothing damaged Lloyd George's reputation more than the honours scandal, that is to say, the sale of honours for cash, which besmirched his 1918–1922 administration. This practice had existed for centuries. Now, however it was systematised and exploited as never before. Lloyd George cynically traded honours for contributions to his personal fund. In Lloyd George's defence it is claimed that the money he received was devoted to political causes. Much Conservative indignation was provoked, because money which could have been expected to have increased Tory funds went instead to the Lloyd George fund. He himself viewed the acquisition of honours with the utmost cynicism, especially peerages, though he did support the award of the DBE (Dame of the British Empire) to Maggie in recognition of the wonderful work she had performed on behalf of Welsh servicemen and their families. Allegedly, Lloyd George knew little about the actual transactions, which remained in the hands of seedy operators such as Maundy Gregory and 'Bronco'

Bill Sutherland. In July 1922, however, the Duke of Northumberland led a damaging assault in the House of Lords when he read out a typical tout's letter: 'There are only five knighthoods left for the June list. It is not likely that the next government will give so many honours, and this really is an excellent opportunity'.[63] There was an accepted tariff: £10,000–£12,000 for a knighthood, £35,000–£40,000 for a baronetcy, and a lot more for peerages. Many of those 'honoured' were distinctly shady – tax-dodgers, food-hoarders, fraudsters, men who had traded with the enemy. The King was outraged that honours which he had been persuaded to approve were touted so shamelessly. Here was a new version of 'Lloyd George knew my father'.[64] It did him no good at all.

Admirable and positive achievements, nevertheless, can be attributed to Lloyd George's peacetime administration. Fisher's Education Act raised the school leaving age to 14, while teachers' salaries were increased by the Burnham scale – though women's salaries were disgracefully less than men's. Addison's housing programme involved the subsidising by the government of local authority building programmes. As Minister of Reconstruction, Addison graduated to the Ministry of Health where he introduced reforms which anticipated Bevan's National Health Service. Old age pensions were nearly doubled and the Unemployment Insurance Act now benefited thousands of new workers, though not, unfortunately those in farming and domestic service. Sadly, a slump which succeeded the postwar boom in 1920 curtailed reforms and forced Lloyd George to appoint Sir Aukland Geddes drastically to cut government expenditure, including the armed forces. Addison pleaded in vain for economies to be made in the implementation of Lloyd George's unrealistic foreign policy – the endless conferences; interventions in Russia and Mesopotamia; the absurd vendetta against the resurgent Turkey on behalf of the hopeless Greeks. Addison was rewarded by demotion to the Duchy of Lancaster, a reduced salary and then dismissal. As Lloyd George felicitously explained to his constituents at Pwllheli, 'Dr Addison did not make a success of housing, he got the sack because he was no good and he has now joined the Labour Party'. The relationship between Addison and Lloyd George was soured by this disloyalty, which unfortunately was typical of Lloyd George. Fisher fared no better at Education where Lloyd George maintained that classes of 70 in primary schools were not necessarily to be deplored. Thus, were high hopes of reform dashed by economic catastrophe monitored by political cowardice.

Ireland – an Achievement Greater than Gladstone's?

There was however a real achievement of which the Peacemaker General could be legitimately proud. He came closer than any of his distinguished predecessors to solving the problem of Ireland – closer than Pitt, closer than Peel, closer than Gladstone. What exactly was the problem which Lloyd George had to tackle? The 26 counties of Southern Ireland were economically backward, fervently Catholic and profoundly anti-British. 'Depend upon it', pronounced an Irish judge, 'no Irishman hates another Irishman as much as all Irishmen hate all Englishmen'.[65] It should be added in defence of the judge that the Irish had good reason to hate the English, for instance, the disgraceful Irish famine of the 1840s, when the potato crop failed and England's abysmal response most certainly contributed to the resulting 1 million related deaths. The problem would have been simpler if the judge had been correct in his claim that *all* Irishmen hated the English, but he was wrong. Of the six northern counties, four were, for the most part Protestant, prosperous and pro-British. Not surprisingly there was a fanatical commitment by the northern counties to remain in union with England. Compromise was seemingly not an option when Ireland was heading for civil war immediately before a greater conflict exploded in 1914. Ireland was put on hold – though the Easter Rising (1916) reminded the British government that southern Ireland was not by any means reconciled. The provocative and barbarous suppression of the Easter Rising – despite Lloyd George's and Asquith's well-meant interventions – doomed John Redmond's moderate Home Rule party, which was superseded by the extreme republican Sinn Feiners (meaning 'ourselves alone'). Sinn Fein won all the southern Irish seats in the Coupon Election (1918) and promptly refused to appear at Westminster. Instead, they appealed to the bullets of the Irish Republican Army (IRA). Deadlock ensued. Rebellion faced repression.

For all his devotion to Welsh nationalism, Lloyd George had no time for Irish independence. He had, in fact, moved on from Cymru Fydd. Field Marshal Sir John French was sent out to Dublin Castle as lord lieutenant. The British army mounted a full-scale campaign against the IRA. Because there was a shortage of soldiers due to the British army's demobilisation and commitments elsewhere, the government welcomed the recruitment of soldiers facing demobilisation but not too enthusiastic about a return to 'civvy street' – actually a familiar problem elsewhere such as in Weimar Germany.[66] Such soldiers who wanted to keep marching were incorporated in the forces of the crown and deployed in Ireland. Because there was a shortage of uniforms they were equipped with khaki battledress and the black belts and dark green caps of the Royal Irish Constabulary. Some wit called them the Black and Tans, after a popular hunt from County Limerick but there was nothing funny about the behaviour of the Tans who, together with the 'Auxies'[67] (irregular auxiliary troops) answered atrocity with atrocity. 'We have murder by the throat!', exalted Lloyd George in a notoriously bloodthirsty – and inaccurate – speech.[68] Others were appalled, including George V, who appealed to his subjects on both sides to forget and forgive, and to stop murdering each other.

Gradually, both sides drew closer together. Eventually, Sinn Fein's leader, Eamon de Valera, was prepared to face Lloyd George across the negotiating table, delivering interminable lectures on Irish history which, Lloyd George complained, invariably ended with Oliver Cromwell. Lloyd George, for his part, poked fun at de Valera because there was no word in Gaelic for 'republic'.[69] For the final negotiations in London, 'Dev' elected to stay on the far side of St George's Channel so that he could repudiate any settlement made by his subordinates. The Irish Treaty was thrashed out in London in December 1921. Here Lloyd George can be seen at his most impressive. The essence of the deal was as follows: dominion status involving more or less complete self-government for the 26 southern counties to be called the Irish Free State, swearing allegiance to the crown and permitting harbour facilities to the Royal Navy and permission for the British army to recruit; the six northern counties to remain in union with England, but the fate of the two most Catholic, Fermanagh and Tyrone, to be entrusted to a Boundary Commission which would probably award them to the south in due course, leading eventually to Irish union. Only with this concession could the southern Irish negotiators be persuaded to accept a settlement, strictly speaking, short of Irish unity – and in the event de Valera refused to accept such a compromise.

Civil war therefore ensued between accepters and rejecters of the Treaty. One of the British negotiators, Birkenhead, told his Irish opposite number Michael Collins that he had signed his political death warrant, to which Collins retorted that he had signed his actual death warrant. Such proved to be the case. Collins was murdered. Although the British government was no longer involved, the killing continued. Field-marshal Sir Henry Wilson, who had never concealed his Ulster allegiance, was gunned down outside his London home by IRA assassins in June 1922. Both Orange extremists and the IRA have continued to murder each other ever since.

Nevertheless, the Treaty stood the test of time for over 50 years.[70] Perhaps Tony Blair, Ian Paisley, Gerry Adams and Martin McGuiness eventually cobbled together a better settlement in 2006 – though even they fell short of putting an end to the violence entirely. Ireland is still a somewhat old-fashioned society, so some would argue. The tragic death of an Indian dentist in Galway in 2012 because she was not permitted a life-saving abortion showed what still remains to be done in 'romantic Ireland' (Yeats).[71] Nevertheless, EU money has underpinned real progress, based on Lloyd George's settlement which proved to be more lasting than Gladstone's. No wonder Frances Stevenson remembers him coming into her room with the treaty document, 'exhausted but triumphant'. 'Lock it up carefully', he said. Frances found it there in a drawer after his death.[72]

Lloyd George succeeded in tackling the Irish problem because of his insight into human nature, his flexibility and his deceitful exploitation of the vulnerability of his opponents – was there really a train waiting at Euston to convey the news to Sir James Craig in Belfast if the Irish refused to sign?[73] Still, a modern biographer, Peter Rowland, has a case when he writes that 'the Irish settlement was the greatest triumph of Lloyd George's career'.[74]

The Fall of the Peacefinder

Whether one agrees with Rowland or not, unfortunately plenty of influential people preferred the continued use of the sword to the implementation of the Irish Treaty – on both sides. Now, Lloyd George himself was to trigger the collapse of the coalition by a really unjustifiable piece of sabre-rattling. In at least one respect, he was a faithful follower of W. E. Gladstone, in that he was profoundly, viscerally anti-Turk. He displayed his low opinion of the Ottoman Empire in 362 eloquent pages of his *The Truth About the Peace Treaties*. Lloyd George was bitingly sarcastic about Tory claims that the Turk 'is the gentleman of Europe'.[75] He quotes with approval the dismissal of the Grand Vizier's allegation, in the presence of the allied powers, that Turkey in no way caused the war, and in general was a force for good. Arthur James Balfour counterattacked: 'Ottoman rule always entails the repression of culture and material decline of its subjects.' Lloyd George agreed. He was proud of his government's defence of Greek interests and achievements. He roundly condemned the French government led by Poincaré for treacherously rearming the Turks.

Unfortunately, the Turks, led by Mustafa Kemal Atatürk, fought well, though hardly in a gentlemanly way. They expelled the Greeks from Asia Minor and massacred thousands of civilians in Smyrna while the sailors of the Royal Navy looked on in impotent disgust. Atatürk's successes culminated in the summer of 1922, when only a British garrison, under General Sir Charles Harington, prevented a Turkish invasion of mainland Greece. For weeks, the outcome remained in the balance: Lloyd George's gung-ho irresponsibility in London contrasted with Harington's cool professional common sense in the Aegean. Lloyd George horrified Frances Stevenson with a telegram to the Dominions asking for their support in starting what was obviously liable to become another world war.[76] In the event, only New Zealand replied positively. Conservative allies were dismayed by their prime minister's irresponsibility. Lloyd George had left office when the logical outcome was ultimately achieved, the Treaty of Lausanne (1923), which surrendered all the gains of the Treaty of Sèvres four years before. According to Lloyd George, 'The first backward stagger was the humiliating Treaty of Lausanne, negotiated by Lord Curzon, which left the Christian populations of Asia Minor at the mercy of their old oppressors'.[77] But the rot had set in before then – and on his watch.

It all began with a pet monkey's bite. The victim was King Alexander of Greece, who was mortally wounded. As a result, his pro-western prime minister, Venizelos, was sacked. The French supported the Turks, who were now too strong for Alexander's inept successor. The Greeks were driven out of Asia Minor. Only the admirable Harington stood between Lloyd George and humiliation.[78] Bonar Law, whose health had broken down, wrote from his sick bed to *The Times*: Britain can no longer act as the 'policeman of the world'[79] – in other words, Lloyd George had got it wrong. The Conservative Party does not enthuse over leaders who look likely liabilities in a general election – as Margaret Thatcher was to discover to her cost. As a result, Austen Chamberlain agreed to a meeting of Conservative MPs at the Carlton Club. Stanley Baldwin made a damaging speech when he maintained that a 'dynamic force was a terrible thing'.[80] He was clearly referring to Lloyd George, who had wrecked the Liberal Party and, given half a chance, might well do the same to the Conservative Party. Even more influential than Baldwin's speech was Bonar Law's contribution, which indicated that he was now well enough to lead the Party – and the Government. The motion was carried by 187 votes to 87 that the Party should fight the forthcoming general election under its own colours and not as part of a coalition. Bonar Law and Curzon jumped ships, for slightly different reasons. 'We must resign, LG', Austen Chamberlain reported to the Prime Minister.[81]

The end of Lloyd George's coalition was a strange business. He himself had been outmanoeuvred, just as Asquith had been in December 1916. Both men did not believe that their colleagues could manage without them. In truth, Lloyd George was quite laid back about his fall from power. For one thing he was tired. For another he wanted to write his memoirs, visit America and 'spend more time with his family'. As they prepared to pack up and leave Downing Street, Lloyd George was positively frivolous, amusing his staff with impersonations of himself presenting a Welsh petition to Bonar Law's cabinet. Tom Jones impersonated Bonar Law, his head in his hands in as miserable a posture as possible. When Lloyd George imagined himself being invited to be seated, he replied, 'I could hardly sit in the presence of Lord Curzon'.[82] Everyone laughed, except Frances Stevenson, who realised that a wonderfully exciting chapter in her life had ended.

What is one to make of Lloyd George's peacetime premiership? While historians have found it easy to name faults, there were certainly positive achievements. Addison's houses and Fisher's schools were uncontroversial positives. The peace treaties at Versailles and with Sinn Fein were more controversial, but undoubtedly major achievements in statesmanship. Lord Morgan argues of Lloyd George's premiership 'that it passed measures of social reform, it brought eventual peace to Ireland, it promoted naval disarmament, it extended some self-government to India and to Egypt, it tried to diffuse labour unrest, it sought peace in foreign affairs'.[83] In many respects, Lloyd George proved to be a worthy successor to Gladstone, but perhaps Lloyd George's *style* looked increasingly inappropriate. It was not just the suspicion of sleaze involved in cash for honours; there were also reservations about Lloyd George's apparent monopoly of power, his manipulation of the press, his marginalisation of the House of Commons. Had he wrecked the Liberal Party in his pursuit of personal power? Should he have been more self-critical over the hands he shook? George V remonstrated with his Prime Minister before he set off for the Genoa Conference: 'I suppose you will be meeting Lenin and Trotsky?', asked the King. 'Unfortunately, Sir, I am not able to choose between the people I am forced to meet in your service. A little while ago I had to shake hands with Sami Bey, a ruffian who was missing for the whole of one day, and finally traced to a sodomy house in the East End. He was the representative of Mustafa Kemal, a man who I understand has grown tired of affairs with women and has lately taken up unnatural sexual intercourse. I must confess I do not think there is very much to choose between these persons whom I am forced to meet in Your Majesty's service.'[84] The King laughed, though others were less tolerant of Lloyd George's homophobia.

Lord Morgan has argued that Abraham Lincoln was even more a role model for Lloyd George than Gladstone.[85] While Gladstone was no warmonger, Lincoln boasted that he made his enemies his friends. That was as much Lloyd George's style as involvement in sleaze. Apart from the unfortunate Chanak Affair,[86] Lloyd George could almost deserve the title 'Peacefinder General'.[87] While Keynes was keen to attribute proficiency in the black arts to Lloyd George, more damaging because more plausible is his claim that Lloyd George represented 'final purposelessness, inner irresponsibility, existence outside or away from our Saxon good and evil, mixed with cunning, remorselessness, love of power that lend fascination, enthralment, and terror to the fair-seeming magicians of North European folklore'.[88] While this may be plausible, it is really not fair.

A thorough examination of Lloyd George's record at Versailles and subsequent conferences, his dealings with labour and his heroic tussles with Irish problems, must command respect. Indeed, his devotion to the cause of peace and the removal of grievances do entitle him to be called 'the Peacefinder General.'[89] As we have seen, Lloyd George made serious tactical mistakes, especially in bungling the Chanak Affair, which alienated his Conservative allies, but he did have ideals and worthwhile objectives which his Conservative and Liberal opponents lacked. Not the least of his achievements between 1918 and 1922 was to keep out of power some thoroughly unattractive and uninspired politicians. Morgan is therefore able to argue that the Coalition fell because British politicians, accurately reflecting the British people, rejected Lloyd George's vision of social harmony and international reconciliation, sadly a world we have since lost. Morgan argues that British democracy in October 1922 was healthier than American or French, to say nothing of Italian or German. It survived 'because of the discretion and calm judgement of those who governed it in those difficult years 1918–1922'.[90] David Lloyd George was, in more senses than one, our last Liberal prime minister; his 'was not a bad government'.[91]

8

The Mighty Pen: A Criticism of Lloyd George, the Author

The Pen is Mightier than the Sword

— Edward Bulwer-Lytton

LLOYD GEORGE's major works on the War and the Peace Treaties throw additional light on the two crucial episodes in his career. They also reveal fascinating truths about his abilities and values. Long before his involuntary retirement in July 1931 (caused by severe prostate problems necessitating surgery), Lloyd George saw his political life in a literary context. Even as far back as his last days as prime minister he had begun research for his memoirs. Now, as he recovered from his operation, he really got down to business. While he protested early on in his memoirs that he was not really a professional writer, this was disingenuous false modesty.[1] For one thing, he had been drawn to journalism since his teens, while in the 1920s when he no longer had a ministerial salary he took up political journalism in a big way, soon establishing himself as the most highly paid operator on either side of the Atlantic. He had also written one book already: William Heinemann published his *Truth about Reparations and War Debts* in March 1931 – described by Peter Rowland as 'a slim volume' which 'did not receive much more than polite attention'.[2] Even so, by this time he had proved that the pen was not only mightier than the sword but better paid.

Lloyd George realised that writing the major, authoritative works of which he believed himself capable was a new venture. True, he had collaborated on documents which the Liberal Party had produced before the 1929 election, and had published collections of his speeches. But now he planned a detailed account of his role as warlord during World War I and a vindication of his contribution to world peace between the end of the war in 1918 and his fall from power in 1922. These two works are massive in scale – 2,043 pages on the war (two volume popular edition) and 1,414 pages on the peace treaties, plus appendices and indexes which are logically integrated parts of the works as a whole. The text is supported by photographs and maps, usually, alas, without scales. The two books are well written and full of interesting pen-portraits and anecdotes, for instance, when the Kaiser insulted King Ferdinand of Bulgaria by belabouring his bottom.[3] These are major works, crucial to an evaluation of Lloyd George's life in politics. They contain valuable documents not published elsewhere. They show us how his mind worked as well as clarifying the motives and contributions of his contemporaries. From our viewpoint in the summer of 2016 they are a highly relevant contribution to debates about the tragic and controversial events a hundred years ago.

How much use to the historian are Lloyd George's blockbusters, given his somewhat ambivalent relationship with truth? Could he be trusted as a witness? To answer these questions involves a discussion of Lloyd George's motives for going to so much trouble as a recorder of his times. We must ask ourselves whether he was serious in his commitment to objectivity and factual accuracy, as opposed to the pursuit of his enemies and the achievement of massive sales with consequent massive profits.

According to Dr Johnson, 'only a blockhead does not write for money'.[4] Lloyd George was no blockhead. When he first envisaged writing his memoirs in 1922, he showed a keen interest in making money, signing up a deal with Funk and Wagnall in the United States and Cassell and Co. in Britain for £90,000. There was widespread condemnation of Lloyd George for making 'blood money' as a result of which he first announced that profits would go to war charities and then on second thoughts withdrew all plans for authorship. Maggie was provocatively triumphant: 'I did tell you not to take the money didn't I? That's a feather in my cap. You can write another book to make money, but not on the war. I could not touch a penny of it.'[5] When he revived the project in 1931, enough time had passed for a profit-making deal to be renegotiated. His house at Churt became a vast, chaotic document centre, managed with some difficulty by his secretaries A. J. Sylvester and Frances Stevenson. Expert advisers such as Captain Liddell Hart and Malcolm Thomson were recruited. Lloyd George examined the documentary evidence which his secretaries mobilised during the day and wrote in the early morning next day, usually between 6.00 and 7.30. He scrawled in pencil, writing left-handed. There could therefore be no doubt that the result was his own work. Later in the day, his long-suffering secretaries would type Lloyd George's rough work for his inspection. He worked very hard indeed. As a result he made about £50,000 in Britain and £12,000 in the United States out of *War Memoirs* and £11,000 for the *The Truth about the Peace Treaties* – by no means eye-catching profits but respectable enough at the time.

Money is not everything, as they say. Lloyd George wrote to vindicate himself against his enemies and critics, who had published hostile descriptions of his policies and achievements, and to attack people who had opposed him during his years in office. He once described himself as not really a historian, but more a lawyer, writing as a solicitor would to defend his client. This attitude explained Lloyd George's selection of evidence. He marshalled documents which backed his cause and ignored or suppressed those which did not – Not that he ever admitted falsifying evidence, any more than a clever solicitor would do. Dr J. Graham Jones represents the more or less unanimous views of professional historians that 'students of the Great War should use them (the *War Memoirs* and the *The Truth about the Peace Treaties*) liberally, but certainly with great caution'.[6] My own view is that Lloyd George writes so persuasively about various crucially important controversies that it is necessary to prove him wrong where he is wrong. We shall examine some important examples.

My other contention is that there can be no possible quibble with the massive and decisive evidence in both works about the sort of man Lloyd George was and of his role in politics. For better or for worse, he was the major player in the political direction of Britain's contribution to the World War I and the peace treaties. Part of his motivation in writing at such length is to prove the scale and the quality of his contribution. Asquith wrote: 'Winston has written a huge book about himself which he has called *World Crisis*.'[7] Lloyd George was equally self-absorbed and self-propelling. As Margot Asquith wrote: 'I realised that Lloyd George was the man who won the war, but I had not appreciated that he did it all on his own.' There he is, warts and all, for our assessment, whether we fully accept his claims or not.

1. The statesman.

2. Lloyd George and Mair.
A handsome pair.

3. The buttoned-up ankle-high boots
were always a feature, as was the dog.

4. Lloyd George, Margaret and Megan. The Welsh invasion of Downing Street.

5. Frances Stevenson at her desk. Trouble!

6. Sir Edward Grey, Liberal Foreign Secretary, 1905–1916. Both Lloyd George and Grey believed that the other was over-rated and instinctively disliked each other.

/. Asquith, Liberal Prime Minister, 1908–1916. 'Squiffy' was a womanising drunkard.

8. Kitchener and Birdwood at Gallipoli, April 1915. Kitchener slightly overdressed.

9. Albert Thomas (French Minister of Munitions), Haig (British Commander-in-Chief) and Lloyd George (British War Minister). Lloyd George wants to know the *raison d'être* of cavalry on the Western Front.

10. With Uncle Lloyd, 7 December 1916. Lloyd George is Prime Minister. 'The man is greater than the office.' 'Tell Uncle Lloyd that he is responsible for putting me in this awful job.'

11. Lloyd George and the Prince of Wales. Instinctive mutual sympathy.

12. Lloyd George and Poincaré. Instinctive mutual loathing.

13. Curzon, Lloyd George's punchbag.
'My name is George Nathaniel Curzon. I am a most superior person. My cheek is pink, my hair is sleek, I dine at Blenheim twice a week.'

14. Stanley Baldwin, feared and detested Lloyd George, 'the Welsh goat'. Succeeded Bonar Law as Prime Minister. In Curzon's view, 'a man of the utmost insignificance'.

15. Lloyd George welcomed back at Victoria by George V, Curzon and the Prince of Wales in attendance. The King gave a wreath to Lloyd George.

16. Golf was Lloyd George's greatest sporting relaxation.

17. Lloyd George about to enjoy some exercise and fresh air.

18. Lloyd George gardening.

19. Lloyd George with Hitler.

20. Welcomed at Berchtesgaden by Hitler. Ribbentrop in attendance.

21. Lloyd George for once did the right thing when he married Frances Stevenson on Saturday 23 October 1943.

22. Lloyd George and Land Girls: the scoundrel.

War Memoirs (1934)

From the very beginning of his *War Memoirs*, we are aware of Lloyd George's willingness to entangle historical controversies with personalities with whom he has issues. Despite his protest that 'I have sternly repressed every tendency to partisan bias',[8] his tone on such occasions is often gratuitously offensive and hurtful. More to the point, he allows his personal prejudices – which for all his protests were certainly marked – to warp his analysis of events. For instance, when he discusses the escalating crisis of July–August 1914, the relevant personality under the spot light is Britain's foreign secretary, Sir Edward Grey. Certainly, Lloyd George had issues with Grey, notably with his trouble-making over Lloyd George's insistence on reform of the Party's organisation in 1929. He therefore had no hesitation in lambasting Grey for his alleged shortcomings in office. His case against Grey is that he could have prevented the war by making it clear to the German government that Britain would intervene if Belgium were to be invaded. His attempt to avert war by summoning an international conference was doomed by his typically insular insistence that it should meet in London. Furthermore, Grey was culpable by failing to keep the cabinet informed of European developments. Lloyd George's criticisms of Grey offended a wide range of readers from the King to his own brother, William. In fact, William asked Megan to intercede with her father, pointing out that Lloyd George's comments on Grey would cause unnecessary offence, but Lloyd George was impenitent and refused to back down. He was sure that he was right to criticise Grey. Sylvester records Lloyd George's low opinion of Grey at dinner on 5 May 1933: 'He never came down into the arena and therefore got a false reputation. He was absolutely worthless. By the second year of the war Grey had completely crumpled up. He was pure funk. Asquith was not a funk. If you had had a Palmerston or Disraeli at the Foreign Office in 1914, there would have been no war.' Or a Lloyd George, perhaps? He incorporated his low opinion of Grey in *War Memoirs*:

> He had qualities, largely of appearance, manner and restraint, which gave the impression of 'the strong, silent man'. Just before 1914 the vogue of the taciturn was still prevalent and no man profited as much by it as Grey. Of one thing there can be no doubt; he failed calamitously in his endeavours to avert the Great War. He was the

most insular of our statesmen, and knew less of foreigners through contact with them than any minister in the government. He rarely, if ever, crossed the seas. When he suggested a Conference of Ambassadors of the Four Powers a few days before the War, he proposed that it should be held in London. Anyone reading with care and impartiality the record of the way in which he missed his opportunities must come to the conclusion that he lacked the knowledge of foreign countries and the vision, imagination, breadth of mind and that high courage, bordering on audacity, which his immense task demanded ... His tiresome hesitancies helped us into the War, but they hindered us when we were well in it ... As to Lord Grey, he was quite futile in any enterprise that demanded decision and energy. I cannot think of any suggestion of his that contributed in the least to the effective prosecution of the War.[9]

When Lloyd George saw William's letter to Megan, he wrote to him:

There are two things you must remember about Grey; his reputation is not based on any achievement. He was a calamitous Foreign Secretary both before and during the war. I think he could have averted the war ... You say that he was a colleague of mine. I would be bound to take that into account if he had behaved in a true spirit of comradeship. Instead of that he was one of the bitterest of those who assailed me when I was made Chairman of the Party. I therefore owe him nothing on the score of friendship or camaradie.[10]

Yet Grey had his admirers. Vansittart, for example, could not understand how anyone could fail to appreciate Grey's integrity: 'I conceived for him something near to hero worship.'[11] Nor has he lacked support from historians, such as his biographer, G. M. Trevelyan. Strangest of all among Grey's admirers must be numbered Lloyd George himself – if we go back to the aftermath of the Agadir crisis, when the pacifists in the cabinet, notably McKenna and Loreburn, were countered by Grey, Haldane and Lloyd George. Most disputable of all is Lloyd George's claim that Grey could have prevented the War. This is, in fact, a colossal 'what if?' While the Kaiser's influence cannot be ignored, he truly conformed to the pressures of his generals, who were convinced that a major European war was inevitable and that Germany's best chance of winning it was to implement the Schlieffen Plan in the summer of 1914. That being the case, could any action, or indeed inaction, by Grey have made any difference? It is worth recalling that the All Highest referred to his British cousin's 'contemptible little army' and that he believed that he had taken the steps to checkmate the Royal Navy.[12] Lloyd George's claim, therefore, that he himself had saved Europe from war by his celebrated Guild Hall speech of August 1911 while Grey dithered, has to be treated with caution, to say nothing of his assertion that the German generals would have been deterred by anything that Grey might have threatened in August 1914.

Lloyd George's inability to be fair to Grey is nothing compared to his bias against Haig. The entries in the Index tell their own story:

> Premature use of tanks ... pays tribute to Geddes's work on transport but omits to mention Lloyd George's part ... his refusal to face unpleasant facts ... his limited vision ... Germans accustomed to his heavy-footed movements ... viciously resists Lloyd George's attempts to get Unity of Command ... his stubborn mind transfixed on the Somme ... a planomaniac ... his misconceptions concerning morale of the German army ... obsessed with Passchendaele ... prefers rather to gamble with men's lives than to admit an error ... fails to appreciate value of tanks ... jealous of Foch ... neglects defences of Fifth Army ... unfairly removed Gough ... gets angry with Lloyd George at Beauvais ... his diaries contain no acknowledgement of Lloyd George's work in production of men and munitions ... obsession with cavalry ...[13]

Clearly we have here a dangerously skewed picture. We have already seen that the chemistry between Lloyd George and Haig was very poor. Haig was an aristocrat with friends at court; a cavalryman with no experience of infantry warfare; a professional soldier who resented the interference of politicians. All this comes across loud and clear in *War Memoirs*. What matters more is the case which Lloyd George puts up against the succession of allegedly futile frontal attacks in which the 'youthful future of Britain' was squandered by Haig and his colleagues. The resulting massacre, particularly of young officers, did indeed amount to a lost generation. One's chief reservation is the monotony of Lloyd George's complaints. There is no hint of the wit or irony which Churchill displayed in his description of the strength of German fortifications on the Somme: 'All these conditions clearly indicated to the Staffs a suitable field for our offensives, and it was certain that if the enemy were defeated here, he would be more disheartened than by being overcome upon some easier battleground.'[14]

Lloyd George was tortured by his success in solving the problems at the Ministry of Munitions which had hitherto impeded the flow of death-bringing weapons. But it seemed that the Germans had solved similar problems. For now, from 1 July 1916 there took place the bloodiest battle in the history of the British army, the Somme; there were 19,000 British deaths on the first day and a total nearing 400,000 during the course of the four-month long battle. By now, Lloyd George had moved from Munitions to the War Office, Kitchener having been drowned when his ship hit a mine off the Orkneys. 'It is claimed that the battle of the Somme destroyed the old German army by killing off its best officers and men. It killed off far more of our best and of the French best.'[15] So Lloyd George wrote:

> The battle of the Somme was fought by the volunteer armies raised in 1914 and 1915. These contained the choicest and best of our young manhood. The officers were drawn mainly from our public schools and universities ... The whole mind of the western strategists was concentrated on one or other of the hamlets along the Somme. They were only waiting, with hand cupped to ear, for the crack which would signify the final break of the German barrier, and they were massing cavalry immediately behind the French and British battle line in order to complete the rout of the tattered remnants of the German Army.[16]

Lloyd George records how the Germans reacted to the rout of their armies on the Somme by detaching the necessary troops for the conquest of Romania.

He was determined that there were to be no more Sommes. His *War Memoirs* show, however, that he was unconvinced that his colleagues shared his determination to control the military. In particular he despaired of the Prime Minister. Asquith and Lloyd George went back a long way, at least to the Liberal victory in 1906. When Lloyd George cheerfully gave up his post as Chancellor of the Exchequer in order to undertake the Ministry of Munitions in May 1915, he received a heartfelt thank-you letter from his chief, which he publishes as a facsimile – perhaps thinking that the reader might doubt the accuracy of Lloyd George's account:

> My Dear Lloyd George, I cannot let this troubled and tumultuous chapter in our history close without trying to let you know what an incalculable help and support I have found in you all through ... I thank you with all my heart. Always your affectionate H. H. Asquith.[17]

This appreciation did not prevent Lloyd George making his famous 'too late' speech in the House of Commons on 20 December 1915, which was a direct criticism of Asquith's (mis)management of the war. Nor did it prevent Lloyd George from writing a critical personal sketch of the Prime Minister as a war leader:

> He gave dignified but not rousing and vigorous leadership to the nation. But a War Minister must also have vision, imagination and initiative ... Mr Asquith at his best did not answer sufficiently to this description to make him a successful chief minister ... Asquith's will became visibly flabbier, tardier and more flaccid under the strain of the War. Then came the personal tragedy which shattered his nerve. The death of his brilliant son, Raymond, came upon him with stunning effect ... For a crisis had arisen where statesmanship had to intervene, decide and direct.[18]

This sketch is a strange mixture of compassion and malice, loyalty and contempt. We cannot forget that Lloyd George pulled strings to get his own sons out of the firing line. There must be no more Sommes – that was the conclusion which Lloyd George drew from these unhappy times. That was the priority which justified Lloyd George in the betrayal of his leader – or at least his cooperation with the other traitors.

To judge, however, from the account of the coup d'etat of 7 December 1916 in *War Memoirs*, Lloyd George behaved with scrupulous loyalty to Asquith, who destroyed his own premiership by failing to come to terms with Bonar Law. He then refused to serve either under Law or, when he refused the chalice, under Lloyd George. Maybe Lloyd George is a little economical with the truth when he insists that he never wanted to be prime minister. He refers to:

> the efforts I made to bring about a new system in the direction of war – efforts which, quite contrary to my intention, culminated in a change of government and the retirement of Mr Asquith ... There was a tragic bitterness about the situation which developed through those days, and which forced a cleavage between me and colleagues with most of whom I had for long years been working in the happiest and most fruitful collaboration – a cleavage later on aggravated and perpetuated by the malice of petty-minded men.[19]

Something like the truth? Lloyd George is more convincing when he describes his negotiations with Labour and with the leading Conservatives who were gratified that the new prime minister 'proposed to make no change in the Army Command for the present'.[20] Lloyd George's comment is highly pertinent: 'Their anxiety that there should be no change in the Army Command was a clear indication of the difficulty I was to experience in controlling the Army Chiefs.'[21]

We have seen in Chapter 6 how Lloyd George was bamboozled by Joffre's successor, General Nivelle, into insisting on the subordination of the British High Command to the French. All was to be sacrificed to Nivelle's master-stroke offensive, which was to result in the total rout of the Germans – the decisive victory which had so far eluded the allies. Haig, Robertson and the King were furious, but Lloyd George insisted to the point of resignation. The Nivelle offensive was a fiasco; Nivelle was sacked, the French army mutinied and Lloyd George was humiliated. His self-confidence and overall credibility were so damaged that later in the year he failed to stop Passchendaele. Not surprisingly, Lloyd George is reticent about the way in which his attempts to dominate the General Staff were defeated by French inadequacy. He is understandably silent about the way that his original *raison d'être* was now threadbare.[22]

What has *War Memoirs* to say about the Flanders offensives which he now sanctioned? Clearly Lloyd George's hostility to Haig results from his humiliation over the 1917 campaigns. He writes as a man overwhelmed by guilt, remorse and anger. As for Passchendaele, Andrew Suttie writes that the chapters covering the notorious mud-bath are 'the most polemical and therefore the most inaccurate of *War Memoirs* and, perhaps because of this, were the most popular'.[23] So what has the Welsh Wizard to say for himself? He argues that the members of the War Cabinet only sanctioned the battle because they were misled. In particular, they were not told that the senior French generals, notably Foch and Petain, were against the offensive, believing that Haig's plans took no account of the Flanders terrain and of the probable weather conditions. Still less were Haig's army commanders, Plumer and Gough, enthusiastic. General Robertson, however, the chief of the Imperial General Staff and therefore the Cabinet's senior professional military adviser, was extremely culpable in failing to report these adverse opinions, and therefore deliberately misleading his political masters, out of a misplaced loyalty to Haig.

Lloyd George correctly implies that Wully was in awe of Haig, on professional and social grounds. This was no excuse, however, for either Haig or Robertson. In the end, Lloyd George, Bonar Law and Milner were opposed by Curzon and Smuts, who successfully argued that the two senior professionals should have the last word. So the attack went ahead, subject to Haig's promise to call it off if it became evident that it was not likely to succeed in its purpose. On 21 June Lloyd George allowed himself to be talked into giving Haig and Robertson the green light:

> I made a final effort to persuade Haig and Robertson to abandon this foolhardy enterprise. I felt they were plunging into a perilous hazard when the conditions demanded unusual circumspection and preparation of men and equipment for the coming year's final attack on the citadel of the Central Powers. Our officers and men needed training. A few months ago most of them were civilians ... I reminded the Committee that during nearly three years of war I had never known an offensive to be undertaken without sure predictions of success ... I was told that the experience of Arras and Messines rendered success more likely. I agreed that both these operations had been very brilliant. In both, however, there had been an element of surprise.[24]

The description of the battle pulls no punches:

> Prolonged and terrific bombardment churned up the soggy ground. A downpour of rain did not improve matters. On the left the first two lines were reached, but not the green line which was the ultimate objective of the first day's attack. On the right little progress was made and the casualties were undoubtedly heavy.[25]

Gough had urged that the Second Army should be ordered to take the high ground on the right of the Fifth Army's assault. His suggestion was not adopted, with the result that his men were overlooked by German artillery and massacred. Lloyd George quotes a competent observer's description of the battlefield:

> After our preliminary bombardment which lasted for 16 days with ever-growing intensity, and the German retaliation thereto, the whole surface of the ground consisted of nothing but a series of overlapping shell craters, half full of yellow, slimy water. *Through falling into these ponds hundreds upon hundreds of unwounded men, while advancing to the attack, lost their lives by drowning.* [Lloyd George's italics]

We are told how this observer was hauled over the coals by a senior staff officer:

> 'You asked me how things really were and I told you frankly.'
> 'But what you say is impossible.'
> 'It isn't. Nobody has any idea of the conditions up there.'
> 'But they can't be as bad as you make out.'
> 'Have you been there yourself?'
> 'No.'
> 'Has anybody in Operations Branch been there?'[26]

Lloyd George describes how artillery became bogged down, tanks stuck in the mire, unwounded men by the hundreds and wounded men by the thousands sank beyond recovery into the filth. In the middle of August – Lloyd George could well have put this date in italics in that this was after a mere fortnight – General Gough advised Haig to discontinue the battle: '*I informed the Commander-in-Chief that tactical success was not possible, or would be too costly, under such conditions, and advised that the attack should be abandoned.*' [Gough's italics].[27] Unfortunately, Haig was too obstinate and too vain to admit that the 'frocks'[28] had been right. When they were reminded that they had promised to cancel the offensive if results were disappointing, the 'brass hats'[29] took refuge in the appalling weather, which would surely improve during September. So it did, but the ground had already been irreparably churned up. Nevertheless, invincible optimism prevailed over inescapable realism. When Lloyd George visited GHQ in late September:

> I found there an atmosphere of unmistakable exaltation. It was not put on. Haig was not an actor. He was radiant. He was quiet, there was no swagger. The politicians had tried to thwart his purpose. His own commanders had timidly tried to deflect him from his great achievement. He magnanimously forgave us all. He received me hospitably and pleasantly, without any of the humiliation of Canossa.[30]

Charteris, who fed his chief with 'faith-based intelligence', as George W. Bush would have put it,[31] was even worse, as was Kiggell, the chief of staff. No wonder Haig's tame press lords echoed his praises, especially Northcliffe whom Lloyd George described as 'Haig's Kettledrum'.[32] 'German Defence Broken', trumpeted *The Times*.[33] 'In short, the particular task which Sir Douglas Haig set his armies, has been very nearly accomplished.'[34] I could produce more of this false triumphalism, which Lloyd George quotes liberally, but I believe the above to offer a fair sample.

Lloyd George would have nothing to do with this nonsense. For him, the supreme condemnation of Passchendaele was afforded by the tragedy of Cambrai, when at last tanks were deployed en masse on suitable ground with electrifying results (19 November–7 December 1917). Indeed, so promising was the immediate outcome that some ill-advised propaganda specialist at the War Office decreed that church bells were to be rung. Alas, this was tragically premature. The Germans counterattacked and recovered the ground. Due to the devastation at Passchendaele, there were no reserves with which to follow up the tanks' success. A court of inquiry into the abortive Cambrai breakthrough inspired General Maxse who, to Lloyd George's justifiable wrath, blamed the wounded for spreading unflattering rumours about the High Command. 'I cannot help thinking that we soldiers with our extreme reticence and horror of all forms of publicity may be somewhat to blame for this result', admitted the General. As Lloyd George pertinently remarks, 'clearly, "we soldiers" does not include those who are wounded in the battle, neither does it comprise the 400,000 officers and men who had survived Passchendaele and Cambrai and gone home on short leave. There is neither reticence nor untruth to be found in them'.[35] Lloyd George concludes: 'Passchendaele was indeed one of the greatest disasters of the War, and I never think of it without feeling grateful for the combination of seamanship and luck which enabled us to survive and repair its unutterable folly.'[36] With due respect to Suttie, the arguments here are emotional rather than inaccurate.

Lloyd George's chapters on Passchendaele were certainly controversial, not least because Haig died shortly before their publication. Several military authorities such as Sir Ian Hamilton alleged that this was no coincidence, but the result of Lloyd George's cowardly refusal to face his critics. He countered by publishing a number of supportive letters as an impressive appendix in the two-volume edition, which emerged in January 1938. Here is a selection:

> Your book about Passchendaele was, if anything, not even severe enough. The conditions were impossible – no staff officer was ever to be seen near the front line, the sheer hopelessness and slaughter shook

the morale of every man who took part. The generals responsible for prolonging the fight should have been shot. (From an ex-captain)

I served in the frontline in France for four years. I feel that I must write a few lines to endorse all that you write on the subject. It is unfortunate of course that your work could not have been published in Lord Haig's lifetime, but when one thinks of the thousands and thousands of lives flung *recklessly* away, without a chance, in that mud, and of those divisions coming up, spick and span, from rest billets, but coming up hopelessly, knowing what they had to face (the only time I have ever seen British soldiers anything but cheery and confident) one is glad that the truth should be made widespread at last. Consideration for no one's feelings should be allowed to muffle the tragedy for ever. (From a lieut.-colonel)

As an ex-artillery officer, one of the thousands of wretched fellows who took part in that most depressing engagement, I heartily endorse every single word you write about that most terrible section of the Great War through which you so nobly and victoriously led this grand old country of ours. During the Passchendaele 'show' it was common talk in every officers' mess that the whole thing was being badly bungled, and that the Higher Command had no clear-cut idea of what was happening; you have said what countless thousands of us are thinking. (From a Captain, R. A.)

Bravo! As one of the survivors of the Passchendaele massacre I should like to add my testimony to the remarks in your recent publication. It is as a breath of fresh air ... (From a private)

I agree with every word you have written and said, although a professional soldier at the time ...

I had a son in the War and he endorses everything you say. It may interest you to know that my gardener was a sergeant-major at Passchendaele and he says that your remarks in your last volume about the battle are completely in accord with all the soldiers. (From a schoolmaster)

Pardon me writing to you, but I do feel annoyed with the President of the British Legion in calling your remarks a lie. My respects to you, Sir, for daring to tell the truth. (From a gunner)

Mr Lloyd George's information is not based on guesswork or hearsay. I remember stumbling across the Canal Bridge at Pilkem into a weary, mud-stained officer who directed me through the slush to the Ypres-Elverdinghe road. He had a Cambrian-Oxford accent and the tiredest-looking eyes I have ever known. His name was Gwilym Lloyd George and he served in the battery of howitzers just behind the canal bank. (From one of Old Chows' company.)

As a member of the Tank Corps, I was an actual witness of the conditions at the battle of Passchendaele which Mr Lloyd George describes as deliberate murder to order men into action in October 1917. As a junior officer I wondered why such senseless slaughter was allowed to continue. (From D. E. Hickey, Captain, late Tank Corps, quoted in the *Daily Telegraph*, 3 July 1934.)[37]

Lloyd George discusses this very point at some length. What should he have done? The most obvious measure was to sack the Commander in Chief. But:

... the campaign had been extolled in the Press and on platforms, and a peremptory dismissal of the victor would have been regarded as if Wellington had been recalled after Badajoz. But apart from that I had to ask and answer another question. Who could be put in his place? It is a sad reflection that not one amongst the visible military leaders would have been any better.[38]

As we saw in Chapter 6, Lloyd George sent Hankey and Smuts round the Western Front in order to 'trawl' for a replacement. An obvious candidate was Plumer whom the soldiers trusted but who, according to Smuts, was 'as stupid as Haig'.[39] Or there was Sir Claude Jacob who, unfortunately, was unknown to the public. Their most interesting discovery was a general from the Dominions whom Lloyd George does not name. He was General John Monash.[40] Not only was he an Australian, he was a Jew. In 1914 he had been a civilian engineer. To promote him over Haig of Bemerside would have been unthinkable.[41] In the event, Lloyd George contented himself by removing Haig's Intelligence specialist, General Charteris, and his Chief of Staff, General Kiggell. An even more distinguished victim of the Prime Minister's wrath, the CIGS Sir William Robertson, was forced to choose between representing Britain at the Chiefs of Staff committee in Paris, which would be able to overrule the CIGS, or remaining as CIGS. Robertson sulked. He was not even won over by an apple turnover at Riddell's house at Great Walstead – which Lloyd George knew was his favourite pudding, though Robertson conceded that it was delicious and sent his compliments to the chef. Lloyd George told the Commons that 'during the whole of the two or three years I had been associated with him, our personal relations had been not merely friendly, but cordial'.[42] Whether Wully would have concurred with this description is to be doubted for he now lent his support to his director of military operations, Sir Frederick Maurice, who attempted to bring down the Government by accusing Lloyd George and Bonar Law of lying about the strength of the army in France.

Lloyd George's coverage of the celebrated Maurice debate is surprisingly muted considering it climaxed with one of his greatest parliamentary triumphs.[43] Asquith made a wretchedly inadequate and misjudged speech during which Lloyd George records that he was urged by a Miners' Member, Mr Stanton, to 'get on with the War'.[44] Lloyd George quotes his own tendentious appeal for the House's support in the national interest: 'I really implore, for our common country, the fate of which is in the balance now and in the next few weeks, that there should be an end to this sniping.' Asquith's motion was defeated by 293 votes to 106. 'General Maurice was dealt with by the military authorities, who forthwith placed him on retired pay.'[45] In fact, Lloyd George executed some typically fancy footwork over the relevant statistics, claiming that the figures which Maurice himself produced, vindicated the Government. 'If there were in fact anything inaccurate in the statement made by me, which General Maurice had challenged, it was based on information and figures supplied by the General's own Department, so that Maurice would himself have been responsible for misleading the Premier and through him, the public.'[46] Lloyd George had, in fact, disregarded revised figures which Maurice subsequently submitted. His enemies were not sufficiently quick-witted to pinpoint the deceit.

Lloyd George was likewise economical with the truth in his description of an even more crucial conflict in which the survival of embattled Britain was at stake – the submarine crisis of spring 1917. Lloyd George is excellent in his portrayal of the issues involved.[47] The adoption of unlimited submarine warfare by the Kriegsmarine in January 1917 was a calculated gamble: could Britain be starved into surrender before the United States was provoked into a declaration of war followed by military and naval implementation? 'Yes!' was the undertaking which the German admirals gave to the 'All-Highest'. They were proved wrong, but only just. The Welsh Wizard now became 'the man who won the War' – with a vengeance. Once again he recounts the tale of the frocks outmanoeuvring the brass hats – though whether 'brass hats' truly applies here is debatable: 'Seadogs in the Manger' might be a better description. Lloyd George's adversary was the First Sea Lord Admiral Sir John Jellicoe, the issue, the desirability of convoys. Jellicoe was a far less formidable opponent than Haig, who, for all his apparent boneheadedness, was a shrewd political infighter. Poor Jellicoe had severe handicaps. He was not very bright. His navy was clearly losing the war. On the question of convoys – the ultimate war-winner – he was plain wrong. Lloyd George quotes with relish the American Admiral Sims' interview with Jellicoe in April 1917, when he was shown statistics proving that U-boats had sunk a staggering 800,000 tons of merchant shipping that month.

> 'What are you doing about it?', I asked.
> 'Everything we can'.
> 'It looks as though the Germans are winning the war', I remarked.
> 'They will win unless we can stop these losses – and stop them soon' the British Admiral replied.
> 'Is there no solution to the problem?', I asked.
> 'Absolutely none that we can see now'.

Lloyd George to the rescue:

> It was clear that the Admiralty did not intend to take any effective steps in the direction of convoying. After first discussing the matter with Sir Edward Carson (who was the First Lord), I informed the cabinet that I had decided to visit the Admiralty and there take peremptory action on the question of convoys.[48]

The news of this forthcoming raid galvanised the Admiralty into re-examining their statistics and realising that their hostility to convoys was indefensible. 'Accordingly, when I arrived at the Admiralty I found the Board in a chastened mood. We discussed the whole matter in detail. We agreed to conclusions which I thus reported to the cabinet.'[49] The Admiralty did not surrender without a fight, remaining convinced to the last that convoys were not only undesirable but impossible. Lloyd George describes how an unlikely ally in his campaign against Jellicoe and Carson was Haig, who greatly respected Jellicoe's professionalism but could nevertheless appreciate that he was losing Britain the war. With Haig's help, all ended happily with Carson's offer of promotion to the War Cabinet and Jellicoe's retirement. They were replaced by Geddes as first lord and Weymss as first sea lord – acceptable to George V because he was 'a complete gentleman'.[50] Unlike Lloyd George, the King would probably have added.

What economies with the truth can be identified here? The most damaging to Lloyd George's reputation is that his nation-saving trip to the Admiralty was postponed for six weeks while he dithered. Our source here is Sir Maurice Hankey, who was convinced that convoys simply had to be imposed. He believed that Lloyd George was reluctant to take on both the generals and the admirals. 'Oh well, I have never regarded the matter as seriously as you have', Lloyd George protested before eventually admitting that Hankey was right. But untold harm had already been done, cargoes sent to the bottom and valuable sailors' lives lost in distressing circumstances.[51]

Lloyd George's *War Memoirs* are a good read, with plenty of lively detail, memorable anecdote and convincing pen-portraits. They are, however, highly self-regarding, and not forthcoming on the subject of his mistakes. He does admit that the appointment of Neville Chamberlain to the newly created Ministry of National Service turned out badly. Typically, however, Lloyd George blames others: 'I had never seen him, and I accepted his qualifications for the post on the recommendation of those who had heard of his business and municipal experience.'[52] Lloyd George, however, was not reassured by Chamberlain's head – definitely the wrong shape, unlike his own. 'Mr Neville Chamberlain is a man of rigid competency. Such men have their uses in conventional times or in conventional positions, and are indispensable for filling subordinate posts at all times. But they are lost in an emergency or in creative tasks at any time.'[53] Chamberlain was sacked, and they never forgave each other.

The book ends strangely. Its penultimate chapter is, surprisingly, an assessment of Fisher's 1918 Education Act – perhaps a belated confession by Lloyd George that he had been wrong to rubbish Balfour's Act of 1902, on which Fisher's Act was based. Now he claimed the credit for Fisher's appointment. The conclusion follows – a somewhat abrupt end with some reflexions on the relationship between civilians and professional fighting men.

> I want to emphasise once more that my differences with great generals were not due to any personal or political motives. I had no personal quarrel with either Lord Haig or Sir William Robertson. My relations with Robertson were always pleasant ... [Such claims were blatantly false, but in any case they are digressions from the real issue.] Ought we to have interfered in the realm of strategy?[54]

Lloyd George waxes eloquent on the shortcomings of the military mind, quoting the suicidal mistakes made by the German high command, especially the invasion of Belgium. The Germans were disagreeably surprised by the intervention of the British Expeditionary Force, thanks to the brilliance of the great civilian strategist, Lord Haldane. 'The way that devoted but intelligent patriot was hounded out of official life by insinuations of treason is one of the most disreputable and stupid episodes in British history.' The Mesopotamia campaign was a striking proof of the limitations of the military mind in that the politicians' input was nil and the disaster total.[55] The provocation of the United States by unrestricted submarine warfare was another blunder which Lloyd George blames on Germany's military leaders. Then why did Lloyd George let the generals get away with it? Why did he not anticipate President Harry S. Truman's dismissal of General Douglas MacArthur (1951) – an act of immense moral and political courage?

"The most difficult decision presented to the Government was that of the Passchendaele campaign.'[56] Lloyd George argues that civilians such as he were better qualified than the brass hats:

> Gutchkoff, the Russian Minister of War, saw the South African War and he told a friend of mine that he thought the experience acquired by our soldiers in that war had actually disqualified them for command in the Great War. The fighting was so essentially different in every respect. All the men who filled the highest commands in our Army in France were veterans of the Boer War.[57]

As was Lloyd George, in a way – but he now evades the issue of the politician's right and duty to overrule the high command.

> Such highly gifted men as the British Army possessed were consigned to the mud by orders of men superior in rank but inferior in capacity, who themselves kept at a safe distance from the slime which they had chosen as the terrain where their plans were to operate.[58]

He thus permits himself a final barb at the generals for not visiting the front:

> No amount of circumspection can prevent war leading to the death of multitudes of brave men, but now that Generals are not partaking in the personal hazards of a fight, they ought to take greater personal

risks in satisfying themselves as to the feasibility of their plans and as to whether the objectives they wish to attain are worth the sacrifice entailed, and whether there is no better way of achieving the same result at less cost of gallant lives.[59]

Actually, this is typical Lloyd George and especially typical of his *War Memoirs*. To be fair to the generals, several lost their lives in close proximity to the front line, nor did Lloyd George, who was a physical coward, visit the front as often as he should have done. In truth he could not accept that he himself was 'the Butcher of Passchendaele' every bit as much as Haig, who proved to be a cleverer politician in outmanoeuvring his prime minister's attempts to get rid of him.

To his self-proclaimed honest and forthright attempts to prevent further world wars, Lloyd George now addressed himself – that is to say, to the peace conferences at the end of the War, which would supposedly make a repeat of Passchendaele unnecessary. Addressing the House of Commons on 11 November 1918, Lloyd George summed up the challenge now facing him: 'Thus at eleven o'clock this morning came to an end the cruellest and most terrible war that has ever scourged mankind. I hope that we may say that thus, this fateful morning, came to an end all wars.'[60] Alas, when he published his second great work, the storm clouds were gathering. His crusade to achieve this goal had clearly failed. To answer the question why this had proved to be the case, he now surveyed the past. To a great extent indeed, *The Truth About the Peace Treaties* follows on from *War Memoirs*.

The Truth About the Peace Treaties (1938)

Lloyd George's magnum opus on the peace treaties is a very different work from his *War Memoirs*, despite the continuity of theme. To be frank, it is quite tedious in places, and not surprisingly it is far less quoted by historians. It is, however, every bit as polemical as *War Memoirs*. In other words, the author is still attacking his critics and defending himself against their assaults. Or rather, he is not only defending himself but his colleagues as well, notably President Wilson of the United States and Prime Minister Georges Clemenceau. His own complacency is not unlimited. Interestingly, in an argument with Charles Hardinge in 1923 about the strengths and weaknesses of the Peace Treaties, Lloyd George admitted: 'If I had to go to Paris again,

I would conclude quite a different treaty.' Nevertheless, he is anxious to prove that the critics of the peace treaties are often malicious and ill-informed. He is eloquent about his own good fortune in the support he enjoyed from the Tory Party, led by his friend and colleague Andrew Bonar Law, which contrasted with the vicious back-stabbing that Wilson and Clemenceau had to endure. He recognises with regret Wilson's mistake in refusing to bring representatives of the Republican Party to Paris with him, notably the formidable Henry Cabot Lodge. Similarly he watched with amusement and sorrow Clemenceau's problems with Marshal Foch and President Poincaré when they accused him of betraying French military security by not insisting on French annexation of the Rhineland or similarly radical anti-Teutonic measures. Clemenceau loathed Poincaré: 'You wish to sleep with Madame Poincaré – it can be arranged'.[61]

While Lloyd George saw no reason to cover the terms of the treaties in detail, he has much to say about the chief players involved. Although Lloyd George was on one occasion invited to choose between pistols and swords during a spectacular row with Clemenceau,[62] he became quite fond of the old bruiser, writing this perceptive sketch:

> The figure and bearing of Clemenceau are universally familiar. At the Council of Four he wore a square-tailed coat of a very good, thick black broad cloth, and on his hands, which were never uncovered, grey suede gloves; his boots were of thick black leather, very good, but of a country style, and sometimes fastened in front, curiously, by a buckle instead of laces ... His walk, his hand, and his voice were not lacking in vigour, but he bore, especially after the attempt on him, the aspect of a very old man conserving his strength for important occasions. He spoke seldom, leaving the initial statement of the French case to his ministers or officials; he sat back in his chair with an impassive face of parchment, his grey gloved hands clasped in front of him. A short sentence, decisive or cynical, was generally sufficient, or a display of obstinacy reinforced by a few words in a piquantly delivered English.[63]

While both respected Woodrow Wilson's idealism, they found him ridiculous in his narrow Presbyterianism, Clemenceau shaking his head and raising his eyebrows at Lloyd George at the onset of another sermon ('He's off again!') and when poor Wilson drove himself to a serious breakdown, Clemenceau passed the latest bulletin to Lloyd George – 'he's worse today!' – followed by hilarious and heartless laughter by both parties. Lloyd George mercilessly pinpoints his weaknesses:

> The President was not a hero or a prophet; he was not even a philosopher; but a generously intentioned man, with many of the weaknesses of other human beings ... Like Odysseus, the President looked wiser when he was seated; and his hands, though capable and fairly strong, were wanting in sensitiveness and finesse.[64]

Both the Welshman and the Frenchman shared fluency in English, though it was not their mother tongue. Both shared an interest in the opposite sex ('Oh to be seventy again!' it will be recalled was Clemenceau's comment when a pretty woman came into the room[65]), both shared a laid-back attitude to doctrinaire Christianity. These traits Lloyd George records, just as he describes Wilson's devotion to peace and Clemenceau's love of France.[66]

Lloyd George defended the treaties from attacks in Parliament and in the media, both British and French. Paradoxically, these alleged both brutal cruelty towards defeated Germany and excessive leniency. To an extent, Lloyd George had himself to blame, for his cynical promises to hang the Kaiser and extract the last penny from German pockets in order to win the Coupon Election. However, in his first ninety pages he argues convincingly that the allies had pursued a statesmanlike peace from 1915 onwards, offering terms uninfluenced by British triumphalism. Furthermore, he insists that the Coupon Election was not won by irresponsible cries for revenge, as opponents of the Coalition have argued:

> Anyone reading these accounts would imagine that the electors went to the poll with one call in their ears from responsible statesmen who wished to be equipped with the mandate to 'hang the Kaiser' and to compel Germany to pay a sum of £24,000,000,000, or some equally astronomical figure, by way of indemnity. If these writers had thought it worth their while, before writing or repeating this kind of slanderous foolishness, to read the Election Manifesto issued by the two Coalition leaders to the nation, or the speeches delivered at the Election, they would have known that they were circulating falsehoods, and silly ones at that. What was our appeal to the nation? There is not a word about Reparations in our Manifesto and the only reference made to it by me was at Bristol [when, it will be recalled, Lloyd George promised to search German pockets for any surviving loose change[67]].

Lloyd George does admit that he would not agree to point two in Wilson's Fourteen Points, which guaranteed the freedom of the seas. The Royal Navy's blockade of Germany had been as effective as the allied armies in defeating Germany on the battlefield. Wilson ultimately came round just as he also accepted that the 'restoration' of Belgium and Alsace-Lorraine was not good enough; there had to be 'reparation' for the wanton destruction. Lloyd George, however, was adamant that the territorial terms imposed on Germany must not sow the seeds of World War II. So he opposed Clemenceau and Foch, who wanted to confine Germany to the right bank of the Rhine, nor would he commit British troops to the enforcement of such provocative terms. Lloyd George records that the British army was only interested in being demobilised soonest. When angry British troops threatened to march on London, the General of Command, Southern Command, who was none other than Field Marshal Wully Robertson, doubted if his troops would fire on the mutineers.

Lloyd George vividly describes the statesmen's attempts to create a new world. Were Germany's colonies to be mandated? Lloyd George hoped that the liquor trade, slavery and the trafficking in arms could thus be outlawed, while the creation of 'big nigger armies'[68] under German officers would no longer be a threat to world peace. It was not just German ambition that he feared. Clemenceau wanted to retain the right to raise troops in mandated territories, for the defence of France. 'Mr Lloyd George said that as long as M. Clemenceau did not train big nigger armies for the purpose of aggression, which was all the cause was intended to guard against, he was free to raise troops.'[69] The United States, meanwhile, refused to undertake any mandates. 'They probably apprehended that, if they undertook the government of thousands of negroes in tropical Africa, it might create some complications with their own coloured population.'[70] So Lloyd George speculated, once again displaying his racist obsession.[71] In the meantime, he describes the wonderful reception in London for Clemenceau and Foch, though Woodrow Wilson offended the King by his callous remarks at Buckingham Palace about the losses of British ships. Lloyd George pressed for disarmament, unsuccessfully in the case of France. Only universal disarmament, he argued, would reconcile Germany to the loss of her own armed forces. He trumpeted the achievements of the International Labour Organisation under the leadership of Albert Thomas, who wore himself out on behalf of women and children in employment. 'Will the critics of the Versailles Treaty have the decency to acknowledge that this humanitarian organisation was set up by this Treaty and that it was promoted by the governments and statesmen who have to bear the brunt of the critical scurrility of the assailants of Versailles?', he demanded.[72] Lloyd George allowed his sympathy with people seeking freedom to accept India's progress towards self-government, although he foresaw the problems that the implementation of the Balfour Declaration, which granted Jews self-government, would cause. Together with Wilson and Clemenceau he tried to negotiate concerning Italy's claims to Fiume at least – until D'Annunzio seized it in autumn 1919.

Pages 1001–1362 are devoted to the Turkish situation. Lloyd George writes with grief and rage about the ruthless behaviour of Mustafa Kemal who tore up the Treaty of Sèvres by invading Greece. Only Britain, led by Lloyd George, protested. The French, led by Poincaré, withdrew their troops from Chanak, the small town on the Eastern side of the Straits, where the British, led by General Harington, dug in. The French, Lloyd George claimed, had secretly negotiated with Kemal behind Britain's back.[73] Lloyd George sent a ridiculously gung-ho appeal to the Dominions. The ensuing row brought down Lloyd George. The Tories had always believed that 'the Turk is a gentleman'; Consequently 'the first backward stagger was the humiliating Treaty of Lausanne, negotiated by Lord Curzon which left the Christian populations of Asia Minor at the mercy of their old oppressors'.[74] To Lloyd George's horror, ships of the Royal Navy anchored impotently off Smyrna while Kemal's troops massacred 120,000 Greeks – all in the most gentlemanly fashion.

Lloyd George was consistent in retaining his civilised, Liberal prejudice against all forms of political tyranny: witness his footnote comment on Bolshevik Russia and Nazi Germany: 'In both countries an autocracy has been established more complete and pervasive than that of Czar or Kaiser – ruthless suppression of all criticism, freedom of thought and expression, the treatment of the government as treason to the state.'[75] Similarly, he defended the Dominion leaders from Clemenceau's outrageous accusations of racial exploitation which provoked the retort: 'Very well, bring your cannibals here to see me this afternoon'.[76] Lloyd George records Clemenceau's insult to Billy Hughes 'Mr Hughes, I hear that you are a cannibal', and Hughes' celebrated retort that such claims were much exaggerated.[77] This was one of the few humorous touches which Lloyd George attempted. Another was an extract from a totally incomprehensible speech by Ramsay MacDonald:

> They clenched their little fists and they piroutted around their enemy and challenged him to take his coat off. The great personality was the person who went through the raving crowd surrounded with that dignity which made it impossible for the blackguard to touch him, even though he talked behind his back. Translate that power of great personality ...[78]

By way of contrast, under the threat of renewed European war Lloyd George wrote nostalgically of General Botha's astonishingly humane and generous speech pleading for cooperation between the powers. Among other points, Botha recorded that his speech was delivered on the anniversary of the Peace of Vereeniging, when Britain offered generous terms to the Boer republics. Could similar generosity not be shown now to Germany and her allies?

> It is difficult to convey the power of General Botha's deliverance by a mere summary of the words, and the attractive and compelling personality of this remarkable man. The President [Wilson] told me immediately afterwards that it was the most impressive speech to which he had ever listened.[79]

This desperate, nostalgic longing for true leadership and statesmanship from the leaders of the civilised world coloured the Conclusion to Lloyd George's works – a self-deceiving document, but in its way a tribute to its author.

Lloyd George begins his Conclusion with an imagined, fanciful discussion in the land of the immortal shades between Clemenceau, Orlando and Wilson. It reads like something out of Virgil's Aeneid; Why has the position of strength achieved by the democracies in 1919 been squandered? Clemenceau blames himself for surrendering to Lloyd George and Wilson over the Rhineland, but he also contemptuously blames Poincaré for sacrificing French interests. Orlando 'would, I think, acknowledge that he made a mistake in being rushed so easily to abandon the substantial gain guaranteed to Italy by the Treaty of Paris'.[80] President Wilson blames everything on the lack of support for the League of Nations. 'If he has met Cabot Lodge in the shades where spirits await their final destiny, he will have pointed out to him the agony of the world today and said "My friend, that is your doing"'. Lloyd George then intervenes:

> We should also all agree that the failure of a great deal of what is best and noblest in the treaties has been entirely due to the fact that there has been no will power or steady resolve behind their execution ... the treaties were never given a chance by the miscellaneous and unimpressive array of second-rate statesmen who have handled them for the last fifteen years [...] And all of us would be equally shocked at the spectacle of the great democratic countries, which in 1919 commanded universal respect and exercised almost irresistible sway on the destinies of nations, now shivering and begging for peace on the door-steps of two European dictators.[81]

Still, Lloyd George had not yet arrived in Hades. When he wrote this Conclusion he had had the misfortune to witness the actual events in the real world since the treaties were signed. He therefore invites his readers to join him in a discussion as to 'whether the Treaties have achieved the aims which their framers strove and hoped to attain'. Had aggression been contained? Sadly not. Had oppressed nations been liberated? The picture here was more cheerful. 'No Peace ever signed had emancipated so many sub-races.'[82] Had there been universal disarmament? The defeated had initially complied, but, 'with the exception of Britain, the victors were guilty of an outrageous breach of faith'. Here the culprits were France, Italy and Japan. With regard to the trial of war criminals, 'we found that the public attitude was not ripe for action'.[83] The nations had subscribed to a covenant that would bind them to combine their forces against any transgressors who violated international right. However, 'the weakness and the vacillation displayed in the direction of the affairs of the League of Nations had frustrated the purpose which the authors of the Treaties had in view in setting up this great and beneficent organisation'.[84] The organisation, however, to humanise the conditions of labour throughout the world 'has been one of the unchallengeable triumphs of the Treaty of Versailles'.[85] The treatment of the German Colonies as an international trust:

> [...] has been achieved and fairly administered, [but] the League has not exercised these powers ... to revise any part of the Treaties where experience revealed that it was unjust or unworkable [...]

Had the stipulations of these Treaties been faithfully and honestly interpreted and fulfilled, the dark military and economic menace hanging over Europe would have been averted.[86]

Unfortunately the victorious powers had not disarmed, nor, paradoxically, had they come to the rescue of victims of wanton aggression. 'The revisionary provisions of the Treaties have been ignored.'[87] All in all, there had been little wrong with the peace treaties as originally created by the Big Four. But they had not been effectively enforced by their contemptible 'little' successors.

Two personal tragedies had doomed the world which the peace treaties had established. First was the departure from the scene of Prime Minister Georges Clemenceau. He was replaced as the dominant French statesman by Raymond Poincaré.

> For several years after the withdrawal of Clemenceau, the policy of France was dominated by this rather sinister little man. Under his influence, which continued for years after his death, the League became not an instrument of peace and goodwill among all men, including Germans; it was converted into an organisation for establishing on a permanent footing the military and thereby the diplomatic supremacy of France.[88]

The other personal tragedy was the collapse of President Wilson and the repudiation of the League by the US Senate. 'The refusal of the United States to enter the Council of the Nations or to take any share of the responsibility for maintaining the Treaty she had negotiated, seriously crippled the influence and the authority.'[89] No American involvement necessitated the dominance of international relations by Britain and France:

> Britain was the nearest approach to impartiality and fair play, but she was not free from resentment and wrath, for thousands of her merchant sailors had been brutally drowned on the high seas by pirates sailing under the German flag and acting under the orders of the German War Lords, and her actual casualties numbered nearly 3,000,000 of her young men.[90]

The decisive blow to the treaties'survival was definitely the enforced abdication of Woodrow Wilson. As a result, the United States pulled out. 'Between the retreat of America and the treacheries of Europe the

Treaties of Peace were never given a fair trial.'[91] Lloyd George ends with intense gloom and pessimism.

> No treaty can guarantee humanity against universal perfidy … No international policy, however wisely and skilfully designed, and however well built it may be, can long endure until humanity digs down to the bedrock of an eternal ideal … We are passing, now, through a bad period of regression owing to selfish, ill-directed and feeble leadership. But one day the World will throw up men whose wisdom, courage and inspiration will lead the nations to another and more sustained effort for rebuilding the toppling and fissured temple of peace.[92]

In other words, the world would eventually be saved by Roosevelt, Truman, Churchill, Attlee and the United Nations Organisation – but it would not happen until the powers of darkness had tried again to destroy the products of Lloyd George's idealism, and by then he himself had gone.

Summary

So back to the question with which this chapter began: What can we learn about Lloyd George from a study of his two great works, his personality and his achievements? I have quoted directly and at length so that readers can decide for themselves. To my mind, he comes across as immensely industrious and anxious to be thought methodical. He may or may not be a genuine idealist, but he certainly wants to be considered as one. This is important. Hitler expressed open contempt for 'the Judo-Christian pity ethic'.[93] Lloyd George, on the other hand, wants to be seen to be on the side of the angels. It is impressive that he so frequently expresses sympathy with the victims of U-boat attacks on merchant ships and liners, where he sees a real massacre of the innocents.

On the other hand, to what an extent does Lloyd George demean himself in these literary effusions? Does he bear false witness? Is he excessively boastful? There are several episodes where he is economical with the truth – Asquith's fall from power, for instance, or the Maurice Debate, or his role in the dispute about convoys. He is unfair to Haig and Robertson. He openly expresses views which today would be condemned as racist – at the expense of Jews or black people, for example. He is grossly unfair to Asquith and McKenna.

He regards Ramsay MacDonald as a buffoon, a figure of fun. Curzon is always good for a dig. He cannot see where he went wrong in his treatment of Arthur Henderson or Neville Chamberlain. He hardly mentions Lord Riddell with whom he had quarrelled, he does not give enough credit to Sir Maurice Hankey, and there is a delightfully opaque and misleading reference to 'Miss F. L. Stevenson who was the first woman secretary to be appointed by a minister'.[94] In both of his literary masterpieces David Lloyd George comes across as self-regarding, untruthful and ungenerous.

However, he also impresses as a dynamic, resourceful, idealistic campaigner for justice and peace. At the very least one has to admire his literary style and devotion to his task. More than that, though, he really makes the case for himself as one who tried hard to save and enrich the lives of his fellow human beings. He shows how he put his ideals on the map – literally. Whether he could have prevented either World War I or World War II, however, is another matter. His literary blockbusters reviewed in this chapter display the blind spots which prevented him from saving civilisation from World War I – its origins, course and after-effects – but show that he certainly tried. Were the efforts which he put into his memoirs a waste of time? He was, in the event, too old and too unlucky to prevent World War II – or so it would seem, so he took up his pen in frustration and rage. He certainly had something to say and he said it effectively.

9

The Higher You Rise ...
(October 1922–July 1931)

Ramsay is just a fussy Baldwin.

– Lloyd George

LLOYD GEORGE fell from the heights of the Premiership to the depths of the back benches in one cataclysmic descent. How well did he handle this, the most dramatic change of fortune in his life in politics? 'The higher you rise, the harder you fall', goes the saying. This rule applies to most professions and not least to politics,[1] though Lloyd George himself expected to return to Number Ten very soon. Not that he enjoyed losing office. 'You're well out of it', a well-wisher assured him. 'You're never well out of it', Lloyd George replied, 'You're just out of it'.[2] Even before his inevitable return to power, he would dominate British politics. As his daughter Megan put it, 'Whatever happens, Tada will be in power. He will be tremendous in opposition – and Bonar knows it'.[3]

Maggie, likewise 'couldn't see Bonar lasting long'.[4] Her prediction was only too accurate as Bonar Law retired with cancer of the throat and died on October 1923, having been succeeded by Stanley Baldwin. Lloyd George's old punch-bag Lord Curzon shed tears of anger and self-pity when Baldwin got the top job (he had been defeated by 'a man of the utmost insignificance',[5] Curzon blubbered). On 21 June 1923, Lloyd George wrote to Balfour: 'I hear tragic news of poor Bonar. All the same Curzon is the real tragedy!' – a letter to Lloyd George's credit, indicating surprising magnanimity towards a man who represented all he despised.[6] Curzon had indeed risen to the heights – and fallen: Viceroy of India, Foreign Secretary, Lord

President of the Council, member of the War Cabinet – and now public humiliation; a hard fall indeed. Lloyd George, on the other hand, was protected by his own flippancy as well as by his expectation of a return to high office.

It rapidly became clear that this was not going to happen, or at any rate, not in the foreseeable future. In the general election which Bonar Law immediately called in November 1922, the Liberals, both Asquithian and Lloyd Georgian, only totalled 115 MPs between them, as against 138 Labour and 330 Tories. In December 1923, the Tory representation fell to 258, but the Liberals only increased to 158, leaving Labour with 191 seats – enough to justify a minority government with Liberal support. In November 1924, the Tories shot up to 413; Labour with 151 were the undisputed opposition, while the Liberals sank to a pathetic 40. Lloyd George's old friend Winston Churchill was defeated after an appendix operation: 'In the twinkling of an eye I found myself without an office, without a seat, without a Party, and without an appendix.'[7] Churchill's Tory critics were ecstatic: 'a WC without a seat!' they crowed. When Churchill responded by returning to the Tory party, Baldwin made him Chancellor to stop him succumbing to Lloyd George's charms. Asquith had lost his seat, but remained cheerful on the way home; 'being a provident man' he was able to lend his daughter one of *two* P. G. Wodehouse books he had in his luggage.[8] He was raised to the peerage as Lord Oxford, still leading the Party, while Lloyd George became Chairman of the MPs in the Commons. Nine of these refused his leadership, calling themselves the 'Radical Group' under Walter Runciman and confining their allegiance to Lord Oxford. Asquith, whom Lloyd George always liked, was quite content with life at home surrounded by books, bridge, wine and the adoring flattery of his women, but Margot vetoed reconciliation with his number two.

Just how had Lloyd George found himself condemned to the chairmanship of an angry and frustrated rump, still subject to the leadership of a remote and apathetic member of the Upper House? He had loyally spoken up for Asquith in his Paisley constituency, prompting the typical and grudging acknowledgement from his chief: 'I have rarely felt less exhilaration'.[9] Part of the problem was that the Liberals were not a happy family. Lloyd George's 'treachery' in December 1916 still rankled, as did the Coupon Election two years later. The Lloyd George Fund was a constant irritant, illegally obtained (so it was believed), immorally exploited for the personal benefit of Lloyd George and grudgingly bestowed on Liberal causes. The only way that the Lloyd George Liberals could be welcomed back by Lord and Lady Oxford, Lord Grey and Sir John Simon was on their knees, proffering their dirty money in their hands. Meanwhile, the Liberal Party apparently had no programme and only a disreputable past record of conscription, exploitation of anti-German feeling and bloodshed in Ireland. As for Lloyd George's hope of a new coalition involving his Liberal followers, sympathetic Tories such as Churchill and Birkenhead and Labour members who were prepared to forswear socialism, personalities played a crucial part. Many Tories, led by Baldwin, Neville Chamberlain and J. C. C. Davidson (the Party Chairman) loathed and feared Lloyd George. Nor could Lloyd George tolerate Labour leaders such as Ramsey Macdonald whom he despised, and the feeling was mutual. When MacDonald was prime minister, photographs and portraits of Lloyd George were removed from the walls of Chequers, while Baldwin savagely defaced pictures of the Welsh Goat. As for the possibility of Neville Chamberlain and Lloyd George becoming colleagues, the idea was laughable. The only factor uniting the second rate politicians of the British establishment was hatred of the Goat. He was, thank goodness, in the wilderness, and must stay there. His return to power must be stopped at all costs.

What was Lloyd George to do in the face of such political isolation? To his credit he showed determination to make the best of a bad job. First, he had to earn enough money to finance himself and the three women in his life, Maggie in Criccieth, Frances at Churt and Megan who had now established herself as her father's favourite and was embarking on a career in politics. Until October 1922 Lloyd George had been prime minister, enjoying a salary of £20,000 a year and free lodging at 10 Downing Street and at Chequers, the country house in Buckinghamshire which a generous Lord Lee of Fareham presented to Lloyd George and his successors. Chauffeurs, servants, police escorts, secretaries served the Prime Minister at the taxpayer's expense, but disappeared when he was no longer in office. Now, Lloyd George was merely an MP on £400 a year. A kind businessman, Andrew Carnegie, settled £2,000 a year on 'the man who had won the war'. Otherwise Lloyd George had to live on his wits. 'After seventeen years in office, I have retired a poor man', he told an American newspaper proprietor.[10] Nevertheless in his first year as a columnist he netted £30,000. Still, he quarrelled with Lord Riddell who had previously been so generous. 'Riddell Pasha', Lloyd George sarcastically called him, because he disagreed with Lloyd George's pro-Greek, anti-Turk foreign policy. Riddell also disapproved of the former Prime Minister's betrayal of Maggie for Frances and could not forgive Lloyd George for laughing at him when a snarling Bill the Airedale pinned him, gibbering with fear, to a chair – not the way to treat a friend and benefactor of many years. Perhaps Riddell was no longer needed.

When he was deposed in October 1922, Lloyd George was not yet 60 and was at the height of his powers: hence the widespread expectation of his return to office and the neurotic dread of his hostile contemporaries who combined to keep him out of power. Very well, if he was not wanted in Britain, he would accept the many invitations he had received from the New World, whose citizens were anxious to acclaim 'the man who won the war'. Lloyd George loved travel, and for the next 17 years was frequently abroad. He was accompanied by an array of chauffeurs, bodyguards, secretaries and family for whom he paid out of his own pocket. When he went to America and Canada in September 1923, he took with him Sutherland the honours broker, Sylvester the secretary, Sarah the cook, Maggie and Megan, though not Frances who was obliged to keep out of Maggie's way. The whole party was organised by Sylvester 'the Principal Secretary', as he insisted on being styled, to Frances Stevenson's disgust. This high-flying typist and shorthand specialist now replaced the Welshman J. T. Davies who had become a Director of the Suez Canal Company. Lloyd George and Frances used to mimic Sylvester's obsequious manner and plebeian accent behind his back, but he was industrious, efficient and loyal when treated properly. From the historian's point of view, he deserves gratitude for writing two rather indiscreet and uncharitable books about Lloyd George's travels and private life. Sylvester both admired and disliked his chief, who consistently treated him with scant courtesy or generosity.

The Trip to the New World

Sylvester is certainly good value on the trip 'across the pond' during which he was driven to distraction by Lloyd George's tantrums and obsessions, while simultaneously recognising his astonishing genius for public relations. 'The Chief' fussed endlessly about absurd details, for example, when they first arrived in New York, should he wear his blue suit, or a grey lounge suit or morning dress with silk hat? Whatever he wore, Lloyd George was welcomed by deputations of Greeks, Jews, Irish – who appreciated the recent settlement – Welsh women – and everywhere enormous, cheering crowds.

Sylvester recorded that his chief was in fine form when he received the Freedom of New York: 'Don't be hard on the old country. We each have our own problems, but we all have one problem in common – and that is PEACE, World PEACE.'[11] Lloyd George was applauded ecstatically, here and at several other meetings on his visit. He took the opportunity to plead with Americans not to turn their backs on Europe and to support his crusade to appease Germany now that she was a genuine democracy, even if this involved alarming the French. When France's supporters criticised Lloyd George for his disloyalty, 'save us from our friends', he responded furiously, pointing out how Britain had suffered 950,000 deaths during the war in support of France. All he was now doing was to criticise Poincaré's mindless intransigence. He flatly refused to see the menace of a secretly rearming and vengeful, even if democratic, Germany. For Lloyd George, European – indeed worldwide – appeasement must include Germany, who would surely be swept along by such a universal campaign of international goodwill. The results of his euphoria were the Dawes Plan and the London Conference.

Lloyd George refused the opportunity afforded by diplomatic immunity to bring his own supply of alcohol. The United States was dry, and so would be their distinguished visitor. An unofficial dram, however might have prevented a series of tempestuous rows when Lloyd George behaved like a spoiled child, as for instance when cheering crowds stopped his train and interrupted his post-prandial nap. 'Look here, Sylvester, you will have to stop this.' 'Yes, sir', replied Sylvester, without the faintest idea how this was to be done. The fact was that Lloyd George was the most popular visitor ever to the United States, and he had to conform to popular expectations. This he did, on the whole with good humour, autographing endless programmes and shaking hands with delegation after delegation. It was all in a good cause. Sylvester was lost in wonder.

The situation became more fraught when the party reached Canada. Three-hundred people awaited Lloyd George at a reception in his Montreal hotel. He hated receptions – 'stupid, formal affairs'. Then he hit the roof when it transpired that he was to speak in the Arena. Max Beaverbrook had warned him on no account to speak in the Arena, even though it held 15,000 people. Mr Crandall, the editor of the *Montreal Star*, promised that he would be audible thanks to the amplifiers which had been fitted. 'Amplifiers!', screamed Lloyd George, 'I certainly will not use them and I will not speak in that place!'[12]

Of course, he did speak in the Arena and thanks to the amplifiers every word of what Sylvester reckoned was the most brilliant speech of his life, came across perfectly. 'Patriotism is concentric; it is not one circle. There are several patriotisms. You have your patriotism in your city – I believe you prefer Montreal to prosper even before Toronto, and I would not be a bit surprised if Toronto returned the compliment; and you are quite right. Your first patriotism is to your city. The next is to your province; that is Quebec. The next is to the dominion – you are Canadians. Your next is to the British Empire. But that is not the end. Your next is to humanity.'[13] Sylvester recorded: 'If there was any city where L. G. scored a triumph, it was Montreal, and that speech in the much despised Arena which was very nearly not made secured in the hearts of all Canadians a love and admiration for L. G. which was unsurpassed by that of any other statesman.'[14]

Back in the United States Lloyd George delighted in ignoring advice that on no account should he address the question of who won the war? For him to claim this title would cause unlimited offence. Sylvester was therefore apprehensive when Lloyd George asked this very question before a huge crowd at the Cadle Tabernacle, Indianapolis. Lloyd George 'paused and looked intently at his audience, a merry twinkle in his eyes ... L. G. walked close to the edge of the platform and leaning over said quietly, "There are many claimants who never saw the war! Now I will tell you who won the war. *The man who won the war was the humble man in the steel helmet. God bless the man in the steel helmet and his children*".'[15] Sylvester thought this 'a masterpiece of oratory'. Lloyd George never missed a trick. When he asked an aged Colonel, a veteran of the Civil War, if he was ever wounded, he got a forthright reply: 'Yes, sir, I sure was, shot in the leg and by a bloody nigger at that.'[16] Lloyd George made no comment, but in Kentucky he caused some surprise by shaking hands with every member of a negro choir just to emphasise his own racial tolerance.[17] At Richmond, Virginia, he had to avoid resentment by graciously accepting the present of a white pigeon called Doodie, which Lloyd George insisted on taking back to England. The long-suffering Sylvester had to carry Doodie around in a cage. Not surprisingly he found it 'an infernal nuisance'. Doodie eventually became a great favourite both at Churt and at Addison Road where she formed a close friendship with Sarah the Welsh cook. Doodie's pet aversion – an inescapable description – was Lloyd George's steel-rimmed pinze-nez which she would toss aside with her beak. Lloyd George tolerated this bossiness with good humour.[18]

The tour reached a triumphant conclusion at the New York Opera House before an audience of five thousand where he was welcomed as 'David Lloyd George, human being'.[19] Sylvester reported: 'I could not help feeling tremendously proud of my Chief that night. Despite the stress and strain of the last month, the number of times he had spoken, and the difficult and delicate topics with which he had dealt, not once had he made a faux pas. When asked for a final message before the liner *Majestic* cast off, he replied, his voice trembling, "My heart is too full; I cannot speak"'.[20]

A massive crowd welcomed the party home at Waterloo station, symbolising the importance of Lloyd George's trip to America and Canada. His prestige as an international statesman rocketed. In the context of party politics, to which we shall shortly turn, he could hardly be marginalised by his enemies, whether Asquithian Liberals, Baldwin or Macdonald. No doubt Lloyd George had also developed his already high opinion of himself: there might well be problems there as well.

A Musical Interlude

On Christmas Day 1920, Dr Richard Runciman Terry, the Organist of Westminster Cathedral, enlivened the rather gloomy proceedings in Downing Street (at least Riddell thought them gloomy) with some cheery piano-playing. Lloyd George took the opportunity of suggesting to Terry that there could well be a need for a new national hymn book, 'containing nothing but the best hymns and hymn-tunes, irrespective of tradition or private influence'. Dr Terry fully agreed.[21]

A follow-up to this occurred at Criccieth, soon after Lloyd George's return from the New World, when in June 1924 he hosted a meeting at Brynawelon attended not only by Terry, but Henry Hadow the Vice-Chancellor of Sheffield University who was reckoned to be a notable expert on hymnody and Walford Davies, the Professor of Music at the University of Wales, Aberystwyth, and the composer of several notable hymn tunes. Riddell tells us how Lloyd George wanted to discuss possible hymns for the new book in a suitable chapel, but Maggie pointed out that the only organ in Criccieth was in the parish church, as opposed to 'American organs' (i.e., harmoniums) in the chapels. Lloyd George gave in: 'Well, I suppose we shall have to go to the church', and so to the church this distinguished quartet of hymn-enthusiasts repaired, for a comprehensive discussion when hymns from all the best compilations were vetted and judged. Eventually they were whittled down to 280 hymns plus 20 anthems arranged by Dr Terry. The visitors were impressed by Dame Margaret's hospitality and by their host's enthusiastic singing. Riddell asked the experts privately 'whether he really understood much about it. They said he had a good natural ear and quite good judgement, although [*sic*] his taste naturally tended to favour the Welsh style of hymn'.[22] Riddell was amused to see them wincing when Lloyd George enjoyed bawling the more vulgar Welsh numbers.[23] But in truth, Terry, Walford Davies and Hadow had no cause to be patronising about Lloyd George's expertise in hymnody which was life-long, despite his ambivalent approach to Christianity.

At any rate, the result of this hymnographers' summit was *Hymns of Western Europe*, published by Oxford University Press in 1925. Walford Davies' biographer H. C. Coles has this to say: 'It contains a number of excellent hymns and tunes not to be found in the recognised hymnals of any community, but probably because it is addressed to no special public it has not been widely used in public worship.'[24] No doubt Coles has a point, though a number of hymn books have survived such a handicap, notably *Songs of Praise*. My own view is that *Hymns of Western Europe* is really a surprisingly dull collection. Lloyd George boasted that the editors had chosen 'the best examples they could find',[25] but 'if in doubt leave it out' is not the best recipe for a lively compilation. The 280 hymns constitute a kind of LCM (least common multiple), allowing no room for eccentricity or surprises, thus comparing badly with the 702 hymns in *Songs of Praise* (1931) which reminds the Almighty of the glories of the English language, or the 735 hymns in the delightfully dotty *English Hymnal* (1906/1935), or even the 984 in the gloriously catholic and comprehensive *Methodist Hymn Book* (1933). As for the tunes, the editors have not even included Walford Davies' and Terry's best compositions, while the Welsh numbers total only 29 and do not include 'Blyaenwern' or 'Cwm Rhondda' which, unbelievably, is not set to 'Guide me, O thou Great Redeemer'. The book is by no means user-friendly: no index of composers or authors, no alphabetical or metrical index of tunes, only an alphabetical index of first lines which reproduces the format of the hymn-book as a whole so that it is very hard to find hymns for a particular season or topic. In other words this is rather an unsatisfactory compilation which on its few merits did not deserve to be popular.[26]

Much the most arresting part is the Preface: its author actually boasts that the book contains only one tune by a living composer. As for the words, 'most hymnals intended for congregational use are far too large and comprehensive ... it is a matter of common experience that this vital portion of our services has been marred by the intrusion of verses and melodies which in point of purity, of dignity, of reverence fall short of the ideal which worship rightly demands'.[27] There follows some forthright advice for organists, aimed at the improvement of hymn-singing by which:

> ... the House of the Lord is filled with His Glory ... The lyric side of worship covers a wide emotional range: praise and meditation, penitence and thanksgiving, all alike have their own place and require their own method of treatment. But there is a tendency to sing almost all hymns too fast.[28]

The tone of the Preface throughout is both devotional and a little sanctimonious, so that it comes as a surprise that it appears over the name D. Lloyd George. Unless one knows about the preliminary discussions described by Riddell, one can hardly believe it. Perhaps he took Christianity more seriously than his biographers allow. Could Asquith or Churchill have written in this way? I suppose the truth is that Lloyd George really was interested in hymns, just as Churchill wrote what he considered-history, painted masterpieces and built walls, while Asquith played bridge. Lloyd George also chased girls. Girls and hymns – a curious combination, perhaps unique among prime ministers, though W. E. Gladsone's interest in London's prostitutes did not prevent him writing a fine Communion hymn, 'O lead my blindness by the hand' (322 in *The English Hymnal*, not included, alas, in *Hymns of Western Europe* or anywhere else for that matter).

As well as 'hymns and hers', Lloyd George was fascinated by politics, to which we now return.

Liberalism – Fall, Rise and Fall (1922–1935)

When Lloyd George disembarked from the *Mauretania* at Southampton on his return from New York in November 1923 he was pressed by Sir Alfred Mond to declare his attitude to free trade. This was because the Conservative Prime Minister Stanley Baldwin had anticipated the dreaded Goat's return by calling a general election and nailing his own Party's colours to the mast of protection, apparently scared that Lloyd George would get in first. Even Baldwin's staunchest admirers admit that this was an amazingly stupid decision which condemned the Tories to relative electoral failure, compared to their triumph in November 1922. Protection was not a popular policy. Furthermore, when Lloyd George unhesitatingly declared for free trade, Baldwin had achieved the impossible by reuniting the Liberal Party. At least so it appeared. Lloyd George professed his willingness to serve under any leader who could give Britain a genuinely Liberal regime – even Lord Asquith who was, likewise, a free-trader. In the event, the results of the election can have brought little joy to any of the three parties. With 258 seats the Tories were still the largest party, but could be out-voted by the 191 Labour and the 158 Liberal MPs. Asquith decided to put Labour in, calculating that he could put them out again if they misbehaved. Lloyd George would have extracted a commitment to proportional representation, but the chance was missed of evading the three party trap which has so damaged the Liberals ever since.

Labour's tenure of office under MacDonald (January–October 1924) marked a new nadir of the Liberal Party. Here was an oppor-tunity for the Liberals to recover from the defeats and humiliations which they had endured since Asquith's fall in December 1916, but there was a wretched failure to establish a Liberal programme based on genuine principles in Parliament; this coincided with an abysmal decline in Liberal Party fortunes in the constituencies. A shortage of funds, the resignation of agents, the fall in membership – all these problems ensured that the Party could not field enough candidates to contest the next general election with the remotest prospect of forming a government. Morale was at rock bottom and Party workers dreaded another election.[29]

Neither Asquith nor Lloyd George came out of this sad story very well, for neither could deny some responsibility for this depressing state of affairs. Asquith was inadequate as a Leader in the House – long-winded, ponderous and ineffectual. He was over 70 and looked older. He was dominated by his closest supporters – McKenna, Runciman, Viscount Gladstone and the inevitable Margot. Lloyd George was surprisingly lacking in recognisable ideas, apart from the purely negative perception that MacDonald was not up to the job. 'Ramsay is just a fussy Baldwin', Lloyd George assured Megan, 'and his socialism is just lather and blather'.[30] He mocked him mercilessly in the House. He believed that MacDonald used words, not to formulate ideas, but simply as sounds. As a result, 'I never have the ghost of an idea what he proposes to do'.[31] On the question of a demilitarised Rhineland: 'The French are entitled to know what we mean. The British people are entitled to know what we mean, and I should not be a bit surprised if the Prime Minister himself would like to know what we mean.'[32] No wonder MacDonald was infuriated by this mockery of his foreign policy, which he regarded as his specialism. His decision to take on the Foreign Office was that of an unrealistic and vain self-dramatist. He worked too hard and refused to delegate. The poor man was stung into grossly offensive counterattacks against his Liberal critics. After Labour had fallen from power, Lloyd George asked in the *Daily Chronicle*: 'How could Asquith have conjectured that the Leader of a great party would have behaved like a jealous, vain, suspicious, ill-tempered actress of the second rank?'[33] Lloyd George resented Labour's condescending attitude, which reflected the leader's prejudices: 'When we support them our support is received with sullen indifference. If we dare to criticise them, we are visited with a peevish resentment ... Liberals are to be the oxen to drag Labour over the rough roads of Parliament for two or three years, and at the end of the journey when there is no further use for them, they are to be slaughtered. That is the Labour idea of cooperation.'[34]

Unfortunately for the Liberal Party, Lloyd George's analysis was to be proved only too accurate at the general election which followed Labour's fall from power in Autumn 1924. The Tories bounced back with 415 seats – enough to guarantee them a secure five years in office, while Labour's 151 seats made them the undisputable opposition given that the Liberals only won a pathetic 40 seats.

What went wrong? Asquith's leadership – if that was the right word – was limited to angry bleats about the Lloyd George fund which could indeed have made all the difference to the number of candidates put in the field. Lloyd George kept these necessary life-belts locked up in his shed, but there was a real doubt about the Liberal Party's ability to produce suitably qualified candidates even if the Lloyd George fund had been available. Could the Liberal Party realistically claim to offer a recognisable alternative to the Conservatives, going back to the Coupon Election and before? The increased electorate included 11 million working class voters of both sexes who saw Labour as the real upholder of their economic interests. More disturbingly, Labour challenged the Liberal Party in traditional strongholds such as the rural outposts where the Tory squirearchy had previously shared the spoils with Liberal gentry such as Sir Edward Grey.

An even more worrying explanation should be considered. Had the Labour government been the disaster that Asquith and Lloyd George liked to claim? After all, the whole point of putting Labour in had been to demonstrate its inability to govern. Had Labour's reasonably satisfactory showing at the polls reflected a not entirely discreditable performance in government, in contrast to the Liberal Party's abysmal performance in opposition? Wheatley's Housing Act encouraged the construction of inexpensive properties which Lloyd George should have welcomed. MacDonald's foreign policy climaxed at the London Conference of August 1924 when the Dawes plan was adopted to enable Germany to pay reparations satisfactorily. Herriot (France) and MacDonald (Britain) negotiated on equal terms with the Weimar Republic's new star, Gustav Stresemann. How could Lloyd George not applaud MacDonald's successful summitry? Indeed, encouraging approval came from an unlikely source, the Permanent Under-Secretary at the Foreign Office, Sir Robert Vansittart:

> Ramsay MacDonald proved a good Foreign Secretary, the only member of his Labour Party whose mind approached the first order. It has long been the fashion to deride him, but he played well in his first innings. The scoreboard speaks. He improved relations with France, though Sidney Webb did not help by telling her that she suffered from "a fear complex unworthy of a great nation". Despite such handicaps at home he bettered our standing with Italy and Germany, and would have done the same for Russia with reciprocity.[35]

Vansittart presumably knew what he was talking about. Lloyd George could only applaud MacDonald's appeasement of Germany while keeping France relatively contented. This was what the Dawes Plan amounted to, implemented by the London Conference.

There followed two years of frustration for Lloyd George. Asquith, or rather Lord Oxford, the title to which he had been elevated, had just enough fire left in his tired old belly to spoil Lloyd George's prospects. It is indeed a sad irony that by the time Lloyd George did obtain the leadership of the Party, Asquith had irretrievably wrecked it. In the meantime, Lloyd George was in a difficult position in that criticism of Asquith would have proved the claims of his enemies with regard to his alleged disloyalty between 1916 and 1918. All he could do was wait for Asquith to do everyone a favour by falling on his sword – again.

This he did when the General Strike (1926) demanded a response from the Liberal leadership. After the Tory government had discontinued state subsidies, the mine-owners imposed punitive conditions on the miners who already worked in dangerous and unpleasant discomfort. There was indeed a problem in that foreign coal – French, German, Polish – was undercutting British. In order to compete, British mine-owners reduced wages and increased working hours. 'Not a penny off the pay, not a second on the day!',[36] retorted the leader of the mine-workers, the Communist A. J. Cook. The miners threatened a national strike, the owners locked them out. The government refused to intervene. Lloyd George had previously remarked when settling a pit strike that he had never met such stupid men as the mine-workers – until he met the mine-owners. Now Baldwin left them to it. So selfish and deplorable had been the owners' conduct, that the TUC intervened and called a nationwide General Strike – the first and possibly the last in British history. On 2 May print-workers at the *Daily Mail* refused to print a leading article condemning the miners. On 3 May Baldwin claimed that their action had inaugurated the General Strike – not strictly true as it was only now that the TUC took decisive measures. So did the government, mobilising police and troops, issuing emergency food supplies, permitting volunteers to man public transport and publishing the *British Gazette*, a grossly tendentious and provocative broadsheet edited by Winston Churchill.

What were Asquith and his colleagues to do? Without any consultation of ex-ministers or MPs, the senior Liberal Party friends and allies of Asquith supported him in backing the government. The TUC's actions endangered law and order. There were to be no compromises with people who threatened British society. There were to be no negotiations until the TUC called off the strike unconditionally. As it happened, Lloyd George had not been consulted. But his position was clear. At a unique meeting of agricultural workers and dons at Cambridge on 1 May Lloyd George agreed with the Party leadership that the government must be supported, while at the same time seeking to negotiate a just settlement. According to Sylvester, the Liberal Shadow Cabinet expressed 'warm approval of the line which L. G. had taken at Cambridge'.[37] While he sympathised with the miners, he thought that the General Strike was a mistake and that the government was justified in taking the necessary steps to protect society. On the other hand he totally rejected the decision to refuse to negotiate until the strike was called off.

In his considerable experience of industrial disputes Lloyd George had always sought compromise solutions and had deplored intransigence. So, in an article which he published for the *United Press Associations*, he emphatically disassociated himself from his notional leader's response. He remained at Churt, awaiting Asquith's reaction. When he was summoned to Party headquarters on 10 May for discussions, Lloyd George could see no useful purpose in attending a slanging match, and so stayed put. On 12 May the TUC surrendered and called off the General Strike, though a million miners remained out until the Autumn. Lloyd George received a letter from Asquith on 21 May rebuking him for his lack of political comradeship in not reporting to Party headquarters. 'The reason for your absence seems to me to be wholly inadequate.' When Lloyd George dined that night with Frances Stevenson, he was clearly in a state of extreme excitement: 'I have been expelled from the party', he exclaimed, showing her Asquith's letter. Lloyd George replied to Asquith at once. 'I appreciate fully the gravity of the unprecedented letter you have sent me ... I propose to take two or three days to consider it before I reply.' Asquith responded with a telegram to the effect that he had released the text of his first letter to the press.[38]

Lloyd George consulted C. P. Scott and Charles Masterman before replying to Asquith. He too sent his reply to the press. Liberals high and low, apart from Grey, Simon, Runciman and McKenna, sided with Lloyd George. His letter was a masterpiece of sweet reason.

'Who would have thought that in such a dispute, Lloyd George would be in the right and Asquith in the wrong!',[39] was the general verdict. After a few days Asquith resigned the leadership. A few months later he was dead.

He bequeathed to Lloyd George a party on the rocks. To his great credit, Lloyd George adopted a stance of 'better late than never' and did his best to retrieve the situation. Now he was tireless in addressing meetings and making funds available. Above all, confronted with Baldwin's vast majority and MacDonald's vast self-esteem, he resorted to the old adage that the pen is mightier than the sword. Masterman, who for several months had been a severe critic of his old boss, went on record that 'when Lloyd George returned to the Party ideas returned to the Party as well'.[40] Lloyd George now sponsored or co-wrote a number of seminal policy documents, establishing the Liberal Party as the party of progress. He backed up the Liberal Summer Schools, founded in 1920 by Arthur Acland, which had established themselves as breeding grounds for new policies with study weekends at Churt, where he proved a generous host with food and drink (cider) produced on his estate. He was a demanding taskmaster, insisting on everyone getting down to work after breakfast and not letting up until after dinner in the evening. 'We have had fourteen professors here', he boasted with only slight exaggeration to Maggie (Keynes was never a professor).[41]

The results were: *Coal and Power* (1924), which proposed better working conditions and state control of pit mergers as a halfway stage towards nationalisation; *The Land and the Nation* (1923–1925), which advocated state supervision of production and a better deal for farm workers; *Towns and the Land: Urban Report of the Liberal Land Committee* (1925), which advocated urban development of by-passes and rural development; and *Britain's Industrial Future* (1928), based on the *Liberal Industrial Inquiry*[42] which sought to implement state direction of investment and production. Perhaps *We Can Conquer Unemployment* (1929) was the most famous and potentially the most influential report of all. There was a real recovery of Liberal morale, of pride and self-respect. When Baldwin went to the country in May 1929 with the slogan 'Safety First' and Macdonald with 'No monkeying with the economy', Lloyd George led a progressive party transformed since 1924.[43]

Alas, the results of the 1929 contest were bitterly disappointing: Labour 288 seats, Conservatives 260 and Liberals 59. The King sent for MacDonald, who formed the second Labour administration. At Euston on his return from North Wales, Lloyd George had this to say: 'It would be silly to pretend that we have realised our expectations. We have once more been tripped up by the triangle. No party has done as well as it expected. It looks as if we shall hold the balance. That is a very responsible position.'[44]

Sadly, this was whistling in the dark. Why had the Party's unquestionably dynamic recovery since Asquith's retirement not produced better results? Possibly, Lloyd George at 66 was not quite the force he had been, though he still drew large crowds when he spoke – 25,000, for example, when he launched the *Land and the Nation* for an hour and a half in heavy rain at Killerton Park, Devon. Perhaps it was simply too long a climb back from the disaster of 1924. Asquith had queered the pitch beyond redemption, even by Lloyd George. Perhaps those impressive treatises produced by the Churt think-tanks were not really vote-winners. Even in Wales the proposed land reforms allowed Tory rivals to decry them as 'socialism decorated up a bit'; Sir Leoline Forester-Walker, for instance, warned Montgomeryshire farmers that if they voted Liberal, Lloyd George's inspectors would turn them off their land.[45]

The most important of all the Party's tracts was the last – *We Can Conquer Unemployment*. This was the result of cooperation between Lloyd George and Keynes. After the publication of Keynes' influential *Economic Consequences of the Peace*, which cast a highly critical light on Lloyd George's peacemaking skills in 1919 immediately after the Conference, the two men had moved apart. However, during the years of economic drift under MacDonald and Baldwin, Keynes had come to appreciate Lloyd George's radicalism and intelligence. As a result the economist had been glad to cooperate with Lloyd George, but later, during the tedium of the National Government's refusal to innovate or experiment, he could not resist having his bit of fun. He had originally deleted his entertaining but libellous pen portrait of Lloyd George from his work on the Peace Treaties. Now he included it in his *Essays in Biography*: 'Who can paint the chameleon, who can tether a broomstick? Lloyd George is rooted in nothing. He is void and without content.'[46] Lloyd George was hurt. The two men never spoke again.

This does not mean that *We Can Conquer Unemployment* was unsound.[47] The argument that a massive system of public works could have reduced unemployment by, say, 744,000 was possibly unrealistic, but somewhere between 346,000 and 484,000 was a fair guess. Keynes and Hubert Henderson produced a pamphlet in May 1929 entitled, *Can Lloyd George do it?* Their conclusion was that he could. Sadly, the electorate was not prepared to give him a chance, so we shall never know.

Labour's second government was a drab affair, as the economy stagnated and unemployment rose. The Wall Street crash (1931) had widespread repercussions in Europe. The Austrian state bank collapsed, the Weimar Republic lurched to the left and then to the right as unemployment approached 6 million. In Britain, 3 million were out of work. Lloyd George could not be completely ignored. A *Punch* cartoon ('Lossiemouth Nights: The Face at the Window' drawn by Frank Reynolds, dated 8 January 1930) shows MacDonald trying to keep a fire burning while Lloyd George glares down at him with fierce disapproval. He was, in fact, invited to submit his ideas, though no doubt MacDonald's aim was to keep him quiet rather than to listen. Lloyd George despaired of making any meaningful contribution: 'Sisyphus is not in it with me, I am trying to roll a melting, slushy snowball up the hill'.[48] Chancellor Snowden's response was to implement the May Report which advocated deflation and economies; according to Keynes, 'one of the most foolish documents I have ever had the misfortune to read'.[49] Strict orthodoxy was the order of the day, in other words cutting government expenditure, reducing the wages of the armed forces, civil servants and teachers, and raising taxes in order to balance the budget. The navy mutinied at Invergordon. In September 1931, George V invited MacDonald to form a national Government. He agreed, preening himself and predicting that despite being the illegitimate son of a Scottish crofter he would soon be kissed by every duchess in town.[50] Labour refused to join with a few exceptions, proclaiming this to be the 'Great Betrayal'.[51] Britain again had a charismatic prime minister reliant on Tory votes in the House. Samuel and Simon with their respective followers supported MacDonald.

There was an even more charismatic figure in the wings, waiting for his chance so long delayed, but fate cruelly intervened. When Lloyd George felt unwell at his house in Addison Road, Frances summoned his son-in-law, Dr Tom Carey-Evans, who diagnosed prostate problems and sent for Lord Dawson. The latter operated a few days later. Lloyd George was out of action for several weeks. One can imagine the relief of the three second-raters in residence, Baldwin, MacDonald and Neville Chamberlain, who now had a clear run to take Britain into recession and World War II. 'You are first in my thoughts',[52] MacDonald wrote. No doubt. It would be an exaggeration to suggest that Lloyd George was now marginalised. When he finally recovered he was intermittently consulted. While still on his sickbed he furiously opposed MacDonald's decision to go to the country in October 1931, which he correctly perceived to be a cynical exploitation of the general desire for a safety-first government. He bitterly assaulted Sir Herbert Samuel for co-operating with MacDonald. Sure enough, the results doomed what was left of the Liberal party, divided as it was into warring factions. Results: 537 seats for the National Government (469 Tories, 33 Samuelite Liberals, 35 Simonites). In opposition: Labour, 52; Lloyd George's 'family party', 4 (Lloyd George, Gwilym, Megan and Goronwy Owen). It was the end. Lloyd George occasionally intervened in the House. He toured the country making speeches. He produced more revolutionary and dynamic pamphlets offering a 'New Deal', but his judgement was failing. He defended Edward VIII's determination to marry Mrs Simpson, he joined Churchill in opposing more self-government in India and he visited Hitler, bestowing embarrassing compliments on the Fuehrer which were similarly reciprocated. The truth was that, in his mid-70s, he was finished. He retired to Churt to write his memoirs and grow fruit and vegetables. The Welsh Cincinnatus was never recalled from the plough, though the creator of the Lloyd George raspberry could never be totally ignored.

Lloyd George had faced political disaster, but how well had he fared? Luck had not always been with him: the incubus of Asquith; the malice of Liberals who could neither forgive nor forget; his crippling illness in 1931. He did not mope, or indulge in self-pity – at least not until the very end of his life – but he had made mistakes, and being Lloyd George, they were great ones. Perhaps his greatest mistake was to remain committed to the appeasement of Germany despite the evidence that all was not well with Weimar, and that there was a great deal wrong with Hitler, a dreadful misapprehension as Churchill perceived. To an extent, Lloyd George's decline and fall were his own fault – 'Great was the Fall Thereof',[53] as Beaverbrook pronounced. Perhaps, the elephant in the room, however, was the progressive demise of the Liberal Party ever since the coup against Asquith in December 1916, the Maurice Debate and the Coupon Election of 1918. Lloyd George would fight under no other banner.[54] As he explained to Snowden when invited to join the Labour Party, he would die fighting on the left, but he would never be a socialist. On his own admission, however, he himself had wrecked the Liberal Party, justifying Lord Morgan's verdict that Lloyd George had been simultaneously the best and the worst of Liberal leaders.[55]

10

Lloyd George's Families and Friends

WOULD 'WINE, Women and Song' be an appropriate title for this chapter, in that Lloyd George, for all his run-ins with Tory distillers and brewers, was by no means teetotal? In truth, while he enjoyed the occasional glass of whiskey and offered his guests home-brewed cider, he was never a big drinker and was, indeed, quite abstemious. Similarly, while he liked nothing more than hymn-singing round the piano played by his daughter, Mair or an impromptu recital by Frances, his mistress, he was not really interested in music as was, say, Edward Heath or even Gladstone. He did love women, and they loved him. On the whole historians tend to be reticent about Lloyd George's sex life, as though such a topic was unworthy of the consideration of self-respecting academics. Yet the biographer's objective should be the whole personality. While prurience, exaggeration and sensationalism are to be deplored, if one is to understand Lloyd George one cannot ignore his interest in women, even in a study of his life in politics. Nor should he be disassociated from his family life – or rather, lives.

Happy Families

Despite the aberrations of its most distinguished member, the Lloyd George family was remarkably close-knit. Lloyd George has been called an outsider, but the real outsiders were people who tried to obtain entry into this inward-looking family circle. Lloyd George's mistress, Frances Stevenson, was the classic example – shunned to a greater or less extent by all Lloyd George's children after she had formed what she certainly regarded as a binding and long-lasting attachment with the 'Great Man'. Not even when she had become his wife was Frances admitted into the family. When she placed a garland of red roses on her husband's grave, his indignant daughter, Megan, silently chucked it over the wall into the road. What right had Frances to intrude into what was a family occasion?

What made this obsessive family loyalty the more remarkable was Lloyd George's persistent disloyalty to the joint head of the family, his long-suffering wife, Maggie. It was a strange marriage, a fraught association which lurched along for 53 years (1888–1941) producing five children – Dick (1889–1968), Mair Eluned (1890–1907), Olwen (1892–1990), Gwilym (1894–1967) and the baby of the family, Megan (1902–1966). Lloyd George was consistently promiscuous throughout his marriage, though whether his associations with other women for the most part amounted to more than one-afternoon-stands is another matter. Malcolm Muggeridge enjoyed describing 'the goat' ambushing vulnerable young women in the grounds of his Churt estate. Biographers who are not members of Lloyd George's family or nationality reckon that there is truth in these stories. They certainly caused his wife much distress and led to furious rows with her husband. What needs to be stressed is that all five children, to a greater or less extent, sympathised and sided with their mother. For instance, when Lloyd George invited first Gwilym and then Dick to join the board of the *Daily Chronicle* at £2,000 a year, both refused when it transpired that Frances Stevenson was a co-director. At the same time, they admired their father and fully acknowledged his exceptional ability and well-deserved worldwide fame.

Lloyd George's relationships with his children ranged from intense mutual devotion to equally intense mutual loathing. He adored Mair by whose death he was devastated, as we noted in Chapter 3. He had a love–hate relationship with Megan. Gwilym was adjudged to be indolent, but was such a nice chap that he was tolerated by everyone, including his father – although he did have a caustic wit, remarking that 'politicians are like monkeys – the higher they climb, the more revolting are the parts they expose'.[1] Having been ruthlessly sacked as Tory Home Secretary in 1954 to make way for R. A. Butler, perhaps he was a trifle disillusioned. Even so, as J. Graham Jones remarks, 'this was a strange remark from a Conservative Home Secretary, and one who was the son of the arch-monkey himself'.[2] Lloyd George left Gwilym Bron-y-de in his will. Olwen maintained an independent attitude in her (ghosted) book *Lloyd George Was My Father*, recognising her father's genius but sympathising with her mother. Once when she was rebuked by her father for returning home late from a night on the town, she retorted, 'That's good, coming from you'. In a splendid moment of family loyalty, Lloyd George excused himself from the War Cabinet on 19 June 1917 in order to rush across London to the East Castle Street Welsh Baptist Chapel in order to give Olwen away to Captain Tom Carey Evans of the Indian Army Medical Corps. Sir Edward Carson and Dr Christopher Addison came too, as did a goodly array of Welsh MPs.

Poor Dick, on the other hand, was left nothing in his father's will. He was the exception, the lame duck or rather the black sheep of the family. He was convinced that his father had never forgiven him for not being a girl, but in truth he was cut out of the will because Lloyd George reckoned that he had already spent enough on his elder son. Dick could not hold a job down. Money ran through his fingers like water. He was a drunk, for which his father despised him, and had to be financed in various sanatoria. Dick was funny and intelligent, with a keen sense of mischief. He was devoted to his mother who laughed at his imitation of upper-class contemporaries at Dulwich College ('Oh I say') before she had him removed to Portmadoc Grammar School because he was bullied. Dick wrote an affectionate book about his mother and a very different account of his father. There is a sad letter in the Welsh National archive from Dick to his father from J. L. Watling Ltd, Builders and Contractors, Glasgow:

> My dear Tada, Just a short letter to thank you for all your kindness to June and myself. I am doing my best to regain my sense of responsibility – which I know I had lost. Work is the only remedy and I am getting plenty of that up here – and congenial work that I understand and can do. Byth [*sic*] Dick.[3]

Only in John Campbell's *If Love Were All* is there the suggestion that Dick was traumatised by his experiences in World War I.[4] His behaviour, shared by millions of other victims of what was then called shellshock, looks exactly like the post-traumatic-stress-disorder experienced by Afghanistan veterans. Was Dick a drunk *before* he was traumatised by World War I? Lloyd George made no allowances for his elder son. Dick made no allowances either. Once he was displeased to meet a lookalike of more or less his age who, it transpired, had been left £400/annum by David Lloyd George. Once, Dick had a fit of sneezing – 'something at least that I have inherited from my father'.

Lloyd George's brother William George supported his brother's career with conspicuous loyalty and generosity, We have noted the financial generosity with which he supported David in London but at the age of 99 he refused to sell his collection of family papers to Lord Beaverbrook: 'I think I have done my share in honouring Dafydd during his lifetime and afterwards, and quite frankly I don't want to be troubled any more.'[5] He lived to be 101, specifying that the hymn for his 100th birthday service of thanksgiving should be the Old Hundredth.

Frances Louise Stevenson (1888–1972)

Lloyd George had another family, perhaps happier than the one presided over by Maggie in Criccieth. In the summer of 1911, Lloyd George and Maggie became concerned about Megan's poor academic record. She was obviously bright, but was spoiled. Megan was making indifferent progress at her school in London, so the obvious solution was a no-nonsense tutor who could bring her up to a satisfactory academic standard during the summer holidays. Lloyd George interviewed two young women at 11 Downing Street, one of whom appealed to his sexual appetite. She got the job. She was Frances Louise Stevenson (1888–1972, and thus 25 years younger than the Chancellor), a Classics graduate of Royal Holloway College, University of London where she had achieved a Third and a teacher at Allenswood, a reputable girls' independent school. Her most impressive skills were in music and in French which she spoke fluently as her mother was French and her father had worked in France. Photographs testify to her beauty and attractive personality. She, for her part, was bowled over by Lloyd George. As Megan's tutor, she was encouraged to visit Downing Street 'for instruction'. For a surprisingly long time, Lloyd George kept his hands off her, but eventually they arrived at a rather peculiar arrangement as outlined in Chapter 4. A further commitment was imposed on Frances when Lloyd George insisted on a mutual pact whereby when one of them died – in the nature of things this was almost bound to be Lloyd George – the other would commit suicide.

While in due course, after at least two abortions, Frances was to
produce a child and consequently a happy family atmosphere of her
own, at first the other families concerned were far from happy. Frances
felt bound to explain to her parents why she had left teaching to work
for the Chancellor of the Exchequer. There was no way in which she
could hide the truth from her perspicacious mother. Louise Stevenson
was appalled, or perhaps 'disgusted' would be more accurate. Armed
neutrality prevailed for several weeks when Frances refused to mend
her ways. Eventually, as we saw in Chapter 4, the enraptured couple
hoped to win the old folks round with a dinner party in Downing
Street. It was a symptom of Frances' insouciance and Lloyd George's
arrogance to think that John and Louise Stevenson would be bowled
over by the glamour of No. 11 or bewitched by Lloyd George's
charm. The dinner was a disaster. Frances was similarly unsuccessful
in bringing happiness to her lover's family. According to Olwen she
was hard as nails. This was probably true. For instance, immediately
after her husband's death, Frances sacked the loyal and efficient but
by no means uncritical A. J. Sylvester – who responded with *The
Real Lloyd George*,[6] described by Frances as 'mean and unlovely'. Her
most vitriolic opponent was Megan. The problem was that the two
young women had been close for several years, witness this letter
from Megan on holiday in Criccieth to Frances (the original is in the
National Library at Aberystwyth):

'Dear Puss', Scuse the notepaper, but the house doesn't boast of any
better – the family having had a craze for letter-writing these last
days. My goodness me, it seems that I have been asleep ever since
I came here. The weather has been too bad for tennis or anything
else really. We have had sunshine, but the rain between-times has
made the ground too wet for play and everything else uncertain ...
Still the weather bucked up considerably since Monday and I have
been basking in the sunshine all day with my dog. It has relieved me
considerably to let off steam. Thank you for being – I hope – a patient
and sympathetic listener. Cheer up. Au Revoir, Megan.[7]

Frances writes this description of Megan in her diary – patronising
but quite affectionate: 'She is an amusing little person, but is getting
rather artificial. D. thinks she is growing selfish, but this is not her
fault, for she has not been taught to be unselfish. I think she is
wonderfully unspoilt, considering the way she has been brought up.'[8]
The real relationship involving Frances and Lloyd George became

apparent, when Frances acted as host in Lloyd George's absence as visiting dignitaries had to be entertained at Chequers. The effect on Megan was devastating. She never forgave Frances for supposedly seducing her father, betraying her mother and making a fool of her. 'Hell hath no fury like a woman scorned.' Strangely Megan attached no blame to her father, the true culprit.

The rest of the family followed suit, largely influenced by Maggie's reaction. We have seen the grief and disappointment with which Maggie was obliged to tolerate her husband's many infidelities, virtually from the start. She had consoled herself with her garden and the companionship of her family and friends in North Wales. She was busily employed in local politics, in fact virtually running the constituency with Uncle Lloyd and Brother William. She never doubted that, in his impossible way, her Dafyd still loved her. He went some way to compensating for his infidelity 250 miles away by writing frequently, if briefly, gently twitting her about her figure and her suspicious nature: 'The fat little woman you saw me with must have been a round little plump thing whom it is said I have got in the family way & packed off to an obscure little Welsh town in the wilds of Carnarvonshire. Do you know her?' (18 March 1902).[9] With the arrival of Frances Stevenson, though, such badinage ceased to suffice. Maggie was no fool and had more experience of Lloyd George's ways than the idol-worshipping Megan, so soon realised that Frances was different from the secretaries, farm-hands, housemaids and colleagues' wives with whom she had previously had to share her husband. When she received the following dishonest and disloyal missive (dated 24 July 1924), she knew exactly what to make of it:

> You talk as if my affection for you came and went. No more than the sea does because the tide ebbs and flows. There is just as much water in it … You like me sometimes when I am nice to you. So do I, when you are nice to me. But if at the worst moment anybody is not nice to you I am as murderous towards him as Patrick Mahon (a famous axe-murderer). I would readily hit them with an axe. You say I have my weakness. So has anyone that ever lived & the greater the man the greater the weakness. It is only insipid, wishy-washy fellows that have no weaknesses. Would you like to marry Tim!! He is sober and sternly good in all respects. You must make allowances for the waywardness and wildness of a man of my type. What if I were drunk as well? I can give you two samples of both the weaknesses in one man. The wives

do their best under those conditions. What about Asquith and Birkenhead? I could tell you stories of both – women and wine. Believe me hen gariad (old darling) I am at bottom as fond of you as ever ...[10]

The extraordinary thing about this letter is its date. If it had been written in, say, 1894 as opposed to 1924, it would have been typical of the untruthful trash which Lloyd George imposed on Maggie in the early days of the marriage. Thirty years later, nothing had changed – only now it wasn't just surreptitious fumblings in the dark with susceptible secretaries or jolly weekends with Mrs Tim. The affair with Frances was lifelong – and Maggie knew it. While Lloyd George's relationship with Frances was not quite marriage, they had gone through a ceremony which they both took seriously and regarded as binding. They remained committed to one another, even when considering a phoney marriage for Frances in order to deceive the media, first to Stuart Brown who genuinely loved her and later to Billy Owen whom Frances could not take seriously as someone to share with her Great Man.

How was Maggie to cope with this? 'I know very well whom you would marry if anything were to happen to me',[11] she told her husband. In the meantime her solution was to ban Frances from family events ranging from Lloyd George's occasional forays into the Welsh mountains, whether holiday visits to Criccieth or to Eisteddfords, or family recreational cruises to Ceylon or the Mediterranean. Frances was quite simply not wanted on voyage, and Maggie got this across to her husband loud and clear. Thus, when Maggie visited Bron-y-dy at Churt which she did now and again, she entered through the front door, while Frances exited hastily from the back. Frances had a flat in London and a cottage – Avalon – a couple of miles away from Bron-y-dy – where she lurked in angry humiliation – until the hated official wife, often accompanied by her minder the polemical Megan, had departed for North Wales. Then Frances would return. Sometimes Maggie was infuriated to find Frances' underclothing lying around. Shortly after Lloyd George's operation in 1931, Maggie discovered flowers which Frances had delivered. 'Who are these from?', she demanded. On being told, she exploded with rage.[12] Lloyd George was actually fonder of Maggie than he admitted to Frances. Nevertheless he was happiest at Churt with his estate, gardens, dogs and Frances for company. Though not a malicious or ungenerous person, Frances was incapable of being fair to Maggie, wrongly blaming her for unnecessarily and selfishly making Lloyd George uneasy:

> I have never seen anyone with such a capacity for making a place uncomfortable as Mrs Lloyd George. Her meanness forces the household to economise on coal & food, and everything that makes for comfort. The servants would be a disgrace to any house, and the P.M. is rightly ashamed of them.[13]

Clearly one must compensate for Frances' bitterness and resentment that Maggie lived so long and that Lloyd George would not do the decent thing and divorce her. In truth, this was never remotely considered by Lloyd George. Nor was he entirely insincere when he raised his glass to marriage at the celebration of their golden wedding, hosted by Churchill at Cannes on 24 January 1938. His speech was filmed; it was obviously a happy occasion. 'We have lived together in perfect harmony for fifty years', he declared solemnly, with difficulty repressing his laughter. 'One of us is contentious, combative and stormy. That is my wife. Then there is the other partner, placid, calm, peaceful and patient. That is me.'[14] Peter Rowland calls this an unblushing performance. Dick was later to record 'the peals of laughter with which my mother met this ridiculous statement'.[15]

When they were apart, Lloyd George and Frances corresponded frequently. Frances kept these letters, which have been edited by A. J. P. Taylor. They are a revealing record of mutual attraction – a combination of apprehension that the other is being unfaithful ('naughty') and protestations of undying love and loyalty:

> My own darling little girl, I loved your letter and beyond everything I loved your letter because it was you – full of sweet gentle passionate true love. After reading it I took you in my arms and assaulted your dear face with kisses – every bit of it – brow – chin – cheeks – ears – eyes and especially your sweet lips. Now get away Puss! (Criccieth, 13 July 1919)[16]
>
> My girl, Your letters are a real joy & a packet of thrills. You beat me leagues in letter writing and you have never written me nicer letters. (Criccieth, 18 August 1925)[17]

From Frances:

> My own beloved sweetheart, Your long letter was so welcome. It is wretched that you can't get a little more seclusion at Criccieth ... Fondest kisses, my darling, darling man, from your little girl who is looking forward to seeing you.[18]

My own darling man, It was just heaven to hear your voice, & it has given me the necessary courage to keep my spirits up until you return. (10 Downing Street, 10 July 1919)[19]

Not surprisingly, Taylor was prompted by what Roy Hattersley calls 'toe-curling' intimacies to ask Frances if she really wanted such letters to be published. 'Of course', she replied, 'that is why I kept them'. Take these for example:

How are you today cariad bach anwyl anwy (Dear little golden sweetheart)? I am in love with two such darlings. One the little sofa girl with the blue dressing gown, the other a little love in pink with braided hair falling on each side of the sweetest face you ever saw nestling on a pillow. (August/September 1918)[20]
        Well how is the dear little girl with the cold in her'dose'? I have been envying that cold & and wishing I were it ... This is to warn you at the earliest possible moment that I have fallen once more desperately in love with an *absolutely new girl*. She is the darlingest girl I ever met. I saw her for the first time yesterday afternoon lying (in the most seductive attitude) on a sofa. Altogether I am clean gone. I hope one day to make her love me as much as if I were a grilled kidney swimming in fat.[21]

In one such blush-making effusion Lloyd George asked 'Pussy' to go away with him for several years so that they could return with some kittens; and indeed a new topic for discussion arose when Frances gave birth to a daughter, Jennifer, on 4 October 1929. Both Lloyd George and 'Pussy' were besotted with the child. When there was business to be transacted, Lloyd George's long-suffering secretary A. J. Sylvester would be driven to distraction by his employer's insistence on playing games with the toddler. 'I sometimes wonder who is the greater baby', he grumbled. Frances' letters were now chock-full of baby-language

Jennifer misses you too. She said, just as she was going to lie down this morning, 'Where is Taid? I want to kiss him. When is he coming back?' I said, 'On Friday'. She said, 'No, Tuesday, I *telled* him, Tuesday'. (1 August 1932)
        She insisted on telephoning you this afternoon, & said 'Is that "oo", Taid? Come back, will "oo." References to Taid on a big ship, "far, far away"' abound. And then, before long, back to further expressions of endearment: 'My dearest Jamaican sweetheart, Where are you?

I always seem to be looking out for you & am on the point of calling you & when I remember I am so sad.[22]

Betrayal

Apart from Lloyd George's not infrequent infidelities even after his second 'marriage', Frances herself became involved in a passionate affair. Her lover was Colonel Thomas Tweed, the Liberal Party's chief organiser, a man of considerable intelligence and ability who had won the Military Cross during the war. Born in 1890 he was about Frances' age, handsome and charming, and unhappily married to a woman ten years older, who had lied about her age. During 1928 and 1929, Frances was receiving love-letters from two worshippers. Here is Tweed:

> Darling, A few moments of peace as we are sailing down the Skatterack towards Copenhagen gives me the long wanted, but hitherto seemingly impossible chance, to get into spiritual communion with you ...[23]

When Frances became pregnant in January 1929, she had no idea which of her two lovers was the father.[24] Nor, indeed, are her biographers and historians, notably John Campbell and Ffion Hague. Lloyd George longed to believe that Jennifer was his daughter, but subsequently claimed that Tweed had acknowledged her to be his, though this affidavit has not survived. Actually, the child did not resemble either man. She certainly did not look like Lloyd George or his daughters, all of them dark-haired, dumpy Celts, where Jennifer was fair and slim. But neither did she resemble Colonel Tweed.

What was in no doubt was Frances' betrayal of Lloyd George. Was she getting tired of the old man's obsessive suspicion and self-centredness? To a great extent, life with Lloyd George became less glamorous and exciting from their departure from Downing Street in October 1922 onwards. Tweed was different – more youthful and fun. When the affair ended she was heartbroken. In her diary, 19 October 1934, Frances wrote: 'Saw the back of my T.F.T. disappearing down the corridor & my heart bled with longing. It is dreadful to be in the same building and not to speak to him ...'[25] The balloon had gone up in December 1932. Rowlands the maid, who had worked for Frances and had then moved on to Olwen, divulged full details about Tweed's visits. A family meeting convened at Churt where Lloyd George was told about Frances' treachery. Obviously this revelation would finish the affair between Lloyd George and Frances. At least, that was the idea. We learn about the fallout from Sylvester, who was summoned to Churt by his boss:

Now you owe your first duty to me.
There has never been any doubt about that on my part, ever.
Do you know about Frances and Tweed?

Sylvester told all.[26] Lloyd George was terribly hurt. Tweed was banished. Yet Lloyd George and Frances continued their relationship, certainly in a lower key but definitely together still. Things could never be the same again, but the family's hopes were dashed.

Tweed, who was never a fit man after his wartime ordeals, died on 30 April 1940. When he was cremated at Golders Green, Sylvester accompanied Frances and her sister, Muriel, both in deep mourning. He had been instructed by Olwen to procure two other seats on the left-hand side of the chapel. Lloyd George duly arrived with Olwen. Sylvester described his appearance as a calculated insult to the dead Colonel:

He wore a blue suit, a blue overcoat, a blue hat, with a dark tie that was not even black. His face was white, knowing him, he was het up. He sat in the front seat, well towards the left. As he looked towards the pulpit on the right, he could see Frances in the second row and watch her every movement and reaction ... What was the motive for this extraordinary behaviour? Jealousy. He is eaten up with it. Afterwards, on the telephone, Frances told me that he was literally persecuting her to death. He had twitted her about being upset. He wondered whether she would be upset when *he* died. He criticised her deep mourning.[27]

No wonder Lloyd George subsequently denied that he owed anything to Tweed.

Don Juan

Affairs in middle age allegedly included a fling with Dick's wife, Roberta. To cuckold your own son might be considered despicable by any standards,[28] but by June 1931 the marriage was in trouble so that Lloyd George was able to move in. According to John Campbell, the whole family, except for Dick, knew all about it.[29] Sylvester drove his boss and Roberta down to Churt, complete with a suitcase containing Lloyd George's underclothes. Another such affair was uncovered with Ethel Snowden, the wife of the Labour Chancellor of the Exchequer. The Snowdens were neighbours of Lloyd George at Churt. Snowden was a cripple, but his wife was not. The couples were friendly. Dick was convinced that there was more to it than that and was tempted to ask his father if he thought there was anything wrong with seducing the wife of a cripple.[30] Lloyd George also slept with the wives of MPs Sir Charles Henry and Tim Davies. John Campbell records Sylvester's descriptions of employees who were seduced – typists, housemaids, land girls.[31] How much choice did these young women have? Frances Stevenson wrote in her diary that she often had to counsel 'distraught young secretaries or farm-workers at Churt that they only had to say no',[32] if they did not want to gratify their employer; the implication is clear, that they might well be propositioned. According to Ruth Longford, 'the trouble sometimes arose because young girls did not know how to say no to this enormously distinguished elder statesman who was also their employer'.[33] Nevertheless Ffion Hague is probably right in arguing that 'Ll G did not coerce his casual lovers'.[34] To be fair to Lloyd George surely he did not have to, possessed as he was with magnetic charm, to say nothing of his physical attributes. Lord Dawson suggested as much when he warned Lloyd George after his prostate operation that he would have to cut out 'the emotional stimulus which any new goddess must promote and to the patient's detriment ... the wise plan is to keep to well tried love'.[35]

Some of Lloyd George's admirers such as the television presenter Huw Edwards have defended Lloyd George against malicious invention. Malcolm Muggeridge, journalist and editor of *Punch*, obviously enjoyed telling stories about young women innocently strolling in the grounds at Churt until they were ambushed by a white-haired monster from the Celtic past. Jean Trumpington was a land girl at Churt at the beginning of World War II: 'Occasionally, Lloyd George would ask me up to the house – where the old goat would stand me up against a wall, take out a tape measure and try to take all my measurements.'[36] Sir Oswald Mosely once expressed surprise at a guest list at a dinner given by Lloyd George which contained several women of doubtful repute: 'This will lift the roof if it gets out', to which Lloyd George replied: 'My dear boy if everything that I have done in this hotel during the last forty years had got out, you have no idea how many times I would have had to retire from politics.'[37] One prime source is Richard Lloyd George's book *My Father Lloyd George*. This is widely claimed to be ghosted, though on what grounds is unclear considering the style is similar to Dick's biography of his mother. He was certainly an eyewitness to much of his father's career. Part of the book is perceptive and affectionate. For instance, father and son together tried to ignite a recalcitrant fire – until the old man planted his boot right in the centre of it. Immediately the thing came to life. 'There you are, Dick. Easy!' Both roared with laughter while Dick accused his father of sheer luck.[38] On the other hand, the book is suffused with malice, and exaggeration of its basic story is certainly possible. Dick accuses his father of mentally undressing every woman who came into the room, and of then taking the matter further. He allegedly ran what was virtually a private brothel in his later years. 'Is the mistress of the house there?', asked a caller. 'Which one?', Dick replied when staying with his father.[39] Like Sylvester, Dick has a thesis. By squandering his time and his energy on women, Lloyd George deprived the country of his great gifts when they were needed. This vignette about him when Chancellor of the Exchequer rings true:

> Later in the day I was strolling in the large grounds and saw Lady J. sitting in a swing, flirtatiously poking father with her pointed shoe. These were days of long skirts and it was rather daring for a lady to be seen in a swing at all; and when sitting in it it was proper to remain comparatively at rest. I saw father catch the heel, draw the lady back, then give a very hefty thrust. She shot away with a shriek and came sailing back over his head with a flurry of petticoats that would have done credit to a can-can expert. Her clear laughter rang out; there was not the slightest suspicion of rebuke in her voice. The old boy looked around quickly, his moustache on end with vitality, and then turned round to give the flying form another mighty push.[40]

Sylvester confirmed that Lloyd George's enthusiasm for the estate at Churt was partly due to his wish to pursue a couple of land girls. 'When L. G. returned from Jamaica, Coles (the fourth farm manager in a very few years) informed him that he wanted to leave; he did not like the moral atmosphere of the place.'[41] Sylvester supports Dick: 'If L. G. gave his mind to thinking out how he could best help his country, instead of thinking of cunt and women, he would be a better man.'[42] This entry from Sylvester's diary is from October 1940, when Lloyd George was 77. Not long before this, Sylvester noted Lloyd George's interest in nubile, scantily-clad young women who frequented the hotel bathing-pool in Jamaica when he was supposed to be writing his memoirs.

In November 1941 Maggie got up too hastily to answer the telephone at Brynawelon and fell on the polished parquet floor. She broke her hip. Hospital, followed by rest at home, proved ineffectual. Pneumonia set in, and despite the best medical attention, she died on 20 January 1942. Lloyd George was – typically – wintering at Churt, but the local GP telephoned and Lord Dawson confirmed his pessimism. Lloyd George, accompanied by Ann Parry, his Welsh Secretary, drove through the winter storms in his Rolls-Royce, accompanied by Frances as far as Shrewsbury. The weather set in and they were soon snow-bound at Cerrig-y-Druidion. On 20 January, Maggie died from pneumonia, aged 74. Dawson telephoned the inn where Lloyd George was holed up. He gently broke the news to Lloyd George who broke down. 'She was a grand old pal', he blubbered to Sylvester who followed Dawson. As with Mair's death, there is no need to accuse Lloyd George of play-acting when he fell into Dick's arms and wept. 'He looked dreadful, poor old fellow, grey and frail and pathetic.'[43] By the same token, however, one can agree with Dick that 'it was as much a sense of guilt towards my mother as sorrow for her that wrung his heart'.[44]

Megan

Lloyd George's relationship with Megan had always been fraught. Perhaps they were too much alike; she was the most political of his children, sharing his wit and his prejudices. 'Are you as good as your father?', shouted a heckler. 'If I'm half as good, I'll be all right!', she replied. Shades of the young Lloyd George could be seen, too, in her response to an Anglesey rowdy: 'What do you know about farming? I bet you don't know how many ribs a pig's got', to which she replied, 'Come up here, and I'll count them for you'.[45] On the return journey from Jamaica in February 1937, father and daughter clashed. Megan arrived 25 minutes late for a drink in the bar.

> 'Well, Tada, thank you very much for a most delightful holiday.'
> 'If you intended to drink my health and thank me for your holiday, you might at least have been here for seven o'clock, instead of being

here twenty-five minutes late. You have never thought me of sufficient importance to be here on time.'

Sylvester records that he worked himself up into a great rage, his face red and his blue-grey eyes flashing:

'You have never once been up to have breakfast with me, either in Jamaica with me or on the boat, still less to walk with me before breakfast which you know I like to do. But your mother has always been there. That is what I would have expected of her. But then *she* is a lady and you are not.'

Megan's face went white with rage, and her eyes filled with tears. She stammered out that she was sorry if she had done anything wrong.

'Anything wrong? That is the first time you have ever apologised to me', snapped Lloyd George. I remarked: 'I have never heard you talk like that to Megan before.'

'It's about time.'

I returned to the sitting-room to find Megan in floods of tears. 'My God', she said to me, 'it will be a long time before I forgive him for that'.[46]

In the aftermath of Maggie's death, a more serious row was to erupt than one caused by Megan's unpunctuality. Lloyd George had always promised to marry Frances in the event of Maggie's death. Frances was quite willing to let matters rest for a while, say, a year, but when the old man made no move, she became alarmed. It soon emerged that the problem was Megan. Much though she loved her father, she loved her late-lamented mother even more. 'Why can't we leave matters as they have been for the past thirty years?', pleaded Lloyd George, anxious to appease both his daughter and his mistress. 'Not good enough!', retorted Frances. 'Honourable people expect you to marry me', 'There are no honourable people', retorted Lloyd George.[47] Eventually, Frances herself took the initiative and made enquiries as to how a wedding could be arranged at Guildford Registry Office. There was no valid impediment, and Frances went ahead and arranged the date. On 21 October 1943, according to Sylvester 'Sir Thomas Carey-Evans told me that Olwen had been to Churt on Monday. L.G. had told her that he intended to marry Frances, probably on Saturday. She had told Megan who was terribly upset. Carey-Evans's own attitude and that of Olwen was that it was a matter for L.G. himself to decide'.[48]

So it was all arranged. Dyer the chauffeur, who was not aware of the plot, was to drive the bridal couple to Guildford, accompanied by the witnesses, Frances' sister Muriel and A. J. Sylvester. But Megan was not finished yet. First she bullied Gwilym, who had promised to attend, into sending back word. Then she telephoned her father at Churt for a last half-hour's vitriol during which she threatened to kill herself if he went ahead. Lloyd George, to his eternal credit, remained adamant. During the long tale of Lloyd George's sexual adventures – many, it might be thought, to his discredit – his determination to marry Frances Stevenson stands out as a real moral achievement. For once, he did the right thing. Next morning off they drove to Guildford. The ceremony went ahead without a hitch. The couple were very contented as they drove back to Churt through the autumn sunshine across the Devil's Punchbowl. At Bron-y-de the bridegroom introduced his bride as Mrs Lloyd George to the staff while Frances practised her new signature. Gwylim and his wife arrived for tea – a happy and relaxed occasion. Lloyd George produced some excellent champagne.

Lord Dawson remonstrated with Megan, imploring her to change her attitude to her father's re-marriage. He pointed out to her how frail her father had become. At the time of his second marriage it was clear that he was not long for this world. Though the truth was hidden from him, his doctors were sure that he was suffering from cancer of the bowel. Frances guessed the truth. Lord Dawson was overwhelmed by her kindness and efficiency as a nurse – which he pointed out to Megan: would *she* like to keep her father clean?[49] Frances was assisted by Ann Parry, but not, alas, by Megan. It is sad that Megan refused to respond to what one would have thought was rather a good letter from Frances, written in November 1944:

> I hope that you will read this letter through as it is written in all sincerity to ask if you will not reconsider your attitude towards your Father's marriage to me ... I am depriving you of nothing in becoming his wife – neither of his affection nor of any material benefits now or in the future ... Even if you cannot see your way to burying the past as far as I am concerned, I hope that that you will make this concession to him and so establish yourself even more firmly in his heart.[50]

Megan ignored the letter, though she did graciously agree to receive her father provided he came alone. They chatted amicably, but Megan never forgave Frances. Hers was a strange and unforgiving nature, especially as she purported to be a devout Christian and lived with a lover who had a wife: the Labour MP and prominent pacifist Philip Noel-Baker was married to a wealthy Greek. He had promised to marry Megan if his wife died but when this happy event occurred in 1956, Noel-Baker ratted on her. Perhaps he lacked sensitivity: as a government minister he displayed a less than felicitous touch when he infuriated the survivors of the Arctic convoy PQ 17 by assuring them that their sufferings had not been in vain. Megan got cancer and died in 1968 at the relatively young age of 64. Her dying words were, 'Tada, I'm coming'.

Although she was not invited, Frances attended Megan's funeral. She was kind to Dick in his impoverished and dishonourable old age. When she financed a beautiful set of railings round Lloyd George's grave, she sent keys to all members of the family. Not one acknowledged. The general atmosphere in Llanystumdwy was so hostile that Frances eventually surrendered and returned to Surrey, where she became a prominent Anglican. She was taken aback when Muriel and Jennifer exploded with laughter when she became Chair of the Guildford Diocese Moral Welfare Committee. In a televised interview with the BBC's Fyfe Robertson she told him that she disapproved of the permissive society. Did she regret that she had never had babies, she was asked. 'Lloyd George was my baby'. Jennifer was hurt, though not surprised.

Does It Matter?

Even if one simply considers Lloyd George's career as 'a life in politics', his friends, relations and enemies influenced the way it went. Frances Stevenson was very much a modern PA. Lloyd George listened to her views on policies and personalities. Maggie (or perhaps in this context she deserves her full title, 'Dame Margaret') virtually ran Lloyd George's constituency while he lived three hundred miles away in North West Surrey. Her distinction was awarded to her for her conspicuous war work for the families of Welsh troops – a political as well as a charitable achievement. This also mattered.

When we review the often rather lurid story of Lloyd George's relations with women, it is tempting to ask ourselves how he was able to get away with it. This too is very much a political issue. To a great extent, as we suggested in Chapter 4, the answer is that the newspaper proprietors of his day led scandalous private lives themselves. They themselves had too much to hide to risk major revelations. Yet, he was vulnerable to exposure, especially if one considers his Free Church supporters whom he attempted to mobilise as late as 1935. One word from Maggie could have sunk him without trace, but she stood by him, sometimes even in the witness box. Curiously enough, Megan ran similar risks by her adulterous affair when her puritanical Anglesey constituents would have rejected her, had they known.

There is more to the story of Lloyd George's private life than the narrow political aspect, in that a biography is concerned with the whole person. Could one correctly evaluate Baldwin without his pigs or Disraeli without his novels? Like him or loathe him, Lloyd George had his women. Ffion Hague empathises with his two wives, experiencing the pain and the privilege of living close to a great man.[51] On the other hand, while there certainly were elements of greatness there if we look sympathetically at Lloyd George, his selfishness and manipulative dishonesty sully his record. Lloyd George exploited men as well – the soldiers, sailors and airmen in the armed forces during the last two years of the War when he was prime minister. His cavalier attitude to his women friends must be considered highly significant, given that women constitute half the population; his willingness to play fast and loose with the mothers, sisters and wives of the men whom he betrayed in the trenches is part of a disturbing picture of overall irresponsibility and insensitivity to the importance of the individual and to human suffering. In the meantime, an interim assessment might be that, yes, he did benefit the British nation by founding the welfare state, by trying to restrain casualties in World War I, and by campaigning for votes for women. Arguably, these were good things accomplished by 'a scoundrel', as Shinwell put it.

I am encouraged to be critical by a letter from Baroness Shirley Williams who accuses Lloyd George of betraying Liberalism in his exploitation of vulnerable women: 'Apart from his own wife, he behaved towards women as if they were objects for exploitation. Both his behaviour and that of Asquith failed to live up to the Liberal principles both men claimed to espouse.' Shirley Williams believes that:

... some of LG's behaviour can be put down to class ... All too often, girls in domestic service were regarded as easy victims for would be seducers, and might lose their jobs if they protested too much. You will be familiar with all the jokes about LG, but for the girls involved they were not joking matters.[52]

Not even Frances was immune to Lloyd George's mental and physical cruelty, as Sylvester recalls her confiding to Evelyn, his wife: 'Frances said that she could not be out of his sight a fraction of an instant without his calling out and looking slyly around for her. She said that he had held her down by force in an endeavour to get her to confess to things she had never done.'[53] A disturbing picture of a bully willing to exploit feminine weakness. On the other hand, one recalls his kindness to Jennifer; he was always at his best with children.[54]

In the end, with adolescent and adult women, just as with their male relations, he was selfish and ruthless, and we must conclude that Shirley Williams is right: he was a disgrace to Liberalism. His biographers, most of them male and/or Welsh, have been too kind to him.

11

An Uneven Old Age (1931–1945)

Old Age Hath Yet His Honour and His Toil.

– Alfred, Lord Tennyson

No fool like an old fool.

– Traditional

ONTROVERSY CLINGS to Lloyd George even in old age. Many historians are dismissive about his record in the years following his prostate operation in August 1931, which ruled him out of involvement in MacDonald's National Government, armed with 'the doctor's mandate' – but he was certainly all there still ('This isn't China tea', he grumbled when he came round from his operation) and he had no intention of retiring. A. J. Sylvester was amused by the way Lloyd George rushed round his estate or the House of Commons in order to give an impression of vigour.[1] On the face of it, however, these years were futile and unproductive in the context of his career in politics. All moves to bring him back into government failed – with ever increasing degrees of inevitability. Not only was he *persona non grata* with MacDonald, Baldwin and Neville Chamberlain, but even Churchill found him an embarrassment. Furthermore, he had ever-decreasing support in the Liberal Party, hopelessly divided between Simonites backing the National Government ('the Vichy Liberals', as Dingle Foot was to call them subsequently)[2] and cautious followers of Sir Herbert Samuel who had left the government in 1932. Lloyd George could count on the loyalty only of his own family quartet in the Commons – himself, Megan, Gwilym and Gwilym's brother in law, Goronwy Owen.

The prominent Welsh Liberal David Davies had not tried to hide his delight when Lloyd George was taken ill, writing to his colleague, Herbert Lewis: 'What have you done with L. G.? ... Having carted everybody in the course of his career, does it now mean that he has been carted himself?'[3] Lloyd George crucified Samuel for agreeing to the National Government's cynical general election in 1932. He had never warmed to Samuel's Jewish/agnostic, po-faced rectitude. Still less did Lloyd George and Simon hit it off, since both emerged as rival crown-princes to Asquith's tottering throne. Simon fell victim to Lloyd George's sarcasm: 'Sir John Simon has sat on the fence for so long that the iron has entered into his soul'.[4] He demolished Simon's abandonment of Free Trade with malicious wit: 'Protection, unfortunately, is one of the questions to which Sir John Simon has lent one of his countenances',[5] and even more viciously, 'I do object to his intolerant self-righteousness ... greater men did not leave behind the slime of hypocrisy in passing from one side to the other'.[6] Not surprisingly, the Liberals lost their self-belief when Lloyd George wrecked his colleagues' reputations. Without the support of a healthy and sizeable Liberal Party, Lloyd George could not *demand* to be included in the cabinets of men who hated and feared him.

While both contemporaries and historians have suggested that Lloyd George was increasingly losing his 'edge', to represent him as senile is dangerous, at any rate until the last few weeks of his life. True, he himself began to display a hitherto untypical boredom with politics, making his priorities the composition of *War Memoirs* and the cultivation of his estate at Churt – the apples, the potatoes, the honey, the raspberries and his young female employees. Mead from the honey was sold at Harrods, labelled 'From the estate of David Lloyd George OM MP'. After his illness, a restorative trip to Ceylon with Maggie in November 1931 reiterated his enduring love of travel. Lloyd George was determined to flag up his commitment to radical solutions to the economic morass in which Britain continued to wallow under the 'leadership' of MacDonald, Baldwin and Neville Chamberlain. Emulating President Roosevelt's New Deal, in 1935 he launched his Council of Action for Peace and Reconstruction. The Cabinet listened politely to Lloyd George's exposition of his ideas, which merely reproduced the various Liberal tracts of the late 1920s – and took no action.

Lloyd George, however, erupted like a volcano after the outbreak of the Abyssinia crisis in October 1935. The government failed to implement an effective policy against Mussolini's pursuit of an African empire. Half-hearted economic sanctions were applied, but only too soon abandoned. The Mediterranean fleet could have blocked the Suez Canal, thus spoiling Mussolini's game – but a 'mad dog attack' by the Italian air-force on Britain's battleships was feared, so once again, nothing was done; a craven decision especially when one recalls the abysmal record of the Italian armed forces in the Mediterranean five years later. Eden, our League of Nations specialist, was dispatched to Geneva to tell the League that Britain could no longer offer effective support [*sic*]. 'Half a League, Half a League, Half a League onward, Into the valley of death',[7] quipped the cynics. Such cynicism was taken a stage further when the foreign ministers of Britain and France conferred in Paris to produce the Hoare-Laval Pact, whereby Mussolini was invited to accept the more desirable parts of Abyssinia if he called off his army, now employing poison gas against the indigenous tribesmen.

The outcry in Britain was deafening, led by George V, who greeted Hoare when he resigned his seals of office somewhat heartlessly: 'Do you know what they are all saying? No more coals to Newcastle, no more Hoares to Paris!'[8] Both pact and Foreign Secretary were disowned, while Hitler exploited his potential enemies' disarray by remilitarising the Rhineland (March 1936). On 18 June 1936 it was announced that Anthony Eden, now foreign secretary, would report to Geneva that the Government had abandoned economic sanctions as they were clearly not working, whereupon Lloyd George tore into the Government, delivering what Churchill called the finest parliamentary oration he had ever heard. It was certainly an effective mugging job, though maybe the right way out of the Abyssinia crisis was not quite so simple as Lloyd George seemed to believe:

> I cannot imagine a more serious debate than that which we are going through now. If the policy of the Government is to materialise, if we are going to Geneva to say 'We are beaten, the League has failed, we do not propose any further sanctions', believe me, that is an end to the authority of the League of Nations. The Foreign Secretary referred this afternoon to the well-ordered ranks of the League. They have not broken away, and he is going there now to break them. He is going to Geneva to smash the League of Nations. This is a unique occasion. I have been in the House for nearly half a century, I am sorry to say, and I cannot recall an occasion quite like this. I have never before heard a British Minister come down to the House of Commons

and say that Britain was beaten. Here is 'the resolute aim; here is the resolute footstep' – running away! The speech of the Chancellor of the Exchequer has been quoted. I am going to do myself the honour of reading a part of it again. 'The choice before us is whether we should make a last effort at Geneva for peace and security or whether by a cowardly surrender we should break all the promises we have made and hold ourselves up to the shame of our children and our children's children.' Tonight we have the cowardly surrender – and *there* are the cowards.[9]

'Germany's Always Right'

Curiously enough, the Welsh wizard always preferred Hitler to Mussolini, at any rate until the outbreak of World War II. Even then he was prone to listen to Lord Haw-Haw (the traitor, William Joyce), whose Nazi enthusiasm was targeted on London, with a strange mixture of approval and disgust. In the late 1930s, Germany called to him with a siren voice. He had always felt an attraction towards German efficiency, ever since his years at the Treasury. Stella Rudman has recorded Lloyd George's procession from remorse at the harsh treatment of Germany at Versailles to appeasement of the democratic Weimar Republic.[10] Nor did his enthusiasm for the appeasement of Germany cease when Hitler came to power on 31 January 1933. Now there were indications that a European Roosevelt was rising from the ashes of the economic bonfire in Germany. Frances Stevenson had visited Germany in 1935 and reported favourably. Meanwhile, Hitler's bias in favour of Lloyd George prompted him to put out feelers for a visit from the British statesman, whom he had admired since the composition of *Mein Kampf* in 1925. As vain a man as Lloyd George could only be attracted by the following adulation of his eloquence: 'The primitive quality itself of those speeches, the originality of his expression, his choice of pure and simple illustration, are examples which prove the superior political capacity of this Englishman [*sic*]'.[11]

The Nazi regime's economic achievements, especially the reduction of unemployment by ploughing state resources into the construction of motorways, could have come straight from Churt before the 1929 general election. Very well, if the British Government refused to listen to Lloyd George, he would repair to Germany where it seemed that he *was* appreciated. Granted, he had to turn a blind eye to Hitler's massive rearmament, though even this could be condoned by the victorious Allies' perverse refusal to disarm, just as he preferred not to notice the disturbing evidence of state-sponsored murders and anti-Semitism. The Roehm Purge had occurred as recently as in June 1934 and the Nuremberg Laws passed in September 1935. Equally disturbing had been Germany's remilitarisation of the Rhineland in March 1936, which negated France's ability to come to the rescue of her allies to the east of Germany. Yet here was Lloyd George heading for the Bavarian Alps in September 1936. No wonder Ivan Maisky the Soviet ambassador was appalled. So too was Maggie, who opposed the venture and refused to accompany her husband; her judgement was seldom wrong.

The go-betweens were, on the German side, Hitler's new ambassador to London, the former champagne salesman Joachim von Ribbentrop, who spoke fluent English,[12] and on the British side, Dr T. P. Conwell-Evans, a Welsh professor at Konigsberg University who acted as interpreter for the visit. The initiative came from Ribbentrop on behalf of the Fuehrer, but Lloyd George was delighted to accept Hitler's invitation. The party consisted of Lloyd George; Megan; Gwilym; Tom Jones, who had worked in the Cabinet Office; Lord Dawson, the distinguished royal physician; and the ubiquitous A. J. Sylvester. Ribbentrop and Conwell-Evans supervised arrangements in Germany. The party travelled by sea and then motored across Germany on the new autobahn (the first motorways in Europe). Lloyd George was fascinated. After lunch with the Ribbentrops, Lloyd George, Conwell-Evans and Ribbentrop were driven to Hitler's retreat high up in the mountains at Berchtesgaden in the Bavarian Alps. Hitler effusively welcomed his visitors. He was dressed in a smart grey suit, wearing no medals or military uniform; this was definitely a meeting between civilians. Hitler gazed adoringly at Lloyd George, hanging on his words, as translated by Dr Schmidt, the German interpreter. Lloyd George had to listen to an excessively long tirade from Hitler about Bolshevism. Hitler was thrilled by Lloyd George's assertion that Germany would never have been beaten in 1918 if Hitler had been in charge. Both men flattered and charmed each other in a really rather nauseating exercise in mutual adulation. It was agreed that the whole of Lloyd George's party would come to tea next day. When Lloyd George returned to his hotel, Megan flippantly saluted her father with 'Heil Hitler!' Lloyd George replied with a Nazi salute: 'Yes, Heil Hitler! He really is a great leader.'[13]

The tea party was a memorable occasion. This time the Fuehrer ran down the steps to welcome his guest whom he clearly regarded now as an old friend. Tea was served in an enormous tunnel-like room which had been dug out of the mountain. There was one huge window, giving a view over the Bavarian Alps stretching away to Salzberg in the far distance. Hitler gave Lloyd George the impression that he was a man of peace, in favour of friendly relations with the British Empire. But what a leader! That was Lloyd George's chief conclusion. Meanwhile the Fuehrer was asked if he would mind Sylvester taking some photographs and some cine film. There was no objection. Sylvester snapped away, astonishing the SS guards by marshalling not only the guests but Hitler himself in order to fit them in artistically. Hitler presented Lloyd George with a large photograph of himself which his guest proposed to place next to the great war leaders Foch, Clemenceau and President Wilson – 'but not I hope with Erzberger and Bauer',[14] Hitler trusted. Not with German democrats, please! Conversation turned to the war, won not by the soldiers in Hitler's view.

> ... but due to one statesman, a great statesman, yourself, Mr Lloyd George. It was you who rallied the people and gave them the determination for victory. If I, instead of being one of many millions of German private soldiers, had been in the position of a Leader instead of being subject at any time to have been shot, even by black troops, matters would have been very different. I am convinced that if I had been in power then, I could have prevented Germany's downfall.[15]

So, these amazingly self-regarding demagogues lavished praise on each other, each having the time of his life. Lloyd George came away convinced of Hitler's pacific intentions and devotion to the British Empire, represented by himself. Hitler solicitously helped the old man down the steps to his car. The rest of the visit was marred so far as Lloyd George was concerned by too many visits to factories and road-works, and he was disappointed not to be allowed to meet Ludendorff who was now so mad that he was not fit to be seen. There was a colourful row with Megan for being late – 'What is wrong with him now?', she asked Sylvester.[16] But Lloyd George was anxious to get home as soon as possible, and was irked by any unnecessary delay. He wanted to broadcast the fantastic merits of his new friend ('the George Washington of Germany' and 'Germany's Resurrection and Light'[17]) which he proceeded to do in a series of enthusiastic articles in the *Daily Express* and the *News Chronicle*. These were not received with universal approbation, concentration camps and anti-semitism having apparently failed to register with him, but Lloyd George took months to recover his intellectual balance once Hitler's real priorities were unmasked.

Truth to tell, the pilgrimage to Berchtesgaden was the logical culmination of Lloyd George's long exercise in the appeasement of Germany. He had been pro-German since his visit there in 1908. He suffered a temporary aberration in December 1918 when he expressed some no-nonsense anti-hun expletives, mainly to win votes, but in an extraordinarily short amount of time, Lloyd George began to backtrack. The Fontainebleau memorandum was a significant exercise in second thoughts. From the signing of the treaty onwards, Lloyd George regretted the size of the reparations demanded, regretted the war-guilt clause and its corollary, the trial of the war-criminals,[18] regretted the way that Germany had been forced to disarm, and regretted the lopping off of great lumps of German territory. This process escalated in Lloyd George's brain during the 1920s and 1930s. Its most significant corollary was hostility towards France's politicians and strategists, whom he cynically betrayed with promises of military assistance dependent on American cooperation which he strongly suspected would not materialise.

Lloyd George refused to sympathise with French fears for the future and damned France wholeheartedly for her refusal to disarm. Nor would he take any notice of the British Chiefs of Staff when they argued that their French colleagues just might have a point. Logically therefore and predictably Lloyd George was not worried by the remilitarisation of the Rhineland in March 1936 nor by the Anschluss with Austria two years later. When Czechoslovakia was betrayed in September 1938, Lloyd George reckoned that Benes had it coming to him. Even after the rest of Czechoslovakia had been devoured in March 1939, Lloyd George devoted his energies not to criticising Hitler's belligerence and bad faith but to condemning Chamberlain for not achieving a military understanding with Russia without which British guarantees of Czechoslovakia was worthless.

What excuse can we offer for Lloyd George's wilful self-deception with regard to Nazi Germany? Is it indeed a case of defending the indefensible? Others were equally gullible – even Churchill hoped that Britain would be led by a similar genius to Adolf Hitler in future times of trouble, while the Webbs and Bernard Shaw were taken in by Stalin. It could be argued that 1936 was not 1938 or 1939; there was still all to play for. Hitler might have been redeemed by further contacts with his role model David Lloyd George though the facts do not really support this outlook.

Anthony Lentin[19] discusses the question of Lloyd George's conduct as a British statesman, even though he was not a member of the government. 'In so far then as Lloyd George made it clear that, however much she desired an understanding with Germany, Britain would not purchase it at the price of abandoning France, he performed a responsible service.' Similarly Lloyd George made it clear to Ribbentrop that Great Britain would never join the Anti-Comintern Pact, that egregious masterpiece of statesmanship. Lloyd George was disgracefully out of line in slagging off President Benes (often dismissively mispronounced by Foreign Office mandarins as 'President Beans'[20]), thus giving Hitler the green light for aggression against Czechoslovakia – which Lloyd George had never supported since Treaty-making days. He belittled Churchill to Ribbentrop. His Nazi salute to Megan was unwise – possibly mere clowning but very public. One wonders what she made of it, as a committed left-winger.

Was the visit necessarily a mistake? Frances Stevenson wrote in 1967: 'I still believe that had L.G. been given a say in the affairs of Britain during these years preceding 1939, with power to approach Hitler and negotiate with him, the Second World War would never have happened.'[21] Frances stresses her man's negotiating skills: 'He was indeed superhuman in the art of persuasion and in understanding the mind of his opponent.' Unfortunately, Lloyd George would have been handicapped by the basic immorality of appeasement; it was always a case of handing over someone else's property, as when he invited Field Marshal Smuts, in one of his moralistic moods, to return German South-West Africa to Germany – with notable lack of success even though 'Germany was always right', as revisionists and appeasers had been proclaiming ever since the Treaty was signed.

The Monarchist (1936)

Now our crusader tried to defend Edward VIII when that feather-brained play-boy opted for an American double-divorcee as opposed to his throne.[22] George V had always doubted 'whether the boy would be able to manage',[23] and now he was vindicated. Actually, Lloyd George's role in the abdication crisis was not wholly discreditable.[24] He comes out of it better than the vindictive Stanley Baldwin, the Prime Minister and Cosmo Lang, the Archbishop of Canterbury, who was excessively motivated by his loyalty to the Christian view of marriage,[25] to say nothing of the British people who exhibited one of their periodical attacks of hypocritical humbuggery. Lloyd George and the new King, it will be remembered, went back a long way. In May 1911 George V persuaded him to coach Edward in a little basic Welsh so that he could be invested as Prince of Wales at Caernarfon Castle, of which Lloyd George was constable. The idea was to encourage the young man to grow up and accept some responsibility. It was hoped that the relationship between the Crown and 'the difficult Mr Lloyd George'[26] might be improved in the process. For Lloyd George had gravely upset the Establishment by his provocative speeches when he defended the economic and social reforms which he had introduced as Chancellor of the Exchequer. For several days, Edward clocked in at 11 Downing Street for one-to-one tuition in Welsh. The two got on fine. The ceremony at Caernarfon was a brilliant success. Everyone was delighted, though a few grumpy Welshmen objected that they had not had an authentic Prince of Wales since LLwelyn the Great (d. 1282). Still, the greatest modern Welshman had a staunch ally in his old sparring-partner, the Bishop of St Asaph, who would be chosen by Lloyd George to become the first Archbishop of Wales in 1920. Even George V approved.

Actually 'the boy'[27] went from strength to strength, dutifully putting in a military appearance on the Western Front and knuckling down to a 41,000 mile tour of the Empire in 1919 when the War had been won, at the behest of the Prime Minister. Lloyd George was sure that the Prince's charm and amiability would bind the Empire together far more effectively than 'half a dozen solemn Imperial Conferences'.[28] He welcomed the Prince home from India with fulsome gratitude: 'There were difficulties, there were menaces, there was an atmosphere which gave concern to everyone. He went indomitably at the call of duty, and whatever the Empire owed him before, it owes to him a debt which it can never repay today.'[29] Not everyone approved. 'The boy' now became 'the little man', patronised and distrusted by stuffy Tory grandees. He was the most eligible bachelor in the world, and would have saved himself and others a lot of trouble if he had settled down with a suitable German princess or a British aristocrat; but he did not want to settle down. He enjoyed several affairs, culminating in a 14-year relationship with the divorced Mrs Dudley Ward. He smoked and drank his way through his twenties and thirties. Every now and again he made gestures to his poorer subjects which enraged the establishment, notably when he visited depressed parts of South Wales and pronounced that 'something should be done to get them at work again', 'The very idea!', muttered Baldwin.

Then he fell in love with Mrs Wallis Simpson, a divorcee and an American (which was the more offensive to Baldwin and Cosmo Gordon Lang). The Cabinet and the churches lined up in opposition. Edward – or 'David', as his loved ones called him – was ordered to dismiss Wallis or abdicate. Baldwin and Lang played a devious, cruel hand with some astuteness. In the Commons, Winston Churchill fought on his own, pleading for a short delay while further negotiations occurred. He had a rough time, and was shouted down. Some believed that if Lloyd George had been there, the two of them could have saved the day, but Baldwin had very possibly timed his assault to coincide with Lloyd George's holiday in Jamaica. Baldwin moved quickly: Lloyd George had already packed and was heading for the berth which Sylvester had hastily booked, but Megan and Gwilym telephoned to say that all was over. Edward VIII had succumbed and abdicated.

Lloyd George was furious with his Party. Even the North Wales Liberal Federation signalled its support for Baldwin and Archbishop Lang, who unwisely broadcast a mean and rather unchristian character assassination of the outgoing King, though he is defended by his most recent biographer.[30] Lloyd George sent a telegram to Edward in his Austrian exile:

> Best Christmas greetings from an old Minister of the Crown who holds you in as high esteem as ever and regards you with deepest loyal affection, deplores the shabby and stupid treatment accorded to you, resents the mean and unchivalrous attacks upon you and regrets the loss sustained by the British Empire of a monarch who sympathised with the lowliest of his subjects.[31]

Lloyd George was delighted to receive the following reply: 'Very touched by your kind telegram and good wishes, which I heartily reciprocate. *Cymru am byth* [Wales for ever], EDWARD'.[32] Who knows how different the future could have been? Presumably, given Edward VIII's childlessness, Elizabeth II would have ultimately acceded in any case, though a few years after her own father died.

Soyez Realistes! Demandez L'impossible[33]

Perhaps Lloyd George was increasingly unrealistic – in cosying up to Hitler and trying to save Edward VIII's throne. He certainly had to endure indignant opposition from his own constituents, especially from devout Nonconformists who did not enthuse over Wallis Simpson. Furthermore, in February 1937 he was again under fire for ancient offences – his alleged sexual peccadilloes. Sylvester records his chief's fury with his holy constituents:

> I once made them pay £1,000 for suggesting that I was capable of anything of the kind, and now I am seventy-four. To bring a charge like this against an old fellow who had a serious operation six years ago, which has taken away some of his vitals, was a preposterous and ridiculous thing. I have a letter from Tweed saying that he was responsible for the child. If they say anything about Frances, you can exaggerate. Tell them she is a graduate of London University with Honours. As long as I am writing these books, Frances is absolutely essential to me. She knows French. She knew Foch, Briand, Clemenceau, Bonar and all the ministers. I am not the sort of fellow to wait to be attacked. The old girl will stand by me. I will spend £10,000 in showing up the whole bloody lot, including Baldwin ...[34]

Meanwhile, Lloyd George took a sardonic interest in Chamberlain's foreign policy, not really knowing what line to take during the Czechoslovakia crisis of September 1938. He was disgusted by the adulation of Chamberlain, but he could hardly fault him for his willingness to trust Hitler. Furthermore Lloyd George had contempt for 'that swine Benes',[35] the courageous democrat who tried hard to stand up to German intimidation of Czechoslovakia. Lloyd George was not proud of his role in creating Czecho-Germano-Magyaro-Rutheno-Romano-Slovakia at Versailles.

However, where he was in absolutely no doubt was in his condemnation of Chamberlain's guarantees of Poland, Greece and Romania without any understanding with Soviet Russia. These guarantees were given immediately after Hitler's occupation of the rest of Czechoslovakia in March 1939. German seizure of the Sudetenland already reduced Czechoslovakia to a pathetic rump, ready for the taking. Only Russia could save the day:

> The Prime Minister treated the matter of getting Soviet Russia into the alliance, or whatever you call it, rather too much as though it were a matter of placating a number of my right honourable friends above the gangway ... Without Russia these three guarantees are the most reckless commitments that any country has ever entered into. They are demented pledges that cannot be redeemed with this enormous deficiency, this great gap between the forces arrayed on the other side and the forces which, at the present moment, we could put in.[36]

Lloyd George remained in close contact with his friend Ivan Maisky, the Soviet Ambassador[37] who was not surprised to hear that the Cabinet did not really want to negotiate a military alliance.

The Molotov-Ribbentrop Pact (26 August 1939) came as no surprise to Lloyd George. He blamed Chamberlain for failing to answer Hitler's enterprise in sending Ribbentrop to Moscow by countering with a 'third-class clerk',[38] Mr Strang of the Foreign Office. This was only too valid a comment. We had got what we deserved, but the Poles paid the price. 'Is incompetence to be accepted as a valid excuse?', Lloyd George demanded. When Hitler followed the collapse of Poland by suggesting peace terms, Lloyd George disastrously misread the opinion of the House by hoping that Hitler should be given a hearing. He was shot down so decisively that Chamberlain smugly noted 'that he got a proper ticking off in the House'.[39] Meanwhile Lloyd George colluded with Maisky, who tried hard to defend his country's pact with the Germans.

Revenge came soon. Disasters climaxed in the catastrophic Norway campaign (April–May 1940), master-minded by Churchill, now First Lord. The parallels with Gallipoli were indisputable and uncomfortable, but an angry House of Commons ignored Churchill's guilt and blamed Chamberlain, who had claimed that 'Hitler has missed the bus'. Harassed and humiliated, 'showing his teeth like a rat in a corner',[40] Chamberlain appealed to his friends in the House in the event of a division, harmless parliamentary jargon but in the context, ill-chosen words. Lloyd George was relaxing in his smoking-room, but Megan and Clement Davies were present when Chamberlain spoke, and knew exactly what to do. They immediately informed Lloyd George, who was predictably outraged by Chamberlain's complacent arrogance, hurried into the House, caught the Speaker's eye and demolished his old enemy, with consummate brutality.[41] Given that this speech lasted a full 20 minutes and was delivered off the cuff, it must count as one of Lloyd George's finest orations – if not perhaps the kindest:

> It is not a question of who are the Prime Minister's friends. It is a far bigger issue. He has appealed for sacrifice. The nation is prepared for every sacrifice provided that it has leadership. I say solemnly that the Prime Minister should give an example of sacrifice, because there is nothing which can contribute more to victory than that he should sacrifice the seals of office.[42]

Immediately after this speech had been delivered, the House did indeed divide: For the Government, 281; Against, 200. The Government's immense majority had almost disappeared. Chamberlain was devastated and resigned two days later.

He was succeeded eventually by Churchill. The King and the Conservative Party would have preferred Halifax and even Lloyd George was not without his supporters, so unpopular was Churchill, but Labour strongly preferred Churchill while a Premier in the Lords was unthinkable. Lloyd George expected his old friend to give him a seat in the Cabinet, but the offer came with the express permission of Chamberlain who remained leader of the Conservative Party. Lloyd George refused promotion if it came by kind permission of his old enemy who, as Churchill explained to Lloyd George, continued to show him total loyalty. The only other promotion which was tentatively offered to Lloyd George was the Washington embassy after his friend Lord Lothian died in office, but Lord Dawson queried Lloyd George's physical fitness, so Churchill happily dumped Halifax on the Americans. Lloyd George now languished at Churt, seldom coming up to London where he was terrified of being bombed. When asked why he was not in Churchill's government, his favourite retort was, 'I'm not going in with that lot', or he would announce his determination to stay out 'until Winston is bust'.[43] Unfortunately, he made a disastrous speech in the Commons indicating that he expected this to happen soon, prompting Churchill to reply devastatingly that 'his old friend the member for Caernarfon Boroughs sounded like Marshal Petain'. Lloyd George was deeply hurt, frequently referring to himself as 'Papa Petain'.[44]

Friends visiting Lloyd George at Churt found him listening to Lord Haw-Haw as well as the BBC, or skulking in a huge air-raid shelter which he had had constructed. After Maggie's death, he bought a farm near Llanystumdwy to which he and Frances eventually retired. He hated leaving Churt with its gardens and vegetable patches, to say nothing of his marvellous library now illuminated by a vast window giving a panoramic view of the West-Surrey heaths, but he became progressively weaker. Though his doctors and Frances kept the truth from him, he guessed that he was dying and so returned to the scene of his boyhood. Sylvester's attempts to persuade the local Conservative and Labour establishments to give Lloyd George a clear run at the imminent general election failed. So he accepted a peerage from his old friend, Winston, vainly believing that he would be able to influence the peace treaties from the Lords.

Lloyd George did not have a good war. While he did not live to see either VE or VJ day, he could not be blamed for failing to anticipate Hitler's invasion of Russia (22 June 1941) or the Japanese attack on Pearl Harbor (8 December 1941) which brought in America. So his pessimism ('I just do not see how Winston can defeat the Dictators') was not unreasonable. Still, he cut a poor figure cowering in his air-raid shelter at Churt or listening to Lord Haw-Haw. While wrongly predicting Churchill's fall, he came dangerously close actually to relishing the prospect. His great moment would then have arrived when he would negotiate peace terms with his Teutonic friends. He also failed to anticipate Churchill's humiliation by the British people in the general election of July 1945 which he would have enjoyed. His last vote in the Commons was in support of the Beveridge Report – which Churchill ignored. Lloyd George's final decade was depressing, culminating in his unnecessary departure to the bottom of the garden – the House of Lords. Widowhood and remarriage did not rescue a sad story: he became progressively more self-pitying and cantankerous.

There are a number of unpublished letters from Sylvester to his wife in the National Library of Wales in which he grumbles about his 'Chief'. On 23 October 1939, the date of an important speech by Lloyd George, Sylvester complains that after he had gone to bed TIRED OUT, Lloyd George summoned him 'though he had been told that I was in bed. I was dragged up there, what for? Merely to telephone round the constituency to find out reactions – in other words get further adulation for the old peacock'. On 22 November 1939:

This morning he 'phoned me again early at home. I would prefer that he would leave me alone. He is a very, very, very unhappy man, feeling all alone, and his very soul is cankered with jealousy and animus because 'they' have got the job of running this war and he is out of it. If he had been in it, there would never have been such a government. Sour grapes.

Sylvester complained: 'It is not the work … it is the man who is so difficult.' Even Frances agreed that, whereas her man had previously been the life and soul of any party that he joined, now his arrival brought dissension and bitterness. He frequently quarrelled with his family; they could not stand him and he could not stand them. It was a pity that he did not die in May 1940 after demolishing 'plain Mr Chamberlain'.[45]

Travis Crosby defends Lloyd George against the accusation of defeatism.[46] But Andrew Roberts, in his analysis of RUSHA, Colonel Walter Schellenberg's list of people to be locked up, writes, 'To their shame, George Bernard Shaw and David Lloyd George were absent from the list because of the public statements they had made in favour of peace after the war had started'.[47] This sounds dangerously like defeatism: in other words, there's no fool like an old fool.

Conclusion

ON 26 MARCH 1945, David Lloyd George, aka Earl Lloyd George of Dwyfor and Viscount Gwynedd, died from cancer of the bowel at his newly acquired farmhouse, Ty Newydd on the Criccieth side of Llanystumdwy. The little old man on the bed was now an emaciated skeleton, having lost much of his hair and speaking with difficulty through ill-fitting false teeth. 'Who is coming today?', he asked Frances every morning. He still wanted to be the centre of attention, and would bawl 'Hello' if he was unattended.[1] There was no senility. As he lay dying, the two women whom he loved most held his hands, Frances his wife and Megan his youngest daughter. Megan observed a temporary truce for her father's sake, though normal hostilities were resumed after the old man's death. Olwyn Carey-Evans and Jennifer, his probable daughter, were also in at the death, while A. J. Sylvester, Sarah Jones and Ann Parry, representing the paid hands, stood behind the bed. Brother William was too upset and remained downstairs. Frances gave him one of his brother's walking sticks so that he could get home safely. Four days later, Lloyd George's body was conveyed on a farmer's cart driven by his old friend Robert Evans, to be buried beneath a great boulder overlooking the Dwyfor, whose music had so often brought him rest. Hundreds of mourners lined the hills, singing the dead man's favourite hymns. The burial service was conducted by the Anglican Rector and two Nonconformist ministers.

Lloyd George's reputation would have benefited if he had bowed out in the immediate aftermath of his demolition of Chamberlain. However, as we have seen, his tragic defeatism caused him to enjoy the broadcasts of the deplorable Lord Haw-Haw: 'I like to hear both sides of an argument'.[2] Perhaps he still felt admiration for all things German. In the meantime, he had failed to attend the deathbed of his long-suffering wife and had alienated his children by doing the right thing for once and marrying his mistress, Frances. Not even the tolerant Gwylym and Olwyn welcomed the new Mrs Lloyd George, while Megan was never reconciled. She had a heart of cement.

Could Lloyd George console himself by looking back on a positive and creditable 'life in politics'? Most spectacular – and most controversial – was his leadership of Britain during World War I. However, too much blood flowed, especially when he was Premier. Granted, the story of Passchendaele should be suitably nuanced, but the actual cost in human terms cannot be ignored. Lloyd George's notable achievements cannot be denied where the peace treaties are concerned; the League was created; Ireland was pacified; and the Welfare State – or at least the Contributary State – was extended. His massive input has been acknowledged in this biography: Old Age Pensions, National Insurance, reforms in the countryside and so forth. He was a giant in the story of justice for the downtrodden He had indeed devoted his career to their advancement. Yet, he wrecked the Liberal Party – on his own admission.[3] This was partly, though not entirely, a matter of personalities. Lloyd George betrayed his leader, H. H. Asquith. He quarrelled with Sir Edward Grey, Sir John Simon, Sir Herbert Samuel[4] and with many others. It was always somebody else's fault. He could never understand what a massive bone of contention his notorious fund had become by the mid-1920s, when parliamentary candidates were desperately in need of financial support. Episodes such as the ejection of Asquith (December 1916), the Maurice debate (May 1918) and the Coupon Election (December 1918) found Lloyd George at odds with the majority of senior Liberal leaders. This last event was the moment of truth. Should he have made it up with Asquith, proffering cash in hand, or continue his love affair with the Tories, dazzled by the continuation of power, more conferences, more guaranteed office cushioned by the hundreds of MPs who had accepted the coupon? Lloyd George forgot that, in a democracy, a leader must have a party: so when the Tories had had enough of him, they dumped him – despite frenetic activity by the Welsh Wizard, there was no way back. A brilliantly successful visit to the United States and Canada flagged up his claims to be a world statesman, but his multicoloured books, star-studded weekend conferences, impassioned speeches, all led nowhere in national politics – except to a disappointing 1929 general election.[5] The Liberals were finished, and it was largely his fault.

Lloyd George's 'life in politics' became a lingering death. Those who admired or loved him watched with grief as their hero was clinically smothered by Macdonald, Baldwin and Neville Chamberlain. His friends and allies – Frances Stevenson, A. J. Sylvester and his son Major Richard, the shell-shocked alcoholic – had little respect or affection for each other, but agreed that Lloyd George let himself and the country down by preferring the pursuit of women to the pursuit of politics. Sylvester in particular continued to admire Lloyd George while despising his lust, his vanity and his selfishness. The contrast with Churchill is irresistible. Churchill's interest in women was limited to his wife, amusement that his mother had changed her stockings around while 'visiting' and jokes about the name 'Bossom' – 'Who is this man whose name means neither one thing nor the other?'[6] Yet politics remained his priority. Perhaps the ten-year gap between the two made all the difference. Lloyd George, weary and exhausted, made himself comfortable in the Surrey uplands, cutting himself off from Wales and Liberalism. When duty called, he was too old, too out of touch to respond effectively.

Indeed, the story of Lloyd George's last days is sombre. He returned to Llanystudwy mortally ill, to die among his own people, but they did not want his new wife, who fell victim to Megan's poisonous campaign of hatred and jealousy. Lloyd George hankered after the house and farm which he had created at Churt in South West Surrey, but his estate there, which resembled the comfortable escapism condemned in the Queen's Hall speech of September 1914, was really no substitute for life in politics, his true interest. 'Gratefully accept', his telegram to Winston Churchill, was sincerely meant: for his earldom held out the possibility of influencing the peace when Germany surrendered. The allegation that Frances dragooned her husband into making her a countess is untrue and unfair – 'Mrs Lloyd George is good enough for me' was her frank comment. Lloyd George's decision was clearly self-centred. His admirers, especially in Wales, were shocked and disappointed.

David Lloyd George was a great little man for the first 60 years of his life in politics.[7] Nor should his leadership of the Liberal Party between the Carlton Club revolt (1922) and the Doctor's Mandate

(1931) be despised. As Lord Morgan observes in his analysis of Liberal leaders, he was indeed 'the best and the worst of them all'.[8] He continued to dominate politics, much feared by the second-raters in Downing Street, but Lloyd George's decline after the appeasers took over was not purely due to his prostate operation. His 'edge' – apart from the few occasions when he savaged Neville Chamberlain and his colleagues – disappeared. Then he befriended Hitler: there is a terrible photograph of the Fuehrer welcoming Lloyd George while Cornwell-Evans doffs his hat and von Ribbentrop smirks in the background ('It beats me how he ever sold champagne never mind the Third Reich', remarked a fellow war criminal). What a contrast with the photograph of the confrontation between Lloyd George and Haig, the cavalry general!

Was this the end of Lloyd George's integrity? Does 'scoundrel' describe our man now, as opposed to 'statesman'? Was he now revealed as the grubby little adventurer who flogged peerages, chased girls and hero-worshipped Hitler? In other words, was Taffy the Welshman now cut down to size, soon to crawl back to Llanystudwy with his ex-mistress and his tinselly earldom? Or was there perhaps a residual loyalty to the Christianity which Uncle Lloyd personified? 'The sign of the Cross', Lloyd George kept repeating as he lay dying. 'Have you been to chapel today, doctor?', he asked his GP.[9] One afternoon towards the end, when Frances thought that he was asleep, Lloyd George opened his eyes and said, 'Play "Who will lead me to the strong city?"'[10] This was a hymn which Frances had often performed for him in times of stress. The last verse begins: 'Christ will lead me to the strong city', as Frances reminded him shortly before the end. Or maybe, like Herman Goering, Lloyd George preferred to take his chance in the next world.[11] As ever, he is elusive.

It would, however, be a shame to end this account of such a great life in politics on a negative note. The most fitting and perceptive eulogy was paid to Lloyd George in the House of Commons by his old colleague, Winston Churchill. Members agreed that it was the best tribute since Churchill had said 'farewell' to Neville Chamberlain, four years before – irony indeed. Now he praised his friend: 'He was the greatest Welshman which that unconquerable race has produced since the age of the Tudors.'[12] Another remarkable Welshman, Aneurin Bevan agreed: 'We have lost our most distinguished member and Wales her greatest son.'[13] We too should salute the most creative politician of the twentieth century. He surely did have integrity – as a Welshman, as a Nonconformist, as a bonnie fighter for little people like himself. As prime minister and international statesman, he never tried to enter the magic circle of the social, intellectual establishment, unlike Asquith, for example. He remained the plebeian, Welsh outsider; all the more reason why he could be proud of his courageous and productive life in politics. Yes, he had faults, but they were outweighed by achievements. Olwen spoke for us all when she thanked her father as she collected her pension, for we are all in his debt.

Chronology

1863 Born in Chorlton-upon-Medlock, Manchester, 17 January
1864 Moved in with Uncle Lloyd at Highgate, Llanystumdwy
1884 Qualified as a solicitor
1888 Married Margaret Owen. Llanfrothen Burial Case
1890 Won by-election for Caernarfon Boroughs by 18 votes
1895 Blamed for the fall of Rosebery's Liberal Government
1896 Shouted down at Newport
1899 Opposed the Boer War
1901 Almost lynched in Birmingham
1902 Led campaign against Balfour's Education Act
1905 President of the Board of Trade
1907 Death of Mair Eluned, 30 November
1908 Chancellor of the Exchequer
1909 The People's Budget; speeches at Limehouse and Newcastle
1910 Conference on the House of Lords; plans for coalition
1911 National Insurance; Mansion House speech; enter Frances Stevenson
1912 Marconi Scandal
1913 Land reforms advocated
1914 Effective campaign to prevent financial panic
1915 Minister of Munitions
1916 June: Secretary of State for War; Prime Minister, 7 December
1917 Nivelle offensive; convoys introduced; Passchendaele
1918 The Maurice Debate; Armistice; the Coupon Election
1919 The Fontainebleau memorandum; the Paris Peace Conference
1920 Civil war in Ireland; the Irish Treaty, 5 December
1922 Honours scandal; Chanak crisis; Carlton Club vote; resignation; Genoa
     conference; Germany and Russia agree at Rapallo
1923 Visit to the United States and Canada
1924–1929 Publication of multicoloured 'Books', including 'Employment'
1926 General Strike; Asquith replaced by Lloyd George as Leader

1929   Liberals secure only 59 seats
1931   Prostate operation; excluded from National Government
1934   *War Memoirs* of David Lloyd George, Odhams
1935   Council of Action for Peace and Reconstruction
1936   Visits Hitler at Berchtesgaden, September
1938   Golden wedding celebration at Cannes, January;
         The Truth about the Peace Treaties, Odhams
1940   Demolishes Neville Chamberlain in Norway Debate, 8 May
1941   Death of Maggie, January; attacks Churchill, May
1943   Married Frances Stevenson, 23 October 1943
1945   Earl Lloyd-George of Dwyfor died at Ty Newydd, 26 March

Notes

Foreword

1 Cited in Robert Blake and William Roger Louis (eds), *Churchill: A Major New Assessment of his Life in Peace and War* (Oxford, 2002), p. 6.
2 *House of Commons Debates*, 5th Series, Vol. 409 (28 March 1945), cc. 1385–86.
3 There is an admirable survey, written from the (now dated) vantage point of the early 1970s, in Kenneth O. Morgan, 'Lloyd George and the historians', Transactions of the *Honourable Society of Cymmrodorion* 1972, pp. 65–85, based on a lecture to the society at the House of Commons on 22 February 1972.
4 J. M. Keynes, *Essays in Biography* (London, 1951), p. 35.
5 The phrase is that used in Morgan, 'Lloyd George and the historians', p. 71. J. Graham Jones, *Lloyd George Papers at the National Library of Wales and Other Repositories* (Aberystwyth, 2001). This booklet contains (pp. 81–4) a list of the most important scholarly monographs on Lloyd George available at that time, but it is now inevitably a little dated.

Introduction

1 Ivor Nicholson and Watson, *Lord Riddell's War Diaries 1914–1918* (London, 1933), p. 32.
2 Frances Lloyd George, *The Autobiography of Frances Lloyd George* (London, 1967), p. 74.
3 Hence the title of the collected speeches of David Lloyd George, *From Terror to Triumph*, arranged by F. L. Stevenson, B. A. (London, 1915).
4 John Grigg, *From Peace to War* (London, 1997), pp. 164–7.
5 Ibid., pp. 169–71.
6 Ibid., pp. 171–2.
7 Cf. Robert Graves, *Goodbye to All That* which is quoted in Chapter 6.

8   Quoted in Ben Novick, *Conceiving Revolution: Irish Nationalist Propaganda and the First World War* (Dublin, 2001), p. 218.

9   Ananias, Acts 5.

10 Quoted in William H. Janeway, *Doing Capitalism in the Innovation Economy: Markets, Speculation and the State* (Cambridge, 2012), pp. 240–1.

11 Quoted in Roy Hattersley, *David Lloyd George: The Great Outsider* (London, 2010), page number unknown.

12 Cf. Donald McCormick, *The Mask of Merlin* (London, 1963), pp. 313–14.

13 Earl Lloyd George, *My Father Lloyd George* (London, 1963), p. 58.

14 Lord Morgan refers to Lloyd George's 'disastrous visit to Hitler', *British Liberal Leaders* (London, 2015), p. 250.

15 Quoted in Hugh Purcell, *Lloyd George* (London, 2006), p. 4.

16 Lloyd George, Diary, 10 October 1878.

17 A fellow Welshman the Very Rev. F. Llwellyn Hughes, Dean of Ripon 1951–1967, once told me how he had chaired a meeting addressed by Lloyd George who told a story about a Welsh Baptist preacher he knew who was buried in an Anglican graveyard and who at the last trump emerged from the grave shouting: 'Give me ELBOW-ROOM!' 'What a splendid anecdote', I remarked. 'Yes', replied the Dean. 'I told it to LG on our way to the meeting.' On Lloyd George's lack of integrity, cf. B. B. Gilbert, *David Lloyd George* (Ohio, 1987), pp. 12–19.

18 For Beaverbrook's assertion that Lloyd George 'was more fun', cf. Chris Wrigley, *Lloyd George* (Chichester, 1992), p. 152.

Chapter 1: The Rise of the Cottage-Bred Man (1863–1890)

1   Peter Rowland, *David Lloyd George: A Biography* (London, 1975), p. 71.

2   'This particular trait was not so far as I observed transmitted in an undiluted state to his son Dafydd' – W. George, *My Brother and I* (London, 1958), p. 7.

3   For instance, this is certainly the view of William's grand-daughter Anita, conveyed to the author over the telephone (21 January 2012).

4   John Grigg, *Lloyd George: The Young Lloyd George* (London, 1989), pp. 26–9.

5   W. George, *My Brother and I*, p. 33.

6   For example, there was a door at 10 Downing Street which Lloyd George never learnt to open. He invariably turned the handle the wrong way and had to shout so as to be 'rescued'. Ffion Hague, *The Pain and the Privilege: The Women in Lloyd George's Life* (London, 2009).

7   Luke, XV, 25–32.

8   The Liberal government dispatched General Sir Garnet Wolseley to win the battle of Tel-el-Kebir against Arabi who was captured, chucked into a swimming-pool and exiled to Ceylon.

9   Bismarck was 'found' as a puppy on a Hamburg quay by Lloyd George's friend John Williams who exported slates from Portmadoc.

10 Emyr Price, *David Lloyd George* (Cardiff, 2006), implies that the young Lloyd George had a drink problem, p. 25.

11 A. J. Sylvester, Diary, June 1931.

12 Earl Lloyd George, *My Father, Lloyd George* (London, 1960), p. 32. See also Grigg, *The Young Lloyd George*, p. 73 for Lloyd George's complaint about rain in Criccieth.

13 Dom G. Civgiei, *Bounder from Wales* (Missouri, 1976) suggests that Welsh Nonconformists were not as judgemental or as puritanical as English, p. 13.

14 J. Graham Jones, *David Lloyd George and Welsh Liberalism* (Cardiff, 2010), p. 31.

15 Earl Lloyd George, *My Father, Lloyd George*, p. 52.

16 Kenneth Morgan (ed.), *Lloyd George Family Letters, 1885–1936* (Cardiff, 1973), p. 14. Ibid. p. 19. Cf. Emyr Price, *David Lloyd George* (Cardiff, 2006) and letter to the author from Kenneth Morgan, 1 January 2014.

17 Quoted by B. B. Gilbert, *David Lloyd George* (Ohio, 1987).

18 Lloyd George's attack on the curate is described by Grigg, *The Young Lloyd George*, p. 50.

19 André Bernard and Clifton Fadiman, *Bartlett's Book of Anecdotes* (London, 2012) page number unknown.

20 H. du Parcq *The Life of David Lloyd George* (London, 1912), p. 167.

21 Earl Lloyd George, *My Father, Lloyd George*, p. 53

22 Quoted by Grigg, *The Young Lloyd George*, p. 47.

23 Roy Hattersley, *David Lloyd George: The Great Outsider* (London, 2010), pp. 33–5.

24 Morgan, *Lloyd George Family Letters*, pp. 18–19.

25 Ibid., p. 20 for Lloyd George's opinion that 'a farmer's wife is only a portion of his stock'.

26 Hattersley, *David Lloyd George*, p. 50.

27 John Grigg: *The Young Lloyd George* (London, 1989), pp. 164–7 and Frances Stevenson, *Lloyd George: A Diary* (London, 1971), p. 188.

28 Lloyd George's alleged trimming tactics are highlighted by Emyr Price, *David Lloyd George* (Cardiff, 2006), pp. 55–64.

29 Grigg, *The Young Lloyd George*, p. 84.

Chapter 2: An Unusual Backbencher (1890–1905)

1   Roy Hattersley, *David Lloyd George: The Great Outsider* (London, 2010).

2   Kenneth O. Morgan (ed.), *Lloyd George Family Letters 1885–1936* (Cardiff, 1973), p. 29.

3   Lloyd George Papers, House of Lords Archives, A/6, 31 October 1890, Liberal Party meeting at Leigh.

4   Peter Rowland, *David Lloyd George* (London, 1975), p. 100.
5   W. R. P. George, *Lloyd George Backbencher* (Llandysul, 1983), p. 94.
6   DLG to Maggie, 27 May 1897, National Library of Wales.
7   DLG to Maggie, 21 August 1897, National Library of Wales.
8   Morgan, *Lloyd George Family Letters*, p. 59. See W. R. P. George, *Lloyd George Backbencher* pp. 207–37 for a defence of Lloyd George's record as a husband.
9   Cf. Ffion Hague, *The Pain and the Privilege* (London, 2008), pp. 111–34, for a more judicious treatment of Lloyd George's alleged infidelities.
10 Earl Lloyd George, *My Father, Lloyd George* (London, 1962), p. 53.
11 Morgan, *Lloyd George Family Letters*, p. 28.
12 Ibid., p. 51.
13 W. R. P. George, *Lloyd George Backbencher*, p. 331.
14 Ibid., p. 299 and p. 343. See also Donald McCormick, *The Mask of Merlin* (London, 1963), p. 54, for P. C. Stonier's reminiscences.
15 Frank Owen, *Tempestuous Journey* (London, 1954), p. 105.
16 John Grigg, *Lloyd George: The People's Champion, 1902–1911* (London, 1978), p. 49.
17 Lloyd George's sympathy with the victim was always an attractive trait.
18 Why single out P. C. Stonier when many others came into contact with Lloyd George? They did not all swap clothes with him.
19 Lloyd George was always touchy over accusations of responsibility for bloodshed.
20 Grigg, *The People's Champion*, p. 49.
21 Cf. Winston S. Churchill, *Great Contemporaries* (London, 1947), p. 191 on Balfour.
22 Gorst was malicious and irresponsible, but great fun.
23 After three British battle-cruisers blew up in the space of half an hour, Admiral Beatty remarked to his flag-captain: 'Chatfield, there seems to be something wrong with our fucking ships today.' And there continued to be something wrong, as 2,000 men on HMS *Hood* discovered on 24 May 1941. The general theme of Britain's educational backwardness in science and technology – hence the collapse of our car industry, ICI, precision instruments, etc. – has been developed in several publications by Correlli Barnett in particular. When he pleaded for greater emphasis on science teaching in independent schools at the Headmasters' Conference of September 1986 he was greeted with stony, hostile silence, while David Newsome, the Master of Wellington and author of several books applauding Victorian classics-based education, was rapturously received. 'I wouldn't have believed it if I hadn't witnessed it'.
24 John Grigg, *The People's Champion*, p. 26.
25 Hansard, 4th Series, Vol. 107, pp. 1102, 1104–5, 8 May 1902. The general tone of Lloyd George's contributions is conveyed by this extract

from Hansard. The issue at stake was whether County Authorities should have the right to intervene in non-provided schools (i.e., voluntary schools, many of them the property of the churches). This was Lloyd George's suggestion, but Balfour was worried by the possible consequences. 'Mr Lloyd George (Carnarvon Boroughs) thought that the difficulty was not so great as the Right Honourable Gentleman imagined. No-one suggested that even if the power were to be given to the county authority, that of the Board of Education would be abrogated' (Education Bill, England and Wales, House of Commons Debate 24 October 1902, vol 113 cc. 78–88). Lloyd George's taunt is quoted by Du Parcq, *The Life of David Lloyd George*, p. 333. Lloyd George at Lincoln, 12 December 1902, quoted by Peter Rowland, *David Lloyd George: A Biography* (London, 1975), p. 168.

26 Lloyd George at Lincoln, December 12 1902, quoted by Peter Rowland, *David Lloyd George: A Biography* (London, 1975), p. 168.

27 Quoted by Roy Hattersley, *David Lloyd George: The Great Outsider* (London, 2010), page unknown.

28 Quoted by Grigg, *The People's Champion*, p. 35 and Du Parcq, *The Life of David Lloyd George*, pp. 411–12.

29 D. H. Elletson, *The Chamberlains* (Birmingham, 1966).

30 Quoted by Grigg, *The People's Champion* p. 35 and Du Parcq, *The Life of David Lloyd George*, pp. 411–12.

31 Quoted by Grigg, *The People's Champion*, p. 35 and Du Parcq, *The Life of David Lloyd George*, pp. 411–12.

32 Sidney Webb, addressing the Annual Institution of Technical Institutes and Hansard, Fourth Series, Vol. CXV, 3 December 1902.

33 Peter Rowland, *David Lloyd George: A Biography* (London, 1975), p. 168.

34 Owen, *Tempestuous Journey*, p. 134.

35 Quoted by G. Searle, *Country Before Party* (London, 2005), p. 40.

Chapter 3: Cabinet Minister

1 For a sympathetic and convincing portrait of Sir Henry Campbell-Bannerman, consult John Wilson, *CB Sir Henry Campbell-Bannerman* (London, 1973), *passim.*

2 Martin Pugh, *Lloyd George* (London, 1988), p. 30.

3 W. George, *My Brother and I* (London, 1958), p. 90.

4 Quoted by B. B. Gilbert, *David Lloyd George* (Ohio, 1987), p. 299.

5 Roy Hattersley, *David Lloyd George: The Great Outsider* (London, 2010), page number unknown.

6 Quoted by Peter Rowland, *David Lloyd George: A Biography* (London, 1975), p. 192.

7 Ibid., p. 189.

8   A brave speech considering the prejudices of his audience.

9   Peter Rowland, *David Lloyd George*, p. 193; H. Du Parcq, *The Life of David Lloyd George* (London, 1912), p. 501.

10   Earl Lloyd George, *My Father, Lloyd George* (London, 1961), p. 89.

11   National Library of Wales, 22521E 62, 2 June 1907.

12   Kenneth O. Morgan, *The Age of Lloyd George: The Liberal Party and British Politics, 1890–1929* (London, 1971), p. 144.

13   Donald McCormick, *The Mask of Merlin* (London, 1963), p. 58.

14   G. R. Searle, *The Quest for National Efficiency* (California, 1971), pp. 69–70 and Du Parcq, *The Life of David Lloyd George*, p. 483.

15   John Grigg, *Lloyd George: The People's Champion, 1902–1911* (London, 1978), pp. 112–19.

16   Rowland, *David Lloyd George*, p. 195.

17   John W. Wheeler-Bennett, *Hindenburg: The Wooden Titan* (London, 1967), p. 17.

18   George, *My Brother and I*, pp. 214–19.

19   Frances Stevenson, *The Years That Are Past* (London, 1967), p. 49.

20   B. B. Gilbert, *David Lloyd George* (Ohio, 1987), p. 322.

21   Quoted by J. Graham Jones, *David Lloyd George and Welsh Liberalism* (Cardiff, 2010), p. 118.

22   Rowland, *David Lloyd George*, p. 200.

23   Grigg, *The People's Champion* (New York, 1978), p. 134.

Chapter 4: The Political Chancellor

1   Hansard, 4th Series, Vol. 191, 29 June 1908, p. 395.

2   Lucy Masterman, *C. F. G. Masterman: A Biography* (London, 1939), p. 150.

3   Charles Booth, *Life and Labour of the People in London* (https://booth.lse.ac.uk/).

4   B. Seebohm Rowntree, *Poverty: A Study of Town Life* (London, 1908).

5   Hansard, Vol. CXCI cols 395–6.

6   Quoted in M. Pugh, *Lloyd George* (London, 1988), p. 44.

7   Bruce K. Murray, *The People's Budget, 1909–10: Lloyd George and Liberal Politics* (Oxford, 1980).

8   Murray, *The People's Budget*.

9   Peter Rowland, *David Lloyd George* (London, 1975), p. 221.

10   NLW manuscript 215, Margot Asquith to Lloyd George.

11   NLW 45 MS letter from J. E. C. Bodley to Lloyd George, 21 July 1909.

12   John Grigg, *Lloyd George: The People's Champion* (London, 1978), pp. 222–9.

13   G. R. Searle, *Country Before Party* (London, 2005), pp. 70–6.

14 Roy Hattersley, *David Lloyd George: The Great Outsider* (London, 2010), p. 287.

15 Grigg, *The People's Champion* (London, 1978), p. 278.

16 Hattersley, *David Lloyd George*, pp. 296–300 for additional comments.

17 The protests of upper class women and their servants, B. B. Gilbert, *David Lloyd George* (Ohio 1987), pp. 444–6.

18 Frances Lloyd George. *The Years That Are Past*. (London, 1967), p. 42.

19 Cf. for example, *Makers of the New World by One Who Knows Them* (London, 1921).

20 Quoted in: David Gilmour, *The Long Recessional: The Imperial Life of Rudyard Kipling* (London, 2003).

21 See J. Graham Jones, *David Lloyd George and Welsh Liberalism* (Cardiff, 2010), pp. 142–57 for a helpful account of the Llanystumdwy affair.

22 Melanie Phillips, *The Ascent of Woman* (London, 2004) is a demolition of the Pankhursts.

23 Quoted in J. Graham Jones, 'Lloyd George and the Suffragettes', *The National Library of Wales Journal* 33/1 (Aberystwyth, 2003), p. 24.

24 J. Graham Jones has written an unpublished summary of Lloyd George's relationship with the Suffragettes. A thought-provoking comparison could be made of the Llanystumdwy atrocity with the sack of Bolton by Prince Rupert (28 May 1644): the same dispute over the numbers of victims, the same allegation of civilians being abused, women being sexually assaulted, the same lack of satisfactory evidence, the same lack of remorse by the authorities who should perhaps have exercised more control.

25 Cf. Roy Douglas, *The History of the Liberal Party, 1895–1970* (London, 1971) and Ian Packer, *Lloyd George, Liberalism and the Land* (Woodbridge, 2001).

26 See Travis Crosby, *The Unknown Lloyd George* (London, 2014), pp. 145–9 for Lloyd George's land campaign, especially his two speeches at Bedford. Cf. also R. Douglas, *Land, People and Politics* (Allison and Busby, 1976); and J. Loades (ed.), *The Life and Times of David Lloyd George*, article by L. Packer 'Lloyd George and the Liberal Land Campaign, 1991'. Grigg, *The People's Champion*, pp. 352–61, provides an excellent discussion of Lloyd George's achievements up to the end of 1911, though some might consider him too sympathetic.

27 Sir Frederick Maurice, *Haldane 1856–1915* (Westport, CT, 1970), p. 168.

28 A. J. P. Taylor (ed.), *Lloyd George, Twelve Essays* (London, 1971), p. v.

29 Derek Fraser, *The Evolution of the British Welfare State* (Basingstoke, 2002), pp. 195–205.

30 Grigg, *The People's Champion* (London, 1978), pp. 352–61, provides an excellent discussion of Lloyd George's achievements up to the end of 1911, though some might consider him too sympathetic.

Chapter 5: The Improbable Warlord

1   Quoted in David Lloyd George, *The Great Crusade: Extracts from Speeches Delivered During the War* (London, 1918), pp. 31–2.

2   Lord Riddell, *More Pages from My Diary, 1908–1914* (Farnborough, Hants, 1934), pp. 21–2 for 'the jackboot'.

3   See John Grigg, *Lloyd George: The People's Champion* (London, 1978), p. 308 for Mansion House speech.

4   Lloyd George's motives were complex, including his concern for the security of France.

5   David Lloyd George, *War Memoirs* (London, 1938), pp. 56–8.

6   Quoted in Keith Wilson (ed.), *Decisions for War, 1914* (London, 2004), Chapter 7.

7   W. George, *My Brother and I* (London, 1958), pp. 237–9.

8   Margaret Macmillan, *The War That Ended Peace* (London, 2014).

9   See Professor Emeritus John C. G. Röhl, https://johnblakey.wordpress.com/page/20/.

10 Quoted by Roy Hattersley, *David Lloyd George: The Great Outsider* (London, 2010), page number unknown.

11 Lord Riddell, *Lord Riddell's War Diaries* (London, 1933), p. 6.

12 Allan Mallinson, *1914: Fight the Good Fight: Britain, the Army and the Coming of the First World War* (New York, 2013), page number unknown.

13 Max Hastings, *Catastrophe* (London, 2013), pp. 39–40.

14 Walter Reid, *Arras, 1917: The Journey to Railway Triangle* (Edinburgh, 2003), page number unknown.

15 Travis Crosby, *The Unknown Lloyd George* (London, 2014), p. 195.

16 Robert Graves, *Goodbye to All That* (London, 1928), p. 168. Cf. also Richard Toye's article 'Lloyd George's War Rhetoric, 1914–1918' in the *Journal of Liberal History*, Issue 77.

17 Hastings, *Catastrophe*, p. 518.

18 J. M. Bourne, *Who's Who in World War I* (London, 2002), p. 268.

19 Quoted by Michael Senior, *Victory on the Western Front: The Development of the British Army 1914–1918* (Barnsley, 2016), p. 128.

20 Quoted in, Maggie Craig, *When the Clyde Ran Red* (Edinburgh, 2011).

21 Quoted in, F. L. Carsten, *War against War: British and German Radical Movements in the First World War* (Berkeley, CA, 1992), p. 61.

22 For Ireland, see Grigg, *The People's Champion* (London, 1978), pp. 342–9.

23 There is an excellent film, *War Women of Britain*, published by the Imperial War Museum, which shows women making shells. Grigg, *The People's Champion*, pp. 294–5 (12).

24 Grigg, *The People's Champion*, p. 350.

25 Lloyd George, *War Memoirs*, p. 323 re. photograph. Cf. *Lloyd George* (London, 1988), p. 93.

26 Richard Wilkinson, *History Review*, September 2008, pp. 31–6 on Lloyd George and the Generals. Lloyd George's speech to his constituents is quoted by Chris Wrigley, *Lloyd George*, (Oxford, 1992), pp. 74–5.

27 Grigg, *The People's Champion*, p. 390.

28 Ibid., pp. 384–5.

29 Clayton Roberts, David F. Roberts and Douglas Bisson, *A History of England, Volume 2: 1688 to the Present* (London, 2016), p. 433.

30 http://www.stboswells.bordernet.co.uk/history/haigs.html.

31 Richard Wilkinson, *History Review* Issue 61, September 2008.

32 Grigg, *The People's Champion*, pp. 404–6.

33 Frances Stevenson, *Lloyd George: A Diary*, 7 December 1916 (London, 1971).

34 Wilkinson, *History Review* Issue 61, September 2008.

35 House of Lords Archives, quoted by Grigg, *From Peace to War* (London, 1997), p. 363.

36 Ibid., p. 390.

37 Stevenson, *A Diary*, pp. 92–3.

38 Earl Lloyd George, *My Father, Lloyd George* (London, 1961), pp. 156–7.

39 To be fair, both Dick and Gwilym came under fire in due course.

40 Grigg, *From Peace to War*, p. 404.

41 George H. Cassar, *Lloyd George at War, 1916–1918* (London, 2011), p. 350.

42 Duncan Brack, *British Liberal Leaders* (London, 2015), page number unknown.

43 Graham Goodlad and Robert Pearce, *British Prime Ministers from Balfour to Brown* (London, 2013), p. 36.

44 Kenneth O. Morgan, 'Lloyd George and the Historians', *The Transactions of the Honourable Society of Cymmrodorion, Part 1* (London, 1971), p. 76.

45 Editor, *Spectator*, 3 June 1932, p. 15, http://archive.spectator.co.uk/article/4th-june-1932/15/to-the-editor-of-the-spectator.

46 Quoted in, Geoffrey Lewis, *Carson: The Man Who Divided Ireland* (London, 2006), p. 193.

47 Grigg, *From Peace to War*, p. 462.

48 *History Today*, March 1959, p. 163.

49 Richard Toye, *Lloyd George and Churchill: Rivals for Greatness* (London, 2012), p. 170.

50 Hugh Purcell, *Lloyd George* (London, 2006), p. 49.

51 The letters are published with commentary in J. Graham Jones' valuable essays, *David Lloyd George and Welsh Liberalism* (Cardiff, 2010), pp. 222–31.

52 Cf. Churchill's parliamentary tribute, quoted in Chapter 12 of this work, when he claimed that Lloyd George seized power. An MP interrupted: 'Seized?' 'Seized' insisted Churchill.

53 J. Graham Jones, 'Lloyd George, Asquith and "the conspiracy myth"': some new evidence', *The National Library of Wales Journal* 28/2 (Aberystwyth, 1993), p. 219.

54 George H. Cassar, *Lloyd George at War, 1916–1918* (London, 2011), page number unknown.

55 Andrea Bosco, *The Round Table Movement and the Fall of the 'Second' British Empire (1909–1919)* (Newcastle upon Tyne, 2017), p. 338.

56 Cf. C. Hazlehurst, 'The Conspiracy Myth' in *Martin Gilbert, Lloyd George* (London, 1968).

57 J. Graham Jones, 'Lloyd George, Asquith and "the conspiracy myth"', p. 219.

58 Duncan Brack (ed.), *British Liberal Leaders* (London, 2015), page number unknown.

59 For Lansdowne, cf. Lord Newton, *Lord Lansdowne* (London, 1929), pp. 450–7.

60 Cf. George H. Cassar, *Asquith as War Leader* (London, 1994), pp. 230–1.

Chapter 6: The Passchendaele Butcher

1 A. J. P. Taylor, *English History 1914–1945* (Oxford, 1965), p. 74.

2 John Grigg, *From Peace to War* (London, 1997), pp. 478–80 and Frances Stevenson, *Lloyd George: A Diary* (London, 1971), p. 134.

3 David Edgerton, *Britain's War Machine: Weapons, Resources, and Experts in the Second World War* (Oxford, 2011).

4 Quoted in, Robert Lloyd George, *David & Winston: How the Friendship Between Lloyd George and Churchill Changed the Course of History* (New York, 2008).

5 Quoted in Robert Self, *Neville Chamberlain: A Biography* (London, 2006), p. viii.

6 Roy Maclaren, *Commissions High: Canada in London, 1870–1971* (Montreal, 2006), p. 188.

7 J. A. Turner, 'The Formation of Lloyd George's "Garden Suburb": "Fabian-like Milnerite Penetration"?', *The Historical Journal* 20/1 (1977), pp. 165–84. H. Cassar, *Lloyd George at War, 1916–1918* (London, 2011), pp. 102–9. Cf. Chapter 9 of this work for Lloyd George's self-exculpation. Cf. David French, *The Strategy of the Lloyd George Coalition* (London, 1995), pp. 70–4.

8 David Lloyd George, *War Memoirs* (London, 1938), p. 674.

9 John Terraine, *Business in Great Waters*, pp. 41–4.

10 W. S. Churchill, *World Crisis* (London, 1938), p. 1281.

11 David R. Woodward, *Field Marshal Sir William Robertson: Chief of the Imperial General Staff in the Great War* (Westport, 1998), p. 98.

12 David R. Woodward, *Lloyd George and the Generals* (London, 2004), p. 138.

13 Walter Reid, *Arras, 1917: The Journey to Railway Triangle* (Edinburgh, 2011), page number unknown.

14 Gary Sheffield, *The Chief: Douglas Haig and the British Army* (London, 2011), page number unknown.

15 Quoted in, Anthony Boden, *F.W. Harvey: Soldier, Poet* (Stroud, 2011), page number unknown.

16 Monika Elbert, *Transnational Gothic: Literary and Social Exchanges in the Long Nineteenth Century* (London, 2016), p. 180. Robin Prior and Trevor Wilson, *Passchendaele: The Untold Story; Third Edition* (New Haven, 2006). For a satirical picture of Passchendaele, cf. Chapter 1 of A. G. Macdonell, *England Their England* (London, 1949), fiction of course but the author was an artillery officer there.

17 Robin Prior and Trevor Wilson, *Passchendaele* (New York, 1996), p. 194.

18 Prior and Wilson, *Passchendaele*, p. 194.

19 Keith Jeffery, *Field Marshal Sir Henry Wilson: A Political Soldier* (Oxford, 2006), p. 218.

20 Michael S. Neiberg, *Fighting the Great War* (Cambridge, 2005), pp. 60, 287.

21 Jeffery, *Field Marshal Sir Henry Wilson*, p. 218.

22 Neiberg, *Fighting the Great War*, pp. 60, 287.

23 David R. Woodward, *Lloyd George and the Generals* (London, 2004).

24 Ibid., p. 109.

25 Quoted by David French, *The Strategy of the Lloyd George Coalition, 1916–1918*, p. 287.

26 Churchill, *World Crisis*, p. 1281.

27 Samuel Lyman Atwood Marshall, *World War I* (Boston, 1964), p. 358.

28 Quoted by Peter Stanksy, *Sassoon: The Worlds of Philip and Sybil* (New Haven, 2003), p. 73.

29 Philip Williamson and Edward Baldwin (eds), *Baldwin Papers: A Conservative Statesman, 1908–1947* (Cambridge, 2004), p. 36.

30 Peter Rowland, *David Lloyd George: A Biography*, p. 470 for the Maurice debate.

31 Cassar, *Lloyd George at War*, pp. 323, 342.

32 Alistair McCluskey, *Amiens 1918: The Black Day of the German Army* (Oxford, 2008).

33 John Terraine, *History Today*, August 1958

34 David Lloyd George, *War Memoirs of David Lloyd George: Volume I* (London, 1933).

35 Quoted in, Peter Hart, *1918: A Very British Victory* (London, 2010), page number.

36 Haig was disgusted by Wilson's admonition not to boast without factual back-up. Haig was widely admired by the general public, possibly because of press coverage. Brian Bond admitted in a letter which he wrote to me about Haig on 16 October 2007: 'I incline to agree with

you that his ceiling may have been an Army Command, but who would
have been better as C. in C?' Cf. Rufus Adams, *David Lloyd George The
Man Who Won the War* (WEA Rhyl, 2008), for a useful summary of
Lloyd George's merits as a warlord and David French, *The Strategy of the
Lloyd George Coalition* (London, 1997), pp. 291–2

37   Lloyd George certainly had his admirers, of whom Hankey was the
most impressive. For Frances Stevenson's loyalty, cf. *The Years that are
Past* (London, 1967), pp. 129–33.

38   George S. Vascik and Mark R. Sadler (eds), *The Stab-in-the-Back Myth
and the Fall of the Weimar Republic: A History in Documents and Visual
Sources* (London, 2016).

39   Quoted in David French, *The Strategy of the Lloyd George Coalition,
1916–1918* (Oxford, 1995), p. 291.

40   Ibid., p. 292.

41   Ibid., p. 289.

42   Quoted in David R. Woodward, *Lloyd George and the Generals* (London,
2003) page number unknown.

43   Walter Reid, *Architect of Victory: Douglas Haig* (Edinburgh, 2011), page
number unknown.

44   For example, Siegfried Sassoon in the poem *The General*.

45   Joan Littlewood, *Oh! What a Lovely War* (1963); Alan Clark, *The Donkeys*
(London, 1963); Richard Curtis and Ben Elton, *Blackadder Goes Forth*
(BBC, 1989).

46   Haig was unfortunately inclined to ignore unwelcome intelligence. Haig
was as capable as Rawlinson, or Plumer, and better than Gough, whose
dismissal he rather heartlessly implemented: 'One of us has to go and
perhaps conceitedly I don't think it should be me'.[37] When Gough was
sacked, he retorted with commendable good humour: 'Good luck, Douglas,
you will have your work cut out.' After Cambrai, as we have seen, Lloyd
George sent Smuts and Hankey round the Western Front to interview
possible replacements for Haig. The most talented was Sir Claud Jacob,
but he was junior in rank to Plumer whom the men trusted – and Plumer
according to Smuts, 'is as stupid as Haig' – so Haig kept his job.

47   Lloyd George was admired perhaps to excess by Du Parcq and Frank
Owen.

48   Adam Tooze, *The Deluge: The Great War and the Remaking of the Global
Order 1916–1931* (London, 2014).

49   Quoted in, Anthony Read, *The Devil's Disciples* (London, 2005), p. 741.

50   Adams, *David Lloyd George The Man Who Won the War*, p. 13. I have
left this quotation in mid air, so to speak, without comment. I am
happy to leave it to my readers to form an opinion. Personally, I am
sceptical about this kind of emotionalism. Would it really have
impressed even Welsh soldiers in the trenches enduring the battle of the

Somme? As an ex-soldier myself, I am doubtful as to the acceptability of this kind of bombast. On the other hand, 'where there is no vision the people perish'. Can one think of any other modern warlord who could have produced this kind of rhetoric – and produced it so well – except Churchill? Perhaps it is relevant to quote the compliment paid to the Nonconformist preacher C. H. Spurgeon: 'Do you believe his message?' 'I don't know, but he does.' See also Harold Macmillan, *The Past Masters* (Macmillan, 1975), pp. 54–60 for Lloyd George's advice to the youthful Macmillan on the art of making a speech.

51 Robert Graves, *Goodbye To All That* (London, 1971), p. 168.

52 The classic example of this principle in action was to be President Harry S. Truman's dismissal of General Douglas MacArthur (11 April 1951).

53 John Bierman and Colin Smith, *Alamein: War Without Hate* (London, 2003).

54 M. S. R. Kinnear, *The Fall of Lloyd George: The Political Crisis of 1922* (New York, 1973), p. 101.

55 Peter Rowland, *David Lloyd George* (London, 1975), p. 470.

56 Quoted in Richard N. Kelly and John Cantrell (eds), *Modern British Statesmen, 1867–1945* (Manchester, 1997), p. 136. The contrast with Churchill's ineptitude in 1945 is striking, when little attempt was made to counter Attlee's offer of a thorough-going welfare state. Churchill memorably blamed the soldiers for voting 'with criminal irresponsibility'. He was furious, mortified and astonished by the outcome. Lloyd George was his master when it came to political footwork.

57 Alan Wilkinson, *The Church of England and the First World War* (Cambridge, 2014).

Chapter 7: The Peacefinder General

1 Letter beginning 'Dear Puss ...' FCF. 2/1 National Library of Wales.

2 Foch was consistently pessimistic.

3 http://news.bbc.co.uk/onthisday/low/dates/stories/july/11/newsid_ 2499000/2499775.stm.

4 V. R. Berghahn, *Modern Germany: Society, Economy, and Politics in the Twentieth Century* (Cambridge, 1982), p. 44.

5 Rüdiger Overmans, 'Kriegsverluste', in Gerhard Hirschfeld, Gerd Krumeich, Irina Renz (eds), *Enzyklopädie Erster Weltkrieg* (Paderborn, 2003), p. 663.

6 Graziella Caselli, Guillaume Wunsch, and Jacques Vallin, *Demography: Analysis and Synthesis, Four Volume Set: A Treatise in Population* (London, 2005), p. 436.

7 Phillips Payson O'Brien, *How the War Was Won: Air-Sea Power and Allied Victory in World War II* (Cambridge, 2015), page number unknown.

8   Philip Ziegler, *Between the Wars: 1919–1939* (London, 2016).

9   Frances Stevenson, *Lloyd George: A Diary* (London, 1971).

10 Handwritten letter dated 4 June 1913, National Library of Wales 22525E.

11 Roy Jenkins, *Asquith* (London, 1919), p. 477. Ibid., p. 279.

12 Frances Stevenson, *Lloyd George: A Diary.*

13 Geoffrey Sherington, *English Education, Social Change, and War, 1911–20* (Manchester, 1981), p. 94.

14 Scott Berg, *Wilson* (New York, 2013).

15 A. Capet (ed.), *Britain, France and the Entente Cordiale Since 1904* (New York, 2006), p. 33.

16 Alexander B. Downes, *Targeting Civilians in War* (Ithaca, 2011), p. 97.

17 J. M. McEwen, 'Northcliffe and Lloyd George at War, 1914–1918', *The Historical Journal*, Vol. 24, No. 3 (Sep., 1981), pp. 651–72.

18 Timothy C. Winegard, *Indigenous Peoples of the British Dominions and the First World War* (Cambridge, 2011), p. 261.

19 W. S. Churchill, *The World Crisis Volume IV: 1918–1928: The Aftermath* (London, 2015).

20 Antony Lentin, *The Last Political Law Lord: Lord Sumner, 1859–1934* (Cambridge, 2009), p. 82.

21 Marshall Dill, *Germany: A Modern History* (Ann Arbor, 1970), p. 272.

22 Note: a milliard is a thousand millions in UK terms, which is a billion in US terms.

23 Stella Rudman, *Lloyd George and the Appeasement of Germany, 1919–1945* (Cambridge, 2011), p. 11.

24 Thomas Garden Barnes, Gerald D. Feldman (eds), *Breakdown and Rebirth, 1914 to the Present: A Documentary History of Modern Europe Volume IV* (Lanham, 1982), p. 42.

25 Adam Tooze, *The Deluge: The Great War and the Remaking of Global Order 1916–1931* (London, 2014), p. 285.

26 Margaret MacMillan, *Peacemakers Six Months that Changed the World* (London, 2011).

27 Adam Tooze, *The Deluge.*

28 Ibid., p. 279.

29 House of Lords records.

30 Riddell, *Intimate Diary 1918–1923* (London, 1933), p. 101.

31 Jon Meacham, *Franklin and Winston: A Portrait of a Friendship* (London, 2016).

32 Alan Sharp, *Journal of Liberal History*, Issue 77, Winter 2012–13, p. 30.

33 John Campbell, *If Love Were All...: The Story of Frances Stevenson and David Lloyd George* (London, 2007), p. 150.

34 Norman Hillson, *I Speak of Germany (RLF Responding to Fascism): A Plea for Anglo-German Friendship* (London, 2010).

35 A. Lentin, *Lloyd George and the Lost Peace: From Versailles to Hitler, 1919–1940* (New York, 2001), p. 21.

36 Patrick J. Buchanan, *Churchill, Hitler, and "The Unnecessary War": How Britain Lost Its Empire and the West Lost the World* (London, 2008), p. 110.

37 The Kaiser was rightly blamed, in that he always favoured naval aggression.

38 Clemenceau was nicknamed 'The Tiger' due to his combative nature. Carl Cavanagh Hodge (ed.), *Encyclopedia of the Age of Imperialism, 1800–1914* (Westport, CT, 2007), p. 153.

39 Roy Douglas, *Between the Wars 1919–1939: The Cartoonists' Vision* (London, 1992), p. 17.

40 John Maynard Keynes, *The Economic Consequences of the Peace* (London, 2010).

41 Alistair Horne, *To Lose a Battle: France 1940* (London, 2007).

42 Edwin A. Weinstein, *Woodrow Wilson: A Medical and Psychological Biography. Supplementary Volume to the Papers of Woodrow Wilson* (Princeton, NJ, 2014), p. 346.

43 Charles Loch Mowat believed that between Lloyd George and Churchill, Britain was led by a succession of political 'pygmies', namely Bonar Law, Baldwin, MacDonald and Neville Chamberlain. Charles Loch Mowat, *Britain Between the Wars* (London, 1972), p. 142.

44 Frank Owen, *Tempestuous Journey: Lloyd George, His Life and Times* (London, 1952).

45 Lloyd George's phrase. Stella Rudman, *Lloyd George and the Appeasement of Germany, 1919–1945* (Cambridge, 2011), p. 65.

46 Lloyd George regarded the U-boats as manned by pirates.

47 Robert Calder, *Beware the British Serpent: The Role of Writers in British Propaganda in the United States, 1939–1945* (Montreal, 2004), p. 103.

48 Count Harry Kessler, *Walter Rathenau: His Life and Work* (Whitefish, Montana, 2010), p. 324.

49 The generally poisonous tone of right-wing proto-Nazi attacks on Rathenau is given by this rhyme which circulated freely in Weimar Germany: 'Knock off Walter Rathenau, the dirty, stinking Jewish sow'.

50 A. J. P. Taylor (ed.), *My Darling Pussy: Letters of Lloyd George and Frances Stevenson* (London, 1975), p. 44.

51 Job 5:7.

52 Lord Hankey, *The Supreme Command, 1914–1918, Volume 2* (London, 2014), p. 578.

53 Margaret MacMillan, *Peacemakers: Six Months that Changed the World* (London, 2011).

54 The Highlands escapade was typical of Lloyd George's selfishness.

55 Howard Grief, *The Legal Foundation and Borders of Israel Under International Law: A Treatise on Jewish Sovereignty Over the Land of Israel* (Jerusalem, 2008), p. 32.

56 Benjamin Rivlin and Joseph S. Szyliowicz, *The Comtemporary Middle East: Tradition and Innovation* (London, 1965), p. 261.

57 Naomi Kramer (ed.), *Civil Courage: A Response to Contemporary Conflict and Prejudice* (Bern, 2007), p. 160.

58 Roy Hatterslay, *David Lloyd George: The Great Outsider* (London, 2010).

59 David Lloyd George, *War Memoirs* (London, 1936), pp. 766–7.

60 Parliamentary Record 1918, p. 104.

61 The detached nameplates can be seen in the Lloyd George Museum, Llanystumdwy.

62 Austin Vernon Mitchell and Sharon Goulds, *Westminster Man: A Tribal Anthropology of the Commons People* (London, 1982), p. 193.

63 Matthew Parris and Kevin MacGuire, *Great Parliamentary Scandals: Five Centuries of Calumny, Smear and Innuendo* (London, 2004), p. 98.

64 'Lloyd George Knew My Father' is a 20th-century English schoolboy folk song. The simple lyrics consist of the phrase 'Lloyd George knew my father/Father knew Lloyd George' sung to the tune 'Onward, Christian Soldiers'.

65 Edgar Holt, *Protest in Arms: The Irish Troubles, 1916–1923* (New York, 1961), p. 12.

66 Mrs Margaret Thatcher's PPS, Airey Neave, was blown up by the IRA before the election campaign in 1979.

67 Edgar Holt, *Protest in Arms* (New York, 1960), throughout.

68 Richard Toye, *Lloyd George and Churchill: Rivals for Greatness* (London, 2012), p. 221.

69 Frank Owen, *Tempestuous Journey: Lloyd George, His Life and Times* (London, 1955), p. 577.

70 With all its defects, Lloyd George's treaty gave Ireland a semblance of peace for 50 years.

71 G. Higgins, *Heroic Revivals from Carlyle to Yeats* (New York, 2012), p. 143.

72 Frances Stevenson, *Lloyd George: A Diary* (New York, 1971), p. 239.

73 Owen, *Tempestuous Journey*, p. 587.

74 Peter Rowland, *David Lloyd George* (London, 1975), p. 555.

75 G. K. Chesterton, *The G. K. Chesterton Collection II* (Kindle edn, 2010).

76 Frances Stevenson, *The Years that are Past* (London, 1967), p. 206.

77 Cf. Adam Tooze, *The Deluge*, p. 437 for a defence of Harington.

78 Rowland, *David Lloyd George*, pp. 578–80.

79 Andrew Roberts, *A History of the English-Speaking Peoples Since 1900* (London, 2010).

80 Martin Pugh, *Lloyd George* (London, 2014), p. 129.

81 Stevenson, *The Years that are Past*, p. 206.

82 Thomas Jones and Keith Middlemas, *Whitehall Diary: 1916–1925* (Oxford, 1969), p. 217.

83 Kenneth O. Morgan, *Dictionary of National Biography*, article on Lloyd George.

84 Stevenson, *Lloyd George: A Diary*, p. 241.

85 Kenneth O. Morgan, 'Lloyd George and leadership, the influence of Gladstone and Abraham Lincoln' in the *Journal of Liberal History*, Issue 77, Winter 2012–13.

86 Michael Kinnear, *The Fall of Lloyd George: The Political Crisis of 1922* (Toronto, 1973), p. 19.

87 Cf. Matthew Hopkins the notorious seventeenth century Witchfinder General.

88 Cf. Donald McCormick, *The Mask of Merlin* (London, 1963), p. 168.

89 Cf. Michael Braddick, *God's Fury, England's Fire* (London, 2008), pp. 429–35 for M. Hopkins.

90 Kenneth O. Morgan, *Consensus and Disunity: The Lloyd George Coalition Government 1918–1922* (Clarendon Press, 1979), p. 373. Morgan is supported by Tooze who contrasts Lloyd George's courageous and idealistic Liberalism with Wilson's obstinate inflexibility. Lloyd George was perhaps one in a long line of British politicians who mishandled Islamic leaders. Cf. Eden's abysmal dealings with President Nasser of Egypt [Laura M. James, *Nasser at War* (Basingstoke, 2006)] and at the moment of writing, the Bush/Blair handling of Iraq looks like blowing up in the West's faces (August 2014).

91 Morgan, *Dictionary of National Biography*.

Chapter 8: The Mighty Pen: A Criticism of Lloyd George, the Author

1 David Lloyd George, *War Memoirs of David Lloyd George New Edition* (London, 1938), p. viii. I am indebted to Dr J. Graham Jones for showing me his article, 'The Lloyd George War Memoirs'.

2 Peter Rowland, *David Lloyd George* (London, 1975), p. 696.

3 Lloyd George, *War Memoirs of David Lloyd George*, p. 246.

4 Albert N. Greco, *The Book Publishing Industry* (London, 2013), p. 4.

5 Rowland, *David Lloyd George*, p. 572.

6 Lloyd George, *War Memoirs of David Lloyd George*, p. 56 for cruel sarcasm about Grey's silent exterior. This is a good justification of Graham Jones' warning to treat the memoirs with caution. See also G. W. Egerton, 'The Lloyd George War Memoirs', *Journal of Modern History*, Vol. 60, No. 1.

7 Dominique Enright, *Wicked Wit of Winston Churchill* (London, 2011).

8 David Lloyd George, *War Memoirs of David Lloyd George*, pp. 231–2.

9 Ibid., p. 639.

10 Ibid.

11 Lord Vansittart, *The Mist Procession* (London, 1958), p. 110.
12 Michael F. Donoghue, *My Kingdom* (British Columbia, 2014), p. 138.
13 Brian Bond and Nigel Cave, *Haig: A Re-appraisal 80 Years On* (Barnsley, 2009), p. 234.
14 Winston Churchill, *World Crisis* (London, 1938), p. 1071.
15 Lloyd George, *War Memoirs of David Lloyd George*, p. 9.
16 Ibid., p. 322.
17 Ibid., pp. 140–1 for photograph of Asquith's letter.
18 Ibid., pp. 602–3.
19 Ibid., pp. 597–8.
20 Lloyd George, *War Memoirs of David Lloyd George*, p. 22.
21 Ibid.
22 David Lloyd George, *War Memoirs of David Lloyd George*, pp. 597–8.
23 Andrew Suttie, *Rewriting the First World War* (Basingstoke, 2005), p. 150.
24 David Lloyd George, War Memoirs of David Lloyd George, p. 1300.
25 Ibid., p. 1305.
26 Ibid., p. 1307.
27 Ibid., p. 1309.
28 'Frocks' were politicians. See Stephen Heathorn, *Haig and Kitchener in Twentieth-Century Britain* (London, 2013), p. 105.
29 'Brass Hats' were military authorities. See Stephen Heathorn, *Haig and Kitchener in Twentieth-Century Britain* (London, 2013), p. 105.
30 Lloyd George, *War Memoirs of David Lloyd George*, p. 412.
31 Alexander Moes, *The Foreign Policy of George W. Bush: Values, Strategy and Loyalty* (Farnham, 2004), p. 206.
32 Lloyd George, *War Memoirs of David Lloyd George*, pp. 1315–18. At Canossa the Emperor Henry IV surrendered to Pope Gregory VII in 1077.
33 Hugh Cudlipp, *The Prerogative of the Harlot: Press Barons & Power* (London, 1980), p. 124.
34 Philip Langer and Robert Pois, *Command Failure in War: Psychology and Leadership* (Bloomington, 2004), p. 139.
35 Lloyd George, *War Memoirs of David Lloyd George*, p. 1341.
36 Ibid., p. 1333.
37 Ibid., pp. 1312–64.
38 Lloyd George, *War Memoirs of David Lloyd George*, p. 448.
39 John Grigg, *Lloyd George: War Leader, 1916–1918* (London, 2013).
40 *History Today*, August 1958, pp. 519–526.
41 Or would it? It is argued in Chapter 6 that there is always someone else.
42 Grigg, *War Leader 1916–1918*, p. 420.
43 Lloyd George, *War Memoirs of David Lloyd George*, pp. 1784–91.
44 Ibid., p. 65.
45 Ibid., p. 72.

46 Stephen Roskill, *Hankey Man of Secrets* (London, 1970), p. 545.
47 Lloyd George, *War Memoirs of David Lloyd George*, p. 671–3.
48 Ibid., p. 690 and Roskill, *Hankey Man of Secrets*, p. 358.
49 Lloyd George, *War Memoirs of David Lloyd George: 1916–1917*, p. 107.
50 Stephen Roskill, *Naval Policy Between Wars. Volume I: The Period of Anglo-American Antagonism 1919–1929* (Barnsley, 2016), p. 41.
51 David Lloyd George, *War Memoirs of David Lloyd George: 1916–1917*, p. 690. Roskill, *Naval Policy Between Wars. Volume I*, p. 358.
52 Lloyd George, *War Memoirs of David Lloyd George: 1916–1917*, p. 275.
53 Lloyd George, *War Memoirs of David Lloyd George*, New Edition, pp. 805–11.
54 Lloyd George, *War Memoirs of David Lloyd George: 1918*, p. 351.
55 Ibid., p. 2035.
56 Ibid., p. 336.
57 Ibid., p. 2038.
58 Virginia Cowles, *Winston Churchill: the Era and the Man* (London, 1953), p. 321.
59 Frank Davies and Graham Maddocks, *Bloody Red Tabs: General Officer Casualties of the Great War 1914–1918* (Barnsley, 2014), p. 16.
60 Quoted by Ffion Hague, *The Pain and the Privilege* (London, 2008), p. 338.
61 *Journal of Liberal Studies*, article by Alan Sharp.
62 Henry Wickham Steed, *Through Thirty Years, 1892–1922: A Personal Narrative, Volume 2* (New York, 1924), p. 330.
63 John Maynard Keynes, *The Economic Consequences of the Peace* (Dover, 2013), p. 15.
64 *Congressional Record: Proceedings and Debates of the 79th Congress First Session, Volume 91, Part 3* (US Government Printing Office: 1945), p. 4064.
65 Susan Ratcliff, *Little Oxford Dictionary of Quotations* (Oxford, 2012), p. 293.
66 David Lloyd George, *The Truth about the Peace Treaties* (Gollanz, 1938), pp. 19–25. Clemenceau's crack about Madame Poincaré comes from Colonel Hankey's memoirs.
67 Lloyd George, *The Truth About the Peace Treaties, Volume 1* (London, 1938), p. 177.
68 Lloyd George, *The Truth About the Peace Treaties*, p. 547.
69 Ibid.
70 Ibid. p. 553.
71 Ibid., p. 671.
72 Ibid., p. 1351.
73 Marian Kent, *The Great Powers and the End of the Ottoman Empire* (London, 2005) p. 183.

74 Lloyd George, *The Truth About the Peace Treaties*, p. 516.
75 Ibid., footnote on p. 408.
76 Ibid., p. 516.
77 Ibid., pp. 734–5.
78 Ibid., p. 546.
79 Ibid., p. 1403.
80 Ibid.
81 Ibid., pp. 1403–4.
82 Ibid., p. 1404.
83 Ibid., p. 1405.
84 Ibid., p. 1406.
85 Ibid.
86 Ibid., p. 1407.
87 Ibid. p. 1408.
88 Ibid, p. 1407.
89 Ibid., p. 1411.
90 Ibid., p. 1412.
91 Lloyd George accuses Clemenceau of interfering with British plans in Palestine by 'sending a few nigger policemen to prevent us stealing the Holy Sepulcre'.
92 Lloyd George, *The Truth about the Peace Treaties*, pp. 1412–13.
93 Joseph R. Mitchell and Helen Buss Mitchell, *The Holocaust: Readings & Interpretations* (New York, 2001), p. 330.
94 Lloyd George, *The Truth about the Peace Treaties*, p. 1414.

Chapter 9: The Higher You Rise ... (October 1922–July 1931)

1 Brian Close, *I Don't Bruise Easily: The Autobiography of Brian Close* (London, 1978), p. 143 for a professional sportsman's inability to accept dismissal. Bishops and headmasters can be equally bitter.
2 This is supposedly a conversation between diplomat and MP Harold Nicolson and Lloyd George in 1940.
3 Kenneth O. Morgan (ed.), *Lloyd George Family Letters* (Cardiff, 1973), p. 197.
4 Ffion Hague, *The Pain and the Privilege: The Women in Lloyd George's Life* (London, 2009).
5 Andrew Marr, *The Making of Modern Britain: From Queen Victoria to VE Day* (London, 2009), p. 227.
6 House of Lords Archives, G box 1 Folder 17.
7 John Perry, *Winston Churchill* (Nashville, 2010), p. 102.
8 Roy Jenkins, *Asquith: Portrait of a Man and an Era* (New York, 1964), p. 505.
9 David Dutton, *A History of the Liberal Party since 1900* (London, 2013).

10 Peter Clarke, *The Locomotive of War: Money, Empire, Power and Guilt* (London, 2017).

11 Albert James Sylvester, *The Real Lloyd George* (London, 1947), p. 109.

12 Ibid., p. 118.

13 Ibid., p. 121.

14 Ibid., p. 134.

15 Lord Riddell, *Lord Riddell's Intimate Diary of the Peace Conference and After* (London, 1933), p. 257.

16 Albert James Sylvester, *The Real Lloyd George* (London, 1947), p. 134.

17 Ibid., p. 132.

18 Ibid., p. 139.

19 Ibid., p. 144.

20 Riddell, *Lord Riddell's Intimate Diary of the Peace Conference and After*, pp. 366–7.

21 R. Terry, Organist of Westminster Cathedral, was a composer of hymn tunes and anthems.

22 John Campbell, *If Love Were All...: The Story of Frances Stevenson and David Lloyd George* (London, 2007), p. 228.

23 Ibid.

24 H. C. Coles, *Walford Davies* (Oxford, 1942), pp. 128–9.

25 John Robert Fleming, *The Highway of Praise: An Introduction to Christian Hymnody* (Oxford, 1937), p. 53.

26 The merits and demerits of hymns and hymn-books are a matter of opinion. I have tried, however, to justify my views. I happen to know a little bit about hymns, based on academic research. I succeeded in tracking down *Hymns of Western Europe* which is nowadays quite elusive. There is a copy in Dr Williams Library, 14, Gordon Square, London WC1H OAR.

27 Sir Walford Davies, *Hymns of Western Europe* (London, 1927).

28 Ibid.

29 It is hard to see how Lloyd George was to blame.

30 Morgan (ed.), *Lloyd George Family Letters*, p. 202.

31 Rowland, *David Lloyd George*, p. 606.

32 Ibid., p. 606.

33 Naomi Levine, Politics, *Religion, and Love: The Story of H.H. Asquith, Venetia Stanley, and Edwin Montagu, Based on the Life and Letters of Edwin Samuel Montagu* (New York, 1991), p. 679.

34 Rowland, *David Lloyd George*, p. 608.

35 Lord Vansittart, *The Mist Procession* (London, 1958), p. 323.

36 Keith Laybourn, *The General Strike of 1926* (Manchester, 1993), p. 37.

37 A. J. Sylvester, *The Real Lloyd George*, p. 147.

38 John Campbell, *Pistols at Dawn: Two Hundred Years of Political Rivalry from Pitt and Fox to Blair and Brown* (London, 2010), p. 189.

39 The New Age Journal, *The New Age: A Weekly Review of Politics, Literature and Art, Vol. 9* (New York, 1911), p. 386.

40 Patricia Lee Sykes, *Presidents and Prime Ministers: Conviction Politics in the Anglo-American Tradition* (Kansas, 2000), p. 112.

41 Michael Bentley, *The Liberal Mind: 1914–29* (Cambridge, 2007), p. 160.

42 Originally 'Enquiry', but given Lloyd George's reputation, LIE was seen as an unfortunate acronym.

43 See John Campbell, *The Goat in the Wilderness* (London, 1977) for the details of Lloyd George's policy publications.

44 Rowland, *David Lloyd George* for MacDonald to Lloyd George, 26 August 1931, pp. 687–8.

45 See J. Graham Jones' article on the impact of the Land and the Nation on Wales.

46 John Maynard Keynes, *Essays in Biography* (New York, 1951), p. 36.

47 Peter Clarke, 'We Can Conquer Unemployment: Lloyd George and Keynes', *Journal of Liberal History*, Issue 77, Winter 2012–13.

48 Ruth Longford, *Frances, Countess Lloyd George: More Than a Mistress* (Leominster, 1996), p. 104.

49 Stephen Lee, *Aspects of British Political History 1914–1995* (London, 2005), p. 102.

50 Zygmunt Bauman, *Between Class and Elite: The Evolution of the British Labour Movement: A Sociological Study* (Manchester, 1972), p. 227.

51 Rosemary Rees, *Britain 1890–1939* (Portsmouth, New Hampshire, 2003), p. 160.

52 Robert Lloyd George, *David & Winston: How the Friendship Between Lloyd George and Churchill Changed the Course of History* (New York, 2008).

53 Max Beaverbrook, *The Decline and Fall of Lloyd George: And Great was the Fall Thereof* (New York, 1966).

54 See John Turner, *British Politics and the Great War* (New York, 1992), passim.

55 Kenneth O. Morgan, 'Essay on Lloyd George', *British Liberal Leaders* (London, 2015), p. 261.

Chapter 10: Lloyd George's Families and Friends

1 Gillian Shephard, *Shephard's Watch: Illusions of Power in British Politics* (Arlington County, VA, 2000), p. 6.

2 J. Graham Jones, *David Lloyd George and Welsh Liberalism* (Cardiff, 2010), p. 561.

3 Letter, National Library of Wales, dated 25 June 1939.

4 John Campbell, *If Love Were All...: The Story of Frances Stevenson and David Lloyd George* (London, 2007).

5 Roy Hattersley, *David Lloyd George: The Great Outsider* (London, 2010).

6 A. J. Sylvester, *The Real Lloyd George* (London, 1947).

7 Welsh Political Archive FCF.2/1.

8 Frances Stevenson, *Lloyd George, A Diary* (London, 1971), p. 157.

9 David Lloyd George, *Family Letters, 1885–1936* (Oxford, 1973), p. 130.

10 Kenneth O. Morgan (ed.), *Lloyd George Family Letters, 1885–1936* (Cardiff, 1973), p. 203.

11 John Campbell, *If Love Were All...*, p. 116.

12 John Grigg, *Lloyd George, from Peace to War: 1912–1916* (London, 1985), p. 85.

13 Stevenson, *Lloyd George, A Diary*, p. 187.

14 Peter Rowland, *David Lloyd George* (London, 1975), p. 748.

15 Richard Lloyd George, *Dame Margaret: The Life Story of His Mother* (Crows Nest, Australia, 1947), p. 224.

16 Campbell, *If Love Were All...*, p. 169.

17 Ibid., p. 310.

18 Ibid.

19 Ibid., p. 168.

20 Ibid., p. 142.

21 Ibid., p. 141.

22 Ibid., p. 448.

23 Ibid., p. 329.

24 Campbell, *If Love Were All...*, pp. 329–31.

25 Ibid., p. 417.

26 Ruth Longford, *Frances, Countess Lloyd George: More than a Mistress* (Leominster, 1996), p. 110. (Date of the letter is 11 December 1932.)

27 A. J. Sylvester, *Life With Lloyd George* (London, 1975), p. 259.

28 Campbell, *If Love Were All...*, p. 364. Roberta was expected to get on with Jennifer, apparently.

29 Ibid., p. 375.

30 Earl Lloyd George, *My Father Lloyd George* (London, 1961).

31 Campbell, *If Love Were All...*, p. 301.

32 Longford, *Frances, Countess Lloyd George*, p. 135.

33 Ibid.

34 Ffion Hague, *The Pain and the Privilege: The Women in Lloyd George's Life* (London, 2008), p. 470 and letter to the author dated 27 August 2008.

35 Ibid., p. 269.

36 Angela Wintle, 'Baroness Trumpington Remembers Being A Land Girl On Lloyd George's Farm, 1939', 28 March 2017 (http://www.telegraph. co.uk/culture/10830818/Baroness-Trumpington-remembers-being-a-land-girl-on-Lloyd-Georges-farm-1939.html).

37 Rowland, *David Lloyd George*, p. 643.

38 Earl Lloyd George, *My Father, Lloyd George* (London, 1960), p. 235.

39 Ibid., p. 222.
40 Earl Lloyd George, *My Father Lloyd George*, p. 110.
41 Sylvester, *Life With Lloyd George*, p. 182.
42 Ibid., p. 281.
43 Earl Lloyd George, *My Father, Lloyd George*, p. 11.
44 Ibid.
45 Mervyn Jones, *A Radical Life: The Biography of Megan Lloyd George* (London, 1991), p. 79.
46 Sylvester, *Life With Lloyd George*, p. 172.
47 Ruth Longford, *Frances, Countess Lloyd George*, p. 481.
48 Sylvester, Life With Lloyd George, p. 316.
49 Roy Hattersley, *David Lloyd George*.
50 Hague, *The Pain and the Privilege*, p. 530.
51 Ibid.
52 Baroness Shirley Williams to the author, 10 September 2013.
53 Sylvester, *Life With Lloyd George*, p. 165.
54 Jennifer married Michael Longford, the son of Lord Twining, Governor of Tanganyika. She died on 5 March 2012. There was a long, appreciative though slightly inaccurate obituary in *The Times*, 24 March 2012.

Chapter 11: An Uneven Old Age (1931–1945)

1 A. J. Sylvester, *The Real Lloyd George* (London, 1947) and *Life With Lloyd George* (London, 1975). The quotation is from Tennyson's *Ulysses*.
2 Mervyn Jones, *A Radical Life: The Biography of Megan Lloyd George* (London, 1991), p. 172.
3 J. Graham Jones, *David Lloyd George and Welsh Liberalism* (Cardiff, 2010), p. 367.
4 Peter Dennis, *Decision by Default: Peacetime Conscription and British Defence, 1919–39* (Durham, North Carolina, 1972), p. 23.
5 Peter Rowland, *David Lloyd George: A Biography* (London, 1975), p. 680.
6 Quoted in, Rowland, *David Lloyd George*, p. 653.
7 Mahesh Kumar Bhargava, *Disarmament From Versailles To Test Ban Treaty* (New Delhi, 1979), p. 62.
8 The Earl of Avon, *Facing the Dictators* (London, 1962), p. 317.
9 Rowland, *David Lloyd George*, p. 730.
10 Stella Rudman, *Lloyd George and the Appeasement of Germany, 1919–1945* (Cambridge, 2011).
11 Roy Hattersley, *David Lloyd George: The Great Outsider* (London, 2010), p. 396.
12 For a brief critique of von Ribbentrop, cf. my article in *History Today*, November 2001.

13 Rudman, *Lloyd George and the Appeasement of Germany* (Cambridge, 2011), p. 224.

14 Ibid., p. 226.

15 Sylvester, *The Real Lloyd George*; cf. Rudman, *Lloyd George and the Appeasement of Germany*, pp. 222–30; Martin Gilbert, *The Roots of Appeasement* (London, 1966) gives T. P. Conwell-Evans' detailed account of the meeting between Hitler and Lloyd George, pp. 197–211.

16 Jones, *A Radical Life* (London, 1991).

17 Rudman, *Lloyd George and the Appeasement of Germany*, p. 227.

18 A. Lentin, *Lloyd George and the Lost Peace: From Versailles to Hitler, 1919–1940* (Basingstoke, 2001), pp. 18–25.

19 Ibid.

20 Michael Burn, *Turned Towards the Sun: An Autobiography* (Norwich, 2003), p. 101.

21 Lentin, *Lloyd George and the Lost Peace*, p. 105.

22 Donald McCormick, *The Mask of Merlin* (London, 1963), pp. 268–70.

23 John Van der Kiste, *George V's Children* (Stroud, 1991), p. 29.

24 Cf. J. Graham Jones, *David Lloyd George and Welsh Liberalism*, p. 426.

25 Cf. Robert Beaken, *Cosmo Lang* (London, 2014), pp. 86–141.

26 Donald McCormick, *The Mask of Merlin: A Critical Study of David Lloyd George* (London, 1963), p. 266.

27 Ibid.

28 Ibid.

29 Ibid., p. 267.

30 Cf. Beaken, *Cosmo Lang*, pp. 86–141.

31 Sylvester, *The Real Lloyd George*, p. 232.

32 Graham Jones, *David Lloyd George and Welsh Liberalism*, p. 432. The Welsh means 'Wales for ever'.

33 Slogan shouted by rioting French students in 1968.

34 Rowland, *David Lloyd George*, pp. 770–2.

35 A. Capet, *Britain, France and the Entente Cordiale Since 1904* (Basingstoke, 2006), p. 35.

36 Donald McCormick, *The Mask of Merlin: A Critical Study of David Lloyd George* (London, 1963), p. 280.

37 Sylvester, *The Real Lloyd George*, *passim*. For Lloyd George's friendship with Maisky see Sidney Aster, *Lloyd George, Twelve Essays*, A. J. P. Taylor (ed.) (London, 1971), pp. 317–57.

38 Rowland, *David Lloyd George* (London, 1976), p. 760.

39 Ibid. p. 764.

40 Nick Smart, *Neville Chamberlain* (London, 2010), p. 276.

41 Rowland, *David Lloyd George*, pp. 771–2.

42 Robert Lloyd George, *David & Winston: How the Friendship Between Lloyd George and Churchill Changed the Course of History* (New York, 2008).

43 Rudman, *Lloyd George and the Appeasement of Germany*, p. 257.
44 Rowland, *David Lloyd George*, p. 786.
45 A. J. Sylvester's diary, collected in the *A. J. Sylvester Papers* which are held in the National Library of Wales.
46 Travis Crosby, *The Unknown Lloyd George* (London, 2014).
47 Andrew Roberts, *The Storm of War: A New History of the Second World War* (London, 2009), p. 91. RUSHA = *Rasse und Siedlungshauptant* (Race and Settlement Office).

Conclusion

1   Peter Rowland, *David Lloyd George: A Biography* (London, 1976), p. 803.
2   http://www.iwm.org.uk/history/the-rise-and-fall-of-lord-haw-haw-during-the-second-world-war.
3   Duncan Brack (ed.), *British Liberal Leaders* (London, 2015), *passim*. See also Lloyd George's conversation with Tom Jones, quoted by Rowland, *David Lloyd George*, p. 776: Churchill 'will not smash the Tory Party to save the country, as I smashed the Liberal Party'.
4   Rowland cannot bring himself to quote Lloyd George's letter about Samuel to Lord Motteston because it is 'too scathing'. Rowland, *David Lloyd George*, p. 765.
5   John Campbell, *The Goat in the Wilderness* (London, 1977).
6   https://en.wikipedia.org/wiki/Alfred_Bossom.
7   Huw Edwards, *City Mission* (Y Lolfa Cyf, 2014), pp. 213–16 and his television life of Lloyd George.
8   Brack (ed.), *British Liberal Leaders*.
9   Rowland, *David Lloyd George*, p. 803.
10 Ibid.
11 Goering refused to accept the help of Pastor Henry Gerecke, the American Lutheran chaplain who ministered to the major war criminals at Nuremberg, much though he respected him. Ribbentrop's closing words, however, to Pastor Gerecke were, 'I'll see you again'.
12 Robert Lloyd George, *David & Winston: How the Friendship Between Lloyd George and Churchill Changed the Course of History* (New York, 2008).
13 Ffion Hague, *The Pain and Privilege: The Women in Lloyd George's Life* (London, 2008), p. 537.

Select Bibliography

Beaverbrook, Lord, *Politicians and the War* (Oldbourne Books, 1960).

―――― *The Decline and Fall of Lloyd George* (Collins 1963).

Birch, R. C., *The Shaping of the Welfare State* (Longman 1974).

Brack, Duncan, Ingham, Robert & Little, Tony (eds), *British Liberal Leaders* (Biteback, 2015).

Campbell, John, *Lloyd George, The Goat in the Wilderness* (Cape 1977).

―――― *If Love Were All* (Cape 2006).

Carey Evans, Olwen, *Lloyd George Was My Father* (Gomer Press 1985).

Cassar, George, *Asquith as War Leader* (Anthem Press, 1994).

―――― *Lloyd George At War* (Anthem Press, 2009).

Churchill, Winston, *World Crisis* (Odhams New Edition, 1938).

Cook, Chris, *The Age of Alignment* (Toronto University Press, 1975).

Cotton, Olivia, *Churt Remembered* (O. M. Cotton, 2002).

Cregier, Don M., *Bounder From Wales* (Missouri University Press, 1975).

Crosby, Travis, *The Unknown Lloyd George* (I.B.Tauris, 2014).

Du Parcq, Herbert, *The Life of David Lloyd George* (Caxton, 1912).

Edwards, Huw, *City Mission The Story of London's Welsh Chapels* (Y lolfa, 2014).

French, David, *The Strategy of the Lloyd George Coalition* (Clarendon, 1995).

George, W. R. P., *The Making of Lloyd George* (Faber and Faber, 1970).

―――― *Lloyd George Backbencher* (Gomer, 1983).

George, William, *My Brother and I* (Eyre and Spottiswood, 1958).

Gilbert, B. B., *David Lloyd George: A Political Life* (Batsford, 1987).

―――― *David Lloyd George: Architect of Change* (Batsford, 1987).

Gilbert, Martin, *The Roots of Appeasement* (Weidenfeld and Nicolson, 1966).

Graham Jones, J., *A Pocket Guide: The History of Wales* (Cardiff, 1998).

―――― *Lloyd George Papers* (National Library of Wales, 2001).

―――― *David Lloyd George and Welsh Liberalism* (National Library, 2010).

Grigg, John, *The Young Lloyd George* (Eyre Methuen, 1973).

―――― *Lloyd George: The People's Champion* (Eyre Methuen, 1978).

―――― *Lloyd George: From Peace to War* (Eyre Methuen, 1983).

———— *Lloyd George: War Leader* (Allen Lane, 2002).

Hague, Ffion, *The Pain and the Privilege* (Harper Collins, 2008).

Haig, Douglas, *War Diaries*, Gary Sheffield (ed.) (Weidenfeld and Nicolson, 2005).

Hankey, Lord, *The Supreme Command* (Allen and Unwin, 1961).

Hattersley, Roy, *David Lloyd George, The Great Outsider* (Little, Brown, 2010).

Jenkins, Roy, *Mr Balfour's Poodle* (Collins, 1954).

———— *Asquith* (Collins, 1964).

———— *Winston Churchill* (Macmillan, 2001).

Keynes, J. M., *The Economic Consequences of the Peace* (Macmillan, 1919).

———— *Essays in Biography* (Macmillan, 1933).

Lentin, A., *Lloyd George, Woodrow Wilson and the Guilt of Germany* (Leicester, 1984).

Lloyd George, David, *War Memoirs* (Odhams, 1938).

———— *The Truth about the Peace Treaties* (Gollanz, 1938).

Lloyd George, Frances (née Stevenson), *Makers of the New World by One Who Knows Them* (Cassell, 1922).

———— *The Years That Are Past* (Hutchinson, 1967).

Lloyd George, Richard, *Dame Margaret Lloyd George* (Allen and Unwin, 1947).

———— *My Father, Lloyd George* (Frederic Muller, 1961).

Lloyd George, Owen, *A Tale of Two Grandfathers* (Bellew, 1999).

Lloyd George, Robert, *David and Winston* (John Murray, 2005).

Longford, Ruth, *Frances: More Than a Mistress* (Gracewing Leominster, 1996).

Macmillan, Harold, *The Past Masters* (Macmillan, 1975).

Macmillan, Margaret, *Peacemakers* (John Murray, 2002).

———— *The War That Ended Peace: How Europe Abandoned Peace for the First World War* (Profile, 2014).

Mallinson, Allan, *1914 Fight the Good Fight* (Bantam Press, 2013).

Masterman, Lucy, *C. F. G. Masterman: A Biography* (Frank Cass and Co., 1968).

McCormick, Donald, *The Mask of Merlin* (MacDonald, 1963).

Mitchell, David, *Queen Christabel* (MacDonald and James, 1975).

Morgan, Kenneth O., *The Age of Lloyd George* (George Allen and Unwin, 1961).

———— *David Lloyd George* (Cardiff University of Wales Press, 1963).

———— *Consensus and Disunity* (Clarendon Press, 1979).

———— *Lloyd George Family Letters* (ed.) (Oxford University Press, 1973).

———— *Dictionary of National Biography*, entry on Lloyd George.

Morgan, Kenneth and Jane, *Portrait of a Progressive* (Oxford University Press, 1980).

Neillands, Robin, *The Great War Generals on the Western Front* (Robinson, 1999).

Owen, Frank, *Tempestuous Journey: Lloyd George, His Life and Time* (Hutchinson, 1954).

Price, Emyr, *David Lloyd George* (University of Wales, 2006).

Prior, Robin and Wilson, Trevor, *Passchendaele* (Yale University Press, 1996).

Pugh, M, *David Lloyd George* (Longman, 1988).

Riddell, Lord, *Lord Riddell's War Diaries* (Ivor Nicholson and Watson, 1933).

—— *Lord Riddell's Intimate Diary of The Peace Conference and After* (Gollanz, 1933).

—— *More Pages From My Diary* (Country Life, 1934).

Roskill, S. W., *Hankey: Man of Secrets* (Collins, 1970).

Rowland, Peter, *David Lloyd George* (Macmillan, 1976).

Rudman, Stella, *Lloyd George and the Appeasement of Germany, 1919–1945* (Cambridge Scholars, 2011).

Sylvester, A. J , *The Real Lloyd George* (Cassell, 1947).

—— *Life With Lloyd George* (Macmillan, 1975).

Taylor, A. J. P., *Politics in Wartime* (Hamish Hamilton, 1963).

—— (ed.) *Lloyd George: A Diary by Frances Stevenson* (Harper and Row, 1971).

—— (ed.) *Lloyd George: Twelve Essays* (Hamish Hamilton, 1971).

—— (ed.) *My Darling Pussy* (Weidenfeld and Nicolson, 1975).

Tooze, Adam, *The Deluge* (Allen Lane, 1914).

Toye, Richard, *Lloyd George and Churchill* (Macmillan, 2007).

Trumpington, Jean, *Coming Up Trumps* (Macmillan, 2014).

Turner, John, *British Politics and the Great War* (Yale, 1992).

—— *Lloyd George's Secretariat* (Cambridge University Press, 1998).

Wilson, John, *Sir Henry Campbell-Bannerman* (Constable, 1973).

Woodward, David R., *Lloyd George and the Generals* (Delaware, 1983).

Wrigley, Chris, *Lloyd George* (Blackwell, 1992).

[Ian Ivatt, *The Financial Affairs of David Lloyd George* (Welsh Academic Press, 2016). I have unfortunately been unable to consult this apparently valuable book, soon to be published.]

Other Sources

Magazines and periodicals:

The Journal of Liberal History is a valuable source of articles. Issue 77, for example, published in Winter 2012–13, contained 11 articles devoted to Lloyd George, based on recent research.

Archives:

Research students are made welcome at the House of Lords Library where the Parliamentary Archive contains Lord Beaverbrook's voluminous correspondence with Lloyd George, a vast amount of material illustrating Lloyd George's career and Frances Stevenson's papers. The Public Records Office at Kew contains much Lloyd George material. Most valuable of all is the original primary material available at the National Library of Wales, Aberystwyth. Not only documents but photographs, films and exhibitions of Lloyd George artefacts make this a unique collection. The Lloyd George Museum at Llanystumdwy is invaluable. All these sources are helpfully surveyed in J. Graham Jones' book detailed in the Bibliography.

Index